A PHILOSOPHY OF COMMUNITY

July 3, 2004

To Kent and Barbara Manning,

Good friends — with warm regards,

Charlie Puig

A PHILOSOPHY

OF COMMUNITY

OHIO UNIVERSITY IN THE PING YEARS
1975–1994

Florence Clark Riffe

OHIO UNIVERSITY SPECIAL PUBLICATIONS   ATHENS

Ohio University Special Publications, Athens, Ohio 45701
© 2004 by Ohio University Special Publications
Printed in the United States of America
All rights reserved

Ohio University Special Publications books are printed on acid-free paper ♾™
11 10 09 08 07 06 05 04   5 4 3 2 1

Library of Congress Cataloging-in-Publication Data

Riffe, Florence Clark.
   A philosophy of community : Ohio University in the Ping years, 1975-1994 / Florence Clark Riffe.
     p. cm.
   Includes bibliographical references and index.
   ISBN: 0-9667644-4-7 (cloth : alk. paper)
   1. Ping, Charles J. 2. Ohio University—Presidents—Biography. 3. Ohio University—History—20th century. I. Title.

LD4191.O817P56 2003
378.771'97—dc21

2003056313

CONTENTS

Foreword	ix
Preface	xvii
Acknowledgments	xxi

THE EDUCATION OF CHARLES JACKSON PING	1

CHAPTER ONE—COLLEGIALLY SPEAKING

Confronting the Present	7
Shaping the Future	9
Governing without a Union	11
Governing within the Circle	14
Educating for Change—The Educational Plan of 1977	17
Summarizing the Themes of the Community	20
Committing to Educational Justice	22
Making Judgments—UPAC	26
Assessing Quality—Institutional Impact	30
Critiquing and Revising—Toward the Third Century	32
Regarding Faculty	38

CHAPTER TWO—DEVELOPING HISTORY

Resolving the Residence Hall Crisis	42
Refinancing—Indebtedness Unbound	45
Trading Present Space for Future Capital	46
Weathering Cold, Coal, and Conflict	48
Promoting Aesthetic and Historical Values	52
175 Years, 1979	52
Northwest Territory Bicentennial, 1987	54
Regaining Alumni Confidence	56

Raising Funds—Two Campaigns, $155 Million	58
1804 Campaign, 1979	59
Third Century Campaign, 1989	65
Capitalizing on The Ridges	70
The Edwin L. and Ruth E. Kennedy Museum of Art	72

CHAPTER THREE—STUDENTS BY THE SCORES

General Education Excellence	75
Quality over Quantity	85
Increasing Hours to Graduate	86
Freshman ABC Grading Scale	86
Selective Admissions	87
The Honors Convocation	91
Commencement	91
The Court Street Scuffle	93
Learning outside the Classroom	95
Code of Conduct	95
Residence Life	96
Student Governance	98
Education for Leadership—The Cutler Scholars	100

CHAPTER FOUR—PIONEERING KNOWLEDGE

Educating Physicians—The College of Osteopathic Medicine	103
A New Home for Health and Human Services	108
Educating Government—ILGARD	112
Learning for Life	114
Transferring Knowledge to the Marketplace	115
Winning the Selective Excellence Sweepstakes	121
Sponsoring Research	127
Uniting Research and Markets—The Edison Biotechnology Institute	130

CHAPTER FIVE—ENLIGHTENING INTERDEPENDENCE

Circumnavigating a Holistic World	135
Educating for Democracy in Southern Africa	139
Orienting Ohio to Asia	144
Improving Access to the World's Knowledge	149
Studying the World's Contemporary History	153

CHAPTER SIX—REBUILDING A UNIVERSITY

Stabilizing Stewardship	158
In for the Duration	166
The Charles J. Ping Student Recreation Center	169
The Charles J. Ping Institute for the Teaching of the Humanities	170
Recognizing Ping's Leadership	171
Rebuilding a Town—Claire Oates Ping	175
An Everyday Citizen	179
APPENDIX A—103 Goals of the Educational Plan of 1977	183
APPENDIX B—Educational Plan II: Toward the Third Century	192
INDEX	235

FOREWORD

The first words I heard Charles Ping utter were "Sweet are the uses of adversity." It was May of 1975 and I was driving home from campus listening to WOUB's broadcast of the news conference he gave after having been named the eighteenth president of Ohio University. He must have been responding to a reporter's question about why he was interested in taking the reins of such a troubled institution. I smiled at our good fortune in finding a president who quoted Shakespeare, but I wondered if any mortal was capable of leading the university out of the morass of debt and desperation it had been plunged into in the previous four years.

Susan and I joined the faculty in the fall of 1970. The university was bursting at the seams with students. By the following fall the enrollment neared 19,000, having more than doubled in less than a decade. We had come from Indiana University, a similarly historic and picturesque institution, but we quickly found that the undergraduates at Ohio were more lively and sophisticated than their Hoosier counterparts. Over 25 percent of the students came from out-of-state, with large contingents from New York, New Jersey, and Pennsylvania, and the mix of students was stimulating and invigorating. But the community also had been traumatized by the events of the previous spring, when the university had been forced to close in response to the prolonged student disturbances that followed the shootings at Kent State.

Our initial experiences with Athens and the university were similar to those of many who had found their way to this handsome and historic campus nestled in the foothills of Appalachia: we were certain we had discovered a hidden treasure. Our own department, English, was big and bustling with almost sixty faculty, a hundred graduate students, and a remarkable group of creative writers with national reputations. Other disciplines seemed equally vital. This was a university on the move. The future seemed limitless.

Then the bottom fell out. In three quick, disastrous years the enrollment plunged from 19,000 to 13,000. The resulting financial crisis led to massive budget cuts, the dismissal of several hundred staff and many tenure-track faculty, and the creation of a raucous, rancorous atmosphere that pitted the faculty against the administration, redirected the student protest movement to internal university issues, and culminated in the resignation of President Claude Sowle in the spring of 1974. Harry Crewson, a long-time professor of economics and former chair of the city council, was appointed acting president, and he and Vice President for Academic Affairs Taylor Culbert managed to hold the university together for a year while Faculty Senate chair Alan Booth led a committee of trustees, faculty, a president emeritus (Vernon Alden), and students in the search for a new president.

The Ohio Board of Regents was not overly sympathetic to our plight. Plans circulated to strip the university of its graduate programs and limit its enrollment to 10,000. Only effective lobbying of Governor James Rhodes and key members of the legislative leadership by several influential alums managed to provide the additional funding necessary to help the university weather the storm as the search for the new president proceeded. On campus a serious effort, led from within, to unionize the faculty gained momentum. Such was the state of the university in the spring of 1975. Only Charlie Ping could have found such adversity "sweet."

My association with Ping as a faculty member, Faculty Senate chair, dean, colleague in the Ping Institute for the Teaching of the Humanities, and friend stretches over four decades. It's been a remarkable experience, on both the personal and institutional levels, and much of the potential Susan and I sensed about Ohio University back in 1970—seemingly dashed by the events of mid-decade—has been not only realized but dramatically exceeded. The university now is widely regarded, on the strength of academic quality and value, research productivity, library holdings, and endowment, as one of the top public universities in the country. Such, certainly in the state of Ohio, was not the perception in 1975. What happened in the Ping years to restore the university's confidence and put it back on the track to excellence?

Well, there was some "sweetness" in the adversity. The university had a long and noble—if neglected—history, a handsome—if poorly groomed—campus, loyal—if discouraged—alumni, an adventuresome and heterogeneous—if nonselective—student body, and a stable and committed—if dispirited—faculty. The three years of fiscal crisis and savage struggle for scarce resources, paradoxically, also created the potential for cooperation.

All this Ping saw or sensed, and it turned out, in retrospect, to be an ideal environment to put into practice his philosophical commitment to developing a comprehensive planning process based on the idea of a university as a community that exceeded the sum of its parts. A more secure or prosperous place might have yawned and gone on with business as usual.

But Charles Ping turned out to be the right man, in the right place, at the right time. John C. Baker and Vernon Alden had created the academic structure and the physical plant for the modern Ohio University; it was left to Ping to shape its vision of the future. Ping did not save the university community; he got the university to save itself—a harder task. He did so in an unusual fashion. He did not try to impose a grand and rhetorically eloquent vision on the university community; rather he tried to establish a process—he called it holistic planning—through which the various parts of the community would contribute to defining goals and setting priorities and then gather the will to act upon them. Many of us were skeptical. "Planning" and "process" are not terms that ring big bells for many academics, particularly those of us educated in the traditional liberal disciplines of the arts and sciences. Leadership was a word that had been discredited by national events in the 1960s and '70s. But Ping led in a unique fashion. He managed to concoct a synthesis of the idealism he admired in Plato and Hegel with the management strategies he had picked up at the Harvard Business School. He used it to create and implement a comprehensive planning process and then stepped aside to allow it to function even though it removed him from the focus of attention.

A personal example will illustrate. Faculty know that in most administrations, whatever their stated budget or planning process, if you really want support for a pet project you go directly to the president to make your case. My department chairman, the head of the university's library committee and a man passionately committed to books, had long secured special funding for the library by so doing. He tried the same thing with Ping. One afternoon he loomed in my office doorway and more in sorrow than in anger muttered through his substantial beard: "The man hates books." Ping obviously, and not for the first or last time, had just said "No." Saying "no" is tough. All presidents and patriarchs want to be the source from which all bounty flows, but Ping was willing to take the abuse to make the planning process work by not making private deals that undermined the system. Ping cherished books and was as much a product of Renaissance humanism as my colleague, but he resisted the challenge of subverting the system he had put in place for the sweet temporary gratification of saying "Yes." I wish my colleague had lived to see Alden Library, some fifteen years later, its budget repeatedly boosted by funding provided by UPAC (the eighteen-member University Planning Advisory Committee created by Ping), invited to join the distinguished association of the greatest research libraries in North America. In Ping's system the community, not the president, had made the library a priority.

It took time, and time and patience were hallmarks of his administration, but gradually the university came to know and, even better, trust Charlie Ping. But it did not happen overnight. I vividly remember a rocky and contentious Faculty Senate meeting during my term as chair when Ping had made a controversial administrative appointment that troubled many senators. At one point in the heated debate a longtime professor of physics and former chair of the Senate rose and stammered: "You presidents are all alike. You make bad decisions like this one. Then you leave the university and we're left with the problem of cleaning up the mess." I saw Ping set his jaw and lower his head and I thought to myself: this Irishman's got a strong stubborn streak and he's not going anywhere. Later, when several attractive opportunities to move on did arise, I silently thanked that physics prof every time Charlie and Claire decided to stay because I knew his challenge rumbled in Ping's memory. And when that appointment did turn out to be messy, Ping cleaned it up himself.

Ping perfected the plain style. He preferred facts and data to rhetorical flourish. He was an offensive lineman, not an open field runner. He gave it to you straight though sometimes with a bit of philosophical abstraction and was not afraid of telling the truth in dark times. He could also take criticism and in spite of his stubborn streak I often have seen him bow to the challenge of a forceful argument and laugh at a jest at his own expense. He shared William Faulkner's suspicion that chatter was cheap and he was more likely to be impressed with the force of a written argument than with a verbal one. He despised gossip—something of a tragedy for a small town university community that thrives on it in the absence of other diversions.

Ping enjoyed a vigorous intellectual debate and never backed down from a fight—particularly with the regents or legislature—but he preferred cooperation to confrontation. Long before "thinking globally" became a necessity (and a cliché) he encouraged education for interdependence; funding guidelines for UPAC and the Academic Excellence grants encouraged interdisciplinary, even cross-college, proposals; his own administrative style stressed that the president and provost shared the office of the presidency and, aided by two accomplished provosts (Neil Bucklew and Jim Bruning) he made that idea—stolen from the corporate world—work. On the personal side he also shared the presidency with his wife. As Charlie went to work to restore the university, Claire Ping became an equally compelling and indefatigable force in leading local citizen groups interested in the restoration of downtown Athens, ravaged by a series of fires in the early '70s and by the flight of many Court Street merchants as new malls were built east of town. They maintained a vigorous entertaining schedule, and Claire tried to whisk Charlie out of town for a weekend every other month or so just to allow him the chance to recharge the batteries away from the fishbowl world they inhabited.

Ping had a good sense of humor and a deep resonant laugh but he did not tell jokes—not even as openers to his annual state of the university addresses. I used to quip that he was Lincolnesque in everything but the length of his speeches. Yet when he chose he could be a tough act to follow. I had been asked to be the keynoter at the banquet of a statewide organization of fraternities meeting on campus. Charlie was also on the program to give a few words of welcome. I had loaded up my talk with what I thought were bawdy jokes and ribald moments from Shakespeare designed to please a group of undergraduate males. Charlie stood up and proceeded to do ten minutes or so of one of the greatest stand-up academic comic routines I had ever heard. He read a series of postcards he had received over the years from Ohio University students misbehaving on spring break and sharing their high spirits with the old president snowbound back in Athens. It was sophomoric humor but it was theirs. He then went on to recount the trials and tribulations of having the Sigma Chis as his neighbors. Each punch line relating to some fraternity prank that had backfired redoubled the laughter. He held a comic mirror up to their world and they roared at what they saw. The crowd was exhausted by the time I reached the mike and I couldn't raise a titter with my limp jokes. Shakespeare and I were dead on arrival; my audience only wanted more tales of the president and the Sigma Chis.

The university's renaissance was a remarkable experience not just to witness but to live. The decade of the 1980s saw applications increase from 6,500 to 12,000; the median high school class rank of the entering class increase from the sixtieth to the eightieth percentile; the freshman to sophomore retention rate increase from 67 percent to 85 percent; the enrollment gradually climb back to almost 18,000; the endowment increase from under two million to almost one hundred million; external research funds more than quadruple; faculty books and research regularly reviewed or discussed in the *New York Times* and other national publications; and the university repeatedly included in the more prestigious college guides.

Like the mythical phoenix, Ohio University had been refashioned out of its own ashes. Amazingly, for the modern public university, none of this was accomplished by hitching a ride on the back of intercollegiate athletics. The basketball team was competitive and reached the NCAA tournament twice but did not advance past the first round to garner any major national exposure. The football team, in the '80s, had the worst decade in its history. This was a particularly sad paradox as Ping was one of the few presidents who had actually played football in college and was a passionate fan of the game. His sense of honor called for letting coaches fulfill their five-year contracts even when it was apparent after a season or two that no turnaround for the program was likely. When queried about this phenomenon late in his tenure he replied: "We're not in the business of public entertainment. We're in the business of human development." True . . . but for the human development of the team members and the pride of some alums a few more victories would have sweetened Ohio University's only remaining adversity.

It is appropriate that Ping's legacy is honored in the two campus institutions that carry his name: The Charles J. Ping Student Recreation Center and the Ping Institute for the Teaching of the Humanities. Ping cherished, even if his old football knees sometimes refused to cooperate, Juvenal's classical ideal of *"mens sana in corpore sano."* The Ping Center is devoted to exercise and the life of the body while the Ping Institute seeks to stimulate the mind's powers of reason and imagination. Ultimately, however, his spirit will be most lastingly served by the Cutler Scholars Program, which he has led for the past decade. When fully endowed by private gifts, the program, modeled on the Morehead Scholars program at the University of North Carolina and the Rhodes Scholarship program at Oxford, will fully fund fifty students a year in one of the nation's most attractive educational opportunities for our best and brightest.

Florence Riffe, working from a lengthy year-by-year narrative of the period from 1975 to 1994 compiled by Peg Black, has fashioned a compact, compelling account of the university and its president during the Ping years. Most of the events I have touched on here she recounts in the full details of their historical unfolding. It's a remarkable story of a man and an institution, and one I think that will be of interest not only to alumni and friends of the university but to all those interested in higher education and institutional leadership.

Samuel Crowl

PREFACE

The view from Charles Ping's office chair in 1975 was the same as it had been for all of Ohio University's previous seventeen presidents: it faced the door through which hundreds of participants in university operations entered to advise, opine, inform, query, or challenge. Ping's setting also echoed that of his predecessors: a backdrop of books whose titles served as guides for his mission as president of Ohio University, the oldest public university west of the Appalachian Mountains. The vantage differed in one aspect, though. That icon of executive status—the desk—was absent. In its place was an antique table broad enough to seat eight people comfortably. Vernon R. Alden, who from 1962 to 1969 served as the fifteenth president of the university, had also used the table in the president's office. Carved in elaborate patterns along its perimeter and around its central pedestal, the walnut-stained, veneered table had been a gift to the university from Mrs. S. M. Evans, mother of Mrs. John Calhoun Baker. When Mrs. Baker's husband retired as Ohio's fourteenth president in 1962, Mrs. Evans presented the table to the university to honor her accomplished son-in-law. It had no drawers for files, no compartments for writing implements, no corner for a phone and wires. Ping kept it clear of the accouterments of mediated communication, preferring instead to establish a preserve for face-to-face communication in the center of his office.

Despite the seeming immutability of the daily mechanics of steering a major university, changes occurred during Dr. Ping's presidency that distinguished his administration from the previous seventeen. In governance, credentials of the student body, structure and quality of academic programs, financial health, and the physical campus beyond the President's Office in Cutler Hall, changes diffused across campus from the table where consensus was modeled.

Merely listing concrete improvements, however, obscures the major points. The explanation for the philosophical legacy of Charles Ping has its roots in a problem he described in his very first Convocation Address—the design of Ohio's organizational structure, which "suggests coordinate and equal functions. This basic flaw produces tension and conflict as a result of the denial of the primacy of the educational function." The answer had become clearer by September 1977; in his third Convocation Address, Ping told the story of a student who had asked him: "How will you judge yourself as president? What's really important to you?" He admitted later that his response had unfolded as an epiphany: "The measure? Whether we can find a basis for community, that is, a convictional and functional consensus for our life together." Thus the search for community elicited by a student evolved into a philosophy of community, a holistic theme of agreement that the university is larger than the sum of its parts, and that this ideal should shape developments in all of the university's segments.

The pages herein chart those developments. Following a brief biography, five chapters detail Ping's major accomplishments. The chapter "Collegially Speaking" begins with an explication of Ping's philosophy of leadership, a model that employs planning for change and decision-making grounded in the best of liberal education. The chapter then chronicles the governance of Ohio University through the Ping years, emphasizing the implementation of a holistic planning process to manage the continual evaluation and reformation Ping saw as the pathway to excellence. The first step, however, was coaxing the faculty away from forming a labor union that would have denied the university its collegiality. The tone was solidified in the President's Office itself in the form of the 11:30 Group. The people who reported directly to Ping met with him every day for thirty minutes at the round antique table to discuss issues before the community. Building on the foundational concept of *planning for change*, members of the university community learned that changes founded on shared goals and steered by facts and figures progressed more successfully than courses launched as mere reactions to external forces. This melding of measures and money with education was implemented via the University Planning Advisory Committee (UPAC), a Ping legacy that continued to operate through the end of the century. Though UPAC was conceived in an era of dwindling resources for the university, its efficacy through flush times as well positioned Ohio to weather the inevitable return of tight money. Faculty fared well in more specific ways, too, as detailed in the discussion on changes in the reward system, faculty leave, and retirement.

Changes at Ohio University that fall outside the purview of collegial centrality are explained in "Developing History." In addition to constructions, demolitions, and acquisition of a new campus at The Ridges, the chapter describes innovations in areas as diverse as the university calendar, the debt structure, and variances from routine generated by forces beyond the university's immediate control, such as blizzards and protracted labor strikes. During Ping's tenure as president, Ohio University also celebrated its 175th anniversary (1979) and the bicentennial of the passage of the Northwest Ordinance (1987). Details of two fund-raising drives complete the look at efforts distinctive to Ohio University. Aiming to endow the university with the means to strengthen its community for years to come, the 1804 Campaign (begun in 1978) and the Third Century Campaign (begun in 1988) increased the university's endowments an astounding forty-fold.

The chapter "Students by the Scores" details the advancements made not only in attracting better students to Ohio University, but also in enriching their educational experience once they enrolled. Selective admissions accounted for the improved profile of Ohio University students, as measured by test scores and high school grades. As essential as raising the admission bar, though, was the elevation of academic excellence as a defining element of Ohio University's identity. Major manifestations of the new academic climate were the creation of General Education requirements, the creation of the Cutler Scholars Program, the expansion of faculty advising of students, and the spike in demands, such as increasing the number of hours to graduate and removing the freshman ABC grading scale. Students also benefited from participatory governance via the revival of Student Senate, implementation of the Code of Conduct, and a variety of learning and leadership opportunities in residence life.

"Pioneering Knowledge" focuses on academic programs and research at Ohio University that augmented the more traditional structures typical of most state universities. The list is headed by the School of Osteopathic Medicine, which moved from idea to reality with a speed unprecedented in medical education. The bill creating the school completed its journey through the Ohio legislature as Ping was packing his bags for Athens in the summer of 1975. Another program unique to the university is ILGARD—known by its acronym instead of its title, Institute for Local Government Administration and Rural Development—which began in 1981. Two other ideas designed to bolster regional development were the Innovation Center (1983), an incubator for converting ideas into profit-making ventures, and the Edison Biotechnology Institute (1984), one of nine in the state of Ohio. Though several Ohio University programs matured without the state's Selective Excellence funding, they clearly improved because of it—a phenomenon that is explained in the chapter. Also unique to Ohio University were new structures that reflected new emphases in society: the College of Health and Human Services and the Division of Lifelong Learning.

Internationalization of the curriculum was achieved through Ping's personal efforts to establish new partnerships or to bolster existing ones with educational centers half a world away, such as the Mara Institute in Malaysia and Botswana's Department of Education. Various exchanges between Ohio and the world, including the Contemporary History Institute, are explicated in the chapter "Enlightening Interdependence." Also included is a description of concomitant internationalization in library acquisitions and collections.

The volume closes with a summary of Ping's achievements. "Rebuilding a University" begins with the budget battles peculiar to public higher education in Ohio and Ping's leadership role therein. The narrative returns to Charles Ping at the end of his tenure as president. Tributes from a variety of people who worked with him reveal the depth of their conviction that he was a paragon among college presidents. The creation of two campus legacies—a recreation center and an institute for the teaching of the humanities—is reported, as well as the movement to name both in his honor. The chapter includes a profile of Claire Oates Ping, who used her talents to make the larger community a better place to live. Last is a look at Ping as Trustee Professor, when the man who had saved the university became one of its everyday citizens.

ACKNOWLEDGMENTS

Several people helped me navigate through nineteen years of Ohio University history, which, though surveyed, had not been mapped. I am grateful to the following people who read portions of the manuscript and provided advice and insight: Charles Ping, Claire Ping, Alan Geiger, Sam Crowl, Betty Hollow, and Jack Ellis. Others patiently answered my questions: Jim Bruning, Bill Smith, Catherine Steiner, and Helen Gray. Elizabeth Story in Alden Library verified names and identifications that were the most difficult to track. Dozens of others bore with me, in the aisles of grocery stores, at social gatherings, at addresses in cyberspace, and via phone as I sought facts, figures, and clarity. The role of David Sanders, director of the Ohio University Press, deserves special mention. As Athens's premier expert on books *per se* and editing in particular, David always had time for my questions.

Special thanks, and love, are reserved for my husband Daniel Riffe, a man who can measure any concept but whose patience is immeasurable; and to our daughter Eliza Riffe, whose senior year in high school and departure for the University of Chicago had to share attention with *A Philosophy of Community;* and to our son Ted Riffe, whose move to Columbus had to be planned around writing deadlines.

Peg Black, author of a year-by-year record of the Ping years, supplied much of the documentation for this book. As director of University News Services at Ohio University from 1970 to 1992, Peg dispatched both visual and verbal information about the university to both internal and external audiences. Beginning with her first post as assistant director of the former campus news bureau in 1963, she was at the epicenter of every newsworthy happening that made its way into the archives of the institution she loved and served until her retirement and beyond. Peg wrote, edited, or assigned many of the first drafts of Ohio University history during the terms of four presidents—Alden, Sowle, Crewson, and Ping. For the past year she has graciously cheered me on as I used her historical compass to manifest the achievements of Charles Ping. The Ohio University community owes a debt of gratitude to Peg for her professionalism, dedication, and generosity. Thank you, Peg.

DeeDee Riffe

THE EDUCATION OF
CHARLES JACKSON PING

A Doctor of Philosophy degree in Philosophy is the hallmark credential of Charles Jackson Ping. It also demarcates an irony in the story of a six-foot-five-inch football tackle who had hoped to launch his college career on a football scholarship in the Southeastern Conference.

Timing of opportunities explains a lot. A college president persuaded the seventeen-year-old graduate of Murphy High School in Mobile, Alabama, to enroll at Rhodes College (then Southwestern at Memphis) in 1947. Rhodes President Charles Diehl had asked, "Do you want a *degree* or an *education*?" the day he met with Charlie and the Ping family at their home in historic Mobile, one of the oldest cities in America. In town to preach at the Government Street Presbyterian Church, President Diehl had heard from parishioners about the football standout who was waiting for an offer.

Long appreciated in the Deep South as a mecca of liberal education, Rhodes provided the setting, the traditions, and the curriculum for the education behind Ping's first academic degree. He played football, too, despite two knee surgeries before he turned twenty. The surgeries, it turned out, were not lifetime cures; his knee problems would recur for decades.

Rhodes supplied Ping with more than a liberal arts education and the chance to play tackle on the gridiron. The college's affiliation with the Presbyterian Church contributed to his goal of studying theology. But before entering the Louisville Presbyterian Theological Seminary, he married fellow Rhodes student Claire Oates in the little Presbyterian church in Kerrville, just north of Memphis, where he had preached as a Rhodes-supplied minister. When Claire was a freshman at Rhodes, he noticed her. She noticed him. Their first date was November 19, 1949, the day before Claire's birthday. Ping graduated from Rhodes and married Claire on the same day in June 1951, twin milestones he described in the 1994 commencement address at the university.

Becoming an ordained minister allowed Ping to officiate at marriages, which he has done only for special friends—with one exception. One hot summer Saturday, Alan Geiger, campus planner and later assistant to the president, came into Ping's office in Cutler with a plea. "Please listen to the request of a recent graduate in the outer office," Geiger said. Both men had been dispatching paperwork chores on a day when the phones did not ring and other offices were closed. Ping agreed. The young man who entreated the president for the next few minutes turned out to be a groom without a minister. The couple, and their two fuming families, all dressed up, had been stood up in Galbreath Chapel and were sweltering there still while the groom roamed the campus in search of help. Finding Cutler the only building open on the College Green, the groom happened upon Geiger and poured out his plight.

"I'm already married," the young man breathlessly explained to Ping. "But my wife and I eloped. So I promised her mother we'd get married in a church with a minister. Well, the Athens minister who agreed to marry us is more than an hour late and we can't find him." Ping walked back to the chapel with the student and found the groom's family upstairs, the bride's family downstairs, and not a smile in sight. After chatting with the bride and her family, then the groom's family, Ping agreed to perform the ceremony, though he had no prayer book and had to improvise some of the language. "Since the couple was already married, I didn't mind drawing on memory for their second round of vows," Ping said. It was not the first time he had saved the day, nor would it be the last, but it is probably the most epigrammatic example.

At seminary after the Oates-Ping wedding, Claire worked as the registrar while Charlie immersed himself in his studies, attaining a level of excellence that earned him a doctoral fellowship to study philosophy at Duke University. In the half-year interim before the Pings moved to Durham, North Carolina, Ping served as both chaplain and football coach at Culver Academy in Indiana. At Duke, Claire worked as administrative assistant to the chairman of the Department of Biochemistry, Dr. Philip

Handler, with whom the Pings maintained a close friendship for years. In fact, Dr. Handler was a guest of honor at Ping's inauguration as president of Ohio University in March 1976. By that time President of the National Academy of Science, Handler delivered a Kennedy Lecture that weekend. In a twist of fate in 1981, detailed in the chapter "Pioneering Knowledge," Handler would save the day for faculty researchers at Ohio University.

Three years of study at Duke ended with Ping's search for a teaching position at a small liberal arts college. In autumn 1957 he accepted a job teaching philosophy at Alma College in Michigan. Three Pings moved to Alma, for son Andy had been born in Durham. Daughter Ann Shelton was born in Alma. At Alma College, the professor completed two academic tasks he would revisit at Ohio University: designing a senior capstone course for the core curriculum and serving on a team that developed a long-range educational plan for the college. Another event before the Pings left Alma became a touchstone in their lives: the purchase of a cottage on the shore of Grand Traverse Bay in northwest Michigan. The Pings bought the house when they lived in Alma from Dr. William Boyd, the man who had hired Ping at Alma College. Every summer—through parents' career moves, children's moves, even grandchildren's activities—the annual rendezvous at the permanent home in Eastport was a constant for the Ping family.

Ping's administrative experience at Alma appealed to the administrators of Tusculum College. The Pings headed back South to the independent liberal arts school that had opened in 1794 as the oldest coeducational Presbyterian college in America. Though the job description was "dean of faculty and vice president for academics" (with some teaching, too), circumstances put Ping in the president's office for one year. One of his accomplishments was coaching the faculty team that represented Tusculum at the Danforth Summer Institute on Liberal Arts Education, an annual event in Colorado Springs that Ping would recommend years later to faculty at both Central Michigan University and Ohio University.

After becoming president of Central Michigan University, Boyd hired Ping again in 1969 to serve as provost. Originally a teachers' college, Central Michigan was finalizing its expansion to university status. President Boyd prevailed over others who were negotiating with Ping, despite the fact that the Tusculum vice president was reluctant to move to a public university. Boyd's appeal was one he knew might work with such a staunch advocate of liberal education: he wanted Ping to help Central Michigan develop a liberal arts core as the centerpiece of its curriculum. After all, Boyd reasoned, 80 percent of America's college students were enrolled in public universities. It was easy enough to head a school whose sole purpose was liberal arts. The real challenge lay in establishing liberal arts as the core in a curriculum making the transition from pedagogy courses to broader purposes.

Ping accepted Boyd's offer. Three weeks later Boyd called and said, "I have to tell you something." The faculty at Central Michigan had voted to unionize. "I wouldn't have gone there if I had known this was coming," Ping said years later. Instead of rising to the challenge of shaping the curriculum in the form he knew and loved, the new provost had to focus first on the details of labor relations. At that time, Central Michigan was the first of the nation's four-year, *state*-supported universities to establish a faculty union. (City College of New York, funded by the city, was first among four-year colleges to unionize, and a few two-year schools had also done so.) The fact that there were few nonindustrial models available on collective bargaining became an advantage, though it did not appear that way at first, in the administration's search for ways to implement the formidable charge. Ping and Boyd opted to form a bargaining committee composed of academic deans, contrary to the advice of others who had pioneered patterns in union relationships. In pivoting the collective bargaining structure on the academic deans, Ping hoped to preserve the best of collegiate decision making despite the inherently adversarial nature of the union structure.

The union specter did not dominate all of Ping's energies at Central Michigan, however. One window of opportunity opened at the end of his first year in Mount Pleasant: eight weeks in the summer of 1970 at the Institute for Educational Management at Harvard University's Graduate School of Business Administration. In Cambridge he learned to apply the philosophies he had always relied upon in teaching and scholarship to administrative chores that seemed wanting of such principles. The task of negotiating with a faculty union, not his happiest job, was his paradoxical ticket to the Harvard Institute for the next fifteen years, for the program needed someone experienced in dealing with faculty unions to teach others. His expertise on the topic grew in demand as American higher education grew, sometimes on an industrial model, in the years after World War II.

Other opportunities to learn new strategies in collegiate problem solving arose at Central Michigan, where rapid growth posed a host of challenges. Chief among these was incorporating one hundred new faculty positions into the fabric of a teachers' college that had evolved into a comprehensive university. More difficult administratively was finding a method for reprioritizing resources that would underwrite programs central to the university's mission, internal politics notwithstanding. Years later the experience translated into the founding of the University Planning Advisory Committee (UPAC) at Ohio and the painstaking work of crafting long-term educational plans to guide the setting of priorities.

The general education task at Central Michigan, his reason for accepting the offer in the first place, did occupy Ping's time and talents eventually. Ping traveled back to Colorado Springs for the Summer Institute for Liberal Arts Education, now sponsored by the Lilly Foundation of Indianapolis, with a team of Central Michigan faculty. The experience of developing a general education curriculum for 18,000 students at a public university did indeed contrast sharply with Ping's earlier trip to Colorado Springs from tiny Tusculum College, with its enrollment of under 1,000.

The rigors of dealing with a faculty union, exponential growth, and a re-centered curriculum earned Ping strong support to succeed Boyd, who had accepted the presidency at the University of Oregon. In the winter of 1975, Boyd therefore urged Ping to go to Harvard for more training while the search developed. Enrolling in Harvard's Advanced Management Program, Ping became a classmate of corporate managers who were poised to become corporate executive officers of the businesses they managed. In the Harvard atmosphere, Ping relished the immersion in management issues with fellow students from outside academia. A major life change seemed distant when envoys from another university appeared on the scene that winter to talk to Ping.

Ohio University was searching for its eighteenth president. Among the names suggested as candidates to the search committee was Charles J. Ping, provost of Central Michigan, who was wintering at Harvard. In nearby Boston lived Ohio's fifteenth president (1962–69), Vernon R. Alden, whose office at the First Boston Corporation was the staging area for the search committee's pursuit of Ping. Present at that meeting were Alden; Alan Booth, chair of Faculty Senate; Jody Galbreath Phillips, chair of the Ohio University Board of Trustees and of the search committee; and Edwin L. Kennedy, an alumnus devoted to his alma mater.

Reminiscences reveal that a match was in the making, and that everyone present sensed it. Phillips said she realized by mid-interview that Ping was an extraordinary candidate. She said she recalled thinking, "He can pull us out, and do it right away." Booth likewise had no doubts and returned to campus saying to other members of the search committee,

"We've found him." Ping, too, was surprised at the outcome. He left Alden's office with a serious interest in Ohio.

One episode made a memorable impact on Ping. "After the others had left, Vernon Alden took me into a back room of his office to show me something he said I'd find interesting," Ping said. On one wall was a plaque with pieces of this and that—a brick, a rock, hunks of metal. "This is my collection of things thrown through windows at me," Alden said, beaming with pride at the heat he had taken while presiding at Ohio. Yet Alden insisted to Ping that the Athens years had been the best of his life.

Charlie and Claire made an unpublicized trip to Athens to see the campus and to meet others on the search committee. Both sides had researched each other and both sides had formed impressions that were validated by the facts. Candidate Ping's strongest suit was his method of long-range planning centered on the academic program. Ohio University's strengths were its history, reputation, beauty, and academic heart. "When I asked academics their impressions of Ohio University, the response was always positive and glowing," he said, "and it was obviously a place many people loved whole-heartedly. When I asked my friends in the corporate world their impressions, I got the negatives." Countering the obvious drawback of the budget and enrollment crisis of the moment was the stalwart support of the trustees, who voted unanimously to offer the forty-four-year-old Ping the presidency of Ohio University effective September 1, 1975. The match was announced April 29.

CHAPTER ONE

COLLEGIALLY SPEAKING

Confronting the Present

The situation at Ohio University while Ping was writing his first Convocation Address stood in stark contrast to the speech's theme of optimism for Ohio's future. Ohio's enrollment had plummeted by nearly one third, from 19,314 in academic year 1970–71 to 12,841 in Ping's first year as president, 1975–76. Twin plunges in tuition and state subsidy sank the budget into deficits that forced hard decisions about what to cut. Hiring for the administrative staff was frozen, increasing the workload (and dismay) of those who were spared. For maintenance staff, every position eliminated demanded negotiations with the union that sought to protect those very jobs. At the core of the university's mission, untenured faculty whose positions had been marked for elimination waited for word of the new president's stance on whether they would be fired or retained.

As if that litany were not woeful enough, the residence hall system was approaching bankruptcy owing to a 40 percent drop in occupancy. Rather than operate half-full dorms, the administration closed several buildings, and later retooled others for different uses, in order to reduce debt service and operating expenses. Compounding the residence hall bust was the priority of the payments due on $48 million in bonds that had financed construction of new residence halls during the university's expansion in the 1960s, when no one could foresee the gestalt of causes that produced the 1970s enrollment drop.

To complicate matters further, the tight money morass of the early 1970s formed the backdrop for the debut of a budgetary process that pitted units against each other, at a time when the university could least afford such divisiveness. Intending to instill a semblance of openness into decision making, the administration proffered open budget hearings as the way to determine which units were most in need of budget infusions. Like shipwrecked crew members arguing to stay in the proverbial overcrowded lifeboat, unit heads pled their cases. One member of Faculty Senate said the process "divided us all into departmental fiefdoms, fighting among ourselves for survival." Then President Claude R. Sowle resigned abruptly. Forced to draft an interim president, the trustees turned to Harry Crewson, professor of economics, who had served as president of Athens City Council for five years. Though the university's size, complexity, and budget dwarfed the city's, Dr. Crewson had earned the respect of a wide range of major players. Despite the respite in tension brought by the interim president, the faculty nevertheless moved toward unionization.

What had caused the calamity Ohio University faced by 1975? Pundits blamed the university's problems on the series of campus demonstrations against the Vietnam War and on misbehaviors that bore no relationship to pacifist idealism, culminating in the closing of Ohio University after the May 1970 shootings at Kent State University. Though the antiwar movement had swept the entire nation, there is no question that its excesses were more extreme at certain universities. Ohio University was one of the campuses that bore the brunt not only of radical behavior, but also of the negative publicity that followed. Admissions counselors reported anecdotal evidence from parents of prospective students that seemed to validate public perceptions of Ohio University students' rowdiness as a cause for the declining enrollments at Ohio well after the war wound down.

A tarnished image, however, was not the sole explanation for Ohio's enrollment debacle. An exacerbating interaction of results from the proliferation in the number of state-supported colleges and universities hurt older residential institutions of higher education. Acting on the premise that students should have educational choices in close proximity to home, particularly in urban areas, the state expanded the number of institutions of higher education. The urban colleges hurt Ohio University in particular. In the 1960s and 1970s, the number of state universities in Ohio doubled, from six to twelve. In addition, the state established a new structure of two-year community and technical colleges. Examples from two of Ohio's largest metropolitan areas tell the story. In Cleveland in 1963, Cuyahoga Community College boasted the largest first-day enrollment ever for a U.S. community college. The next year, Cleveland State University was created as a state-assisted school when it absorbed Fenn College and its facilities. In Dayton in 1966, Sinclair Community College was granted state-assisted status by the Ohio Board of Regents. The next year Wright State University in Dayton received the legislature's approval to become a full-fledged university after the merger of former branches of Miami and Ohio State proved it could attract students. Enrollment figures show that the number of students from Cleveland and Dayton at Ohio University dropped by half in the decade after the higher education market was expanded by the state legislature.

Other states played the university expansion game, too, further siphoning off enrollment at Ohio, which had long attracted out-of-state students. But the real brake on the flow of out-of-state students to Ohio came in the form of tuition surcharges for those who might have crossed the Ohio River from mid-Atlantic states. The surcharge, passed by the legislature in 1977, effectively doubled tuition for non-Ohio residents. At the enrollment peak in 1970, Ohio University's head count of more than 19,000 students included about 8,000 from states other than Ohio. After the surcharge took effect, out-of-state enrollment was halved.

As administrators and faculty rolled up their sleeves to salvage their university's future in the wake of negative publicity, declining enrollments, and new competition, the prospects for recovery seemed slim. Ping, however, said with characteristic optimism that he was not discouraged.

Shaping the Future

In his first Convocation Address September 19, President Ping elaborated on the vision he had showcased while a candidate. Ohio University would need to

1. Define its purpose,
2. Explore methods for a decision-making process that would focus on priorities but keep an eye on long-range planning,
3. Redesign the organizational structure to eliminate the appearance of equal functions among the supporting cast of the university's educational function,

4. Face the reality that enrollment jolts would no longer revive the budget, and
5. Get over the crisis of confidence and the inaccurate perception that Ohio University's future was necessarily bleak.

On the heels of an opening disclaimer about his reluctance to jump to conclusions, Ping revealed the breadth and depth of his research on Ohio University in an elaboration of those five themes. Regarding its purpose, he emphasized the primacy of the educational function. "As a university we do not have an educational program together with all these other programs [residence halls, maintenance, research, athletics, health care, and on and on] because we are an educational program. Whatever we do, whatever resources are invested, the test of legitimacy is their contribution to this mission."

In formulating a process for decision making, he pointed out the need to "de-polarize the process as much as possible and focus clearly on the issue of priorities." To achieve this, Ping cited three requisite steps:

1. Develop a foundation for planning that incorporates the purpose or mission of the university into goals for the future,
2. Build on a broad base of participation *per se* but with narrower responsibility for review of plans, and
3. Rely on sound information—data, analytical studies, objective assessments—to inform judgments. In this way, the university could retreat from the fractiousness of equal "special interest groups" and install accountability along with input from people with a stake in the outcomes.

Discrediting the outmoded organizational structure that had failed to keep pace with rapid change in universities, Ping made two immediate recommendations for change. One was to reinstate the position of provost in order "to emphasize the primacy of our educational mission" and to give the position shared responsibility with the president. The second was the creation of a University Council to serve as a cabinet to advise the president on policy. Not the same as the 11:30 Group, this council included representatives from constituencies who did not necessarily report directly to the president.

He explicated the theme of budgets and enrollment beyond the pale of the current crisis. Citing research on trends, Ping explained that higher education was facing "a leveling of society's support" and that it could not "expect an enlarged share of the nation's wealth given other priorities for public funding." More central to the problem was the relationship between state funding and enrollment in public higher education. Since the state subsidy depended on the number of students enrolled in courses, an obvious piece of the fix was to try to boost enrollment. Studies that might provide clues about enrollment trends contradicted each other in their predictions, both about numbers of future students and about the educational needs of these future student populations. There was, however, agreement on one point—that the number of traditional students (aged eighteen to twenty-two) in traditional programs (full-time, degree-credit) was leveling off and would decline in the 1980s. Ping called for members of the Ohio University community "to adjust our expectations to realistic figures of student populations" and "to recognize that our mission is to serve a broader student body."

The concluding theme, the future of Ohio University, was as positive as it was surprising. Recounting evidence that the image problems of the university had not diffused past Ohio's borders, Ping said that the negative self-perception was simply inaccurate. In other states, academicians thought well of Ohio University. "The place to start is here on campus with an honest and critical but nonetheless firm belief in ourselves and our future."

Yet the address was more than a historical review, more than a recitation of current issues in higher education, more than a blueprint for future tasks. The speech was an invocation to hope, a call to "confront the future, to plan and work together to shape the future." Ping chose a phrase to share with the audience that had sustained him during the anti–Vietnam War crisis in the spring of 1970. Scrawled in chalk on a campus sidewalk, where he saw it only because his head was bent low in despair, were the words: "There are people to be loved and tasks to be done." It was not heady philosophy, more a declaration of faith, but he acted on it and thereby offered the Ohio University community a future no one could have sensed in 1975.

Governing without a Union

One of the more difficult phone calls of Ping's career was the one he received from the president of Central Michigan University shortly after

Ping had accepted the offer to become provost there. The faculty had voted to unionize. Collective bargaining in the mode of labor unions was new to university decision making in the late 1960s. In fact, Central Michigan was the first of the nation's four-year state-supported schools to enact a faculty union. The situation was somewhat different when he accepted the offer to become president of Ohio University. Ping knew that Ohio's Faculty Senate had polled tenure-track faculty and had found that a majority favored a union. Conducted in December 1974 during Dr. Crewson's interim presidency, the poll was informal, tantamount to a straw vote. The results, however, seemed to countervail the exploratory intention of the poll: 75 percent of the faculty voted in favor of a union, and 83 percent of the faculty had voted. In his first decision after being named president, even before he took over the job, Ping asked the trustees to cancel a proposal to terminate the faculty whose positions had been identified as expendable. This was one cost-saving measure, he argued, that would cost much more in the long run in eroded faculty confidence in the new administration. Equally important to him was the centrality of the educational function to the university's mission. Faculty should be the last personnel group to consider for workforce reduction.

When Ping addressed Faculty Senate on the matter in September, he reported that he had already met with representatives of the Ohio Education Association (OEA) and the American Association of University Professors (AAUP), both of which were potential bargaining agents. He further reported that the agenda for the November board of trustees meeting would include a request to authorize a monitored election on the matter, with a follow-up election to select a bargaining agent if the vote was affirmative. He made one request of the faculty for the interval between mid-September and mid-November—study.

He asked Faculty Senate Chair Richard Bald from the political science department to appoint a nonpartisan committee whose assignments began with compilation of a reading list. (In an irony too striking not to mention, the list included items by one of the nation's most widely read authorities on faculty unions—Dr. Charles J. Ping.) Articles pro and con, past and present, were put on reserve in the library in the same fashion as readings for students. Another assignment in the study of unionization was field trips to campuses that already had unions in place, at which study committee members interviewed both faculty and administrators for candid assessments of the union process. The fact-finding missions complete, the study committee presented its findings in open forums on the Athens campus.

Impatience erupted at one forum. Some senators confronted the president on the need for a second vote. When pressed for a reason to conduct a second vote, Ping answered, "Because the vote was not monitored by an outside agency and therefore was too informal to comply with labor relations standards." Furthermore, he continued, collective bargaining was so new to universities that the issue demanded study of the most recent developments so that an informed decision could be assured.

"I could live with a faculty union," Ping said then and later. "I had lived with one for six years at Central Michigan. In some ways, a union makes a president's job easier. It gives the administration greater authority in decision making. The ultimate variable, however, is the very nature of collegiality, for which union polarity is antithetical, and without which a university loses much of its distinctive governance."

The pro-union factions, for there were two, had outside help in the form of state organizations that provided funds and advice (OEA and AAUP). The faction aligned with the OEA was predominantly young, recently tenured, and painfully cognizant that some of their colleagues had had a close call with unemployment. As the financial situation at Ohio worsened in the winter of 1975, a list had actually been compiled of untenured faculty whose contracts would not be renewed. Though Ping had persuaded the trustees not to act on the hit list, those on it did not soon forget how close they had come to getting pink slips, and not the course closeout, override variety.

The vice president of the OEA group, Assistant Professor of Philosophy Donald Borchert, explained reasons for the move toward unionization this way: "Trust and openness between the administration and faculty had broken down." Faculty members were not consulted, leaving them to perceive that "aloof managers were manipulating us." Borchert's quote on the causes of faculty disgruntlement points to *lack of collegiality*, not the paucity of pay raises, as the paradoxical source of faculty interest in a union.

Though the original straw vote on unionization suggested that 75 percent of faculty members were in a disgruntlement mode, there had always been opposition to collective bargaining. The pro-collegiality core evolved into the Committee for Independent Faculty (CIF). Following the dissemination of facts and assessments presented by the study committee, CIF members countered the polished publications of the OEA and AAUP in a simple mimeographed sheet. Disparity between costly publications and homespun broadsides of the opposing groups' literature may even have helped the CIF argument that collective bargaining would introduce outside influences to Ohio's internal affairs. Moreover, collective bargaining might subject the process of faculty merit evaluations to external administrative law review—hardly an ideal for an academic entity functioning to inspire young people to excel. Political science professor Raymond Gusteson said at the time that collective bargaining was "inappropriate for a university faculty" and that forming a union would damage Ohio University's prestige. As one of the authors of the modest, mimeographed one-pager, Gusteson said that CIF members also thought the timing of the union campaign was wrong, that Ping should be given time to demonstrate his leadership abilities.

While the various factions campaigned for or against unionization, Faculty Senate finalized plans for the February 13, 1976, election. Guidelines, which conformed to the recommendations of the American Arbitration Association, won the unanimous approval of the senate and were published in January. In an election that gave substance to the expression "too close to call," faculty cast their ballots. The vote tally of 668 ballots cast by 721 eligible voters was 354 opposed to the union, 314 in favor.

Ping's opinion, veiled throughout the six-month-long campaign, was clear in his official statement when the vote was announced. "I rejoice in the decision. Faculty bargaining—the insertion of an external bargaining agent, the language of a legal contract and the inevitable recourse to the courts—are in direct conflict with the nature of the university as a self-governing community."

Faculty Senate Chair Bald gave Ping much of the credit for the union defeat, despite the president's restraint in public discourse on the matter, or perhaps because of it. Bald's analysis included the opinion that most faculty thought that change would occur without unionization, making such a drastic fix unnecessary. Much of the faculty confidence that change would occur was a direct result of the approval of the way the new president was handling matters. Equally important for the future, faculty divisions healed rather quickly after the vote, to Bald's surprise. What the vote ultimately meant for Ohio University was summarized by Ping years later: "In rejecting bargaining, the faculty actually achieved an enduring authority and a real involvement in decision making."

Governing within the Circle

One of two initiatives Ping had pledged in the first Convocation Address was a university council that would function as an advisory cabinet. Drawn from a broad spectrum of campus constituencies, the representatives had already assembled and met in the fall of 1975. The council, however, would not be the only forum for open exchanges about managing the university. In February 1976 the president presented a diagram to the board of trustees to illustrate the changes in administrative structure he had pledged in his first Convocation Address. The figure Ping drew was a circle. Instead of a pyramid with some levels above others in both symbol and function, Ping's model captured two of the foundation stones of his educational philosophy—shared governance and primacy of the educational function—both enclosed in a holistic geometric figure. In the center of the circle were the president and provost, who shared direction of the general and academic administration and of course planning and allocations. At equidistant points on the circle around the president and provost were three support units: (1) student services, headed by a dean of students; (2) university operations, headed by a vice president; and (3) university relations, also headed by a vice president. An outer concentric circle fused the parts together into a whole in which no one unit could be autonomous.

First, however, the points on the circle had to be embodied. Three national searches were launched—for provost, dean of students, and vice president for university operations. In the provost search, the committee was chaired by Samuel Crowl of the English department, and a majority of its members were faculty. Crowl was one of the newcomers whose position had been on the faculty hit-list rescinded by pre-president Ping. Among the three names sent to the president, with no rankings or preferences attached, was Neil Bucklew, acting provost at Central Michigan University, who had served as vice provost under Charles Ping two years earlier.

"The committee was certainly aware that there was a connection [between Bucklew and Ping], but Charlie didn't say a word to anybody," Crowl recalled. "Once we put him on that list, we were aware that he would be the next provost." Nay-sayers cast aspersions on the integrity of the search, but committee members saw Bucklew's credentials as equal to those of the other two candidates on the short list. In addition, the thirty-five-year-old Ping protégé had mastered the planning and budgeting Ping had commended to Ohio faculty and trustees. The announcement of Bucklew's appointment as provost was made in April. (When Bucklew left Ohio University to become president of the University of Montana in 1981, Vice Provost for Planning James Bruning did the job, then became provost in his own right in 1982. Bruning, who served as acting president for part of the 1991–92 school year when Ping underwent knee surgery, was succeeded by David Stewart in 1993.)

The search committee for a dean of students properly included student representatives. Of the four names submitted to the president, the internal candidate was named dean. Carol Harter had been serving the university as ombudsman since 1974, but had learned about multiple components of university life as an English professor, and an awarding-winning one at that. Harter, too, was one of those spared when Ping asked the trustees not to fire faculty. (She moved to vice president of operations in 1982. Joel Rudy then moved from associate dean to dean of students and joined the circle.)

The third national search, for vice president of operations, also resulted in a designee for announcement in April. Gene Peebles, with twenty-two years of experience directly applicable to his task at Ohio, was hired from Southern Illinois University. (Subsequent holders of the title, which later evolved into vice president for administration, were Carol Harter and Gary North.)

Rounding out the three supporting points on the circle around the president and provost was vice president for university relations. Martin L. Hecht was asked to remain in that job for the time being, a major duty of which was convincing the legislature that Ohio University was a good investment for state money. However, Ping was rethinking the position *per se*, and he convened an advisory group with expertise in media relations to discuss it. A job description emerged from the advisory group's meetings that charged the vice president of university relations with coordinating news services, alumni relations, university publications, and fund-raising. Hired to fill the reconceptualized job in October 1977, Wayne Kurlinski was charged by Ping with "getting a handle on the whole problem of public misperception of Ohio University." (Kurlinski's successor in 1984 was Martha Turnage, who in turn was succeeded by Adrie Nab in 1992.)

The people whose positions marked the segments on Ping's circular model of administration met with him daily, Monday through Friday. At 11:30 each workday they gathered in the President's Office in Cutler Hall at the round antique table. Ping liked the symbolism of the table, "but I liked the functionalism more. At a round table, people can see each other face to face. It encouraged people to talk to each other and not just to me," he said of the team-building effort.

The 11:30 Group, as they soon began to be called, spent the last thirty minutes of each morning in an exchange about issues most important to each person. Substitutes were not allowed at the meetings, and members who missed a meeting were responsible for catching up—not by taking the president's time, but by asking fellow circle members—much like the classroom policy most faculty demanded of students. The rules were unwritten, but Rudy later said everyone understood that negative comments were unacceptable and that presenting problems without recommending solutions was prohibited.

The team assembled, Ping designated an even broader circle of key players to participate in crafting the first educational plan for Ohio University.

Educating for Change—The Educational Plan of 1977

Throughout the 1976–77 academic year, members of the Ohio University community worked together on the first Educational Plan of the Ping administration. Dozens of faculty and staff worked for hundreds of hours to write a Mission Statement, an Environmental Statement (which described current and future conditions in higher education), and a long-range Goals Statement for Ohio University. Some wrote, some critiqued, all did their homework. A few on the sidelines grumbled, using words like "pointless," "ridiculous," and "overkill" to describe the creation of the three-part plan. Formalizing statements of what some viewed as obvious was not the point. Provost Bucklew captured the effort's face validity this way: "By having goals established, we can determine how to move toward them. It will mean that University decisions will be based on a vision of the future that can be realized."

The finished product, a ten-year plan, was presented to the board of trustees for approval in October 1977. The Mission Statement, written by a committee appointed by Ping, stated the overall purpose of the university before specifying the institution's functions in undergraduate education; in graduate and professional education; in scholarship, research, and creative activity; and in the extended community.

> Mission Statement
> Ohio University is a public university providing a broad range of educational programs and services. As an academic community, Ohio University holds the intellectual and personal

growth of the individual to be a central purpose. Its programs are designed to broaden perspectives, enrich awareness, deepen understanding, establish disciplined habits of thought, prepare for meaningful careers and, thus, to help develop individuals who are informed, responsible, productive citizens.

Surveying the environment of higher education demanded research, including a close reading of the Ohio Board of Regents 1976 Master Plan for the decade. Six study topics yielded findings that informed the Educational Plan's Environmental Statement:

1. Forecasts on financing for the next decade,
2. Alternative sources of revenue,
3. Recommendations for higher education distilled from state and national reports,
4. Projections for educational trends,
5. The changing characteristics of students, and
6. Job prospects for graduates.

Authors of the six reports were Joseph Tucker, James Perotti, and Edward Baum from the provost's office and three deans—Sam Goldman, College of Education; Gerald Silver, College of Business; and Donald Flournoy, University College.

Appendix A contains the complete list of the 103 goals included in the first educational plan. Though tucking them away is an invitation not to read them, it would be useful to peruse them at this point to get a sense not only of the issues important in 1977, but also of the thoroughness with which participants completed the task. Moreover, portions of the remainder of this book explain how many of the goals were indeed reached. In addition, Ping himself commented on progress toward the goals time and time again in his Convocation Addresses, those annual state-of-the-university speeches that showcased the progress of the institution. For here and now, summaries will suffice. The goals were divided into nine categories, five focused on academic matters and four focused on supporting units:

- Liberal and Fine Arts Education, by Samuel Crowl, English
- Graduate and Professional Education, by Sven Linkskold, Psychology

- Science and Technology, by Nicholas Dinos, Chemical Engineering
- Health and Human Services, by Donald Fucci, Hearing and Speech
- Lifelong Learning and Regional Higher Education, by George Klare, Psychology
- Residence Life Programs and Services, by James Hartman, Teacher Education
- Academic Support, by William Allen, Associate Dean, University College
- General Administration, by Dale Mattmiller, Hudson Health Center Director
- Student Services, by John O'Neal, Registrar

Though specificity was essential within each category, certain refrains are repeated throughout the lists. From the five academic areas, goals pertaining to teaching and scholarship emphasized the importance of a liberal arts education, a core of general education courses, and careful advising of students as fitting and proper, regardless of a unit's primary mission. Also appearing in different words in different places are references to methods that permit students to apply what they have learned, whether in the classroom or beyond. Another overriding goal mentioned by all the authors was that of assessment—not only to comply with someone else's notion of accountability, but also to measure performance and progress as well as to stay abreast of changes, whether in academic trends or in student needs. The concept of flexibility emerges from several goals: the expressed determination to be ready to combine forces with other units, to forge partnerships with those outside the university, or to make whatever changes might be necessary for improvement. Authors can be forgiven in many instances for crafting some goals that seem like a wish list—for new facilities, new configurations, new administrative support—in order to achieve state-of-the-art status in their respective fields.

In the four categories not directly aimed at teaching and scholarship, the goals reflect a sense of community, of a partnership with faculty, in helping students learn and develop, albeit in a supporting role that complements teaching. The necessity for adequate library holdings and services, computer hardware and networks, and student residential programs and activities pervades the lists. As on the academic side, the support units' goals include assessments and evaluations.

Of course "getting better" was the ultimate goal of all the faculty and staff who helped write the educational plan, but the lists of narrower targets in categories within closer range would distill decision making and make achievements more discernable. As important as the product was the process, one that had encouraged participation by any member of the university community willing to lend a hand in writing a prescription for Ohio University's health.

Summarizing the Themes of the Community

In September 1977, while he was writing his Convocation Address, Ping read and reread the goals, pondered the view of a community they drew, and extracted six major themes, which became the text of his 1977 address. Two years later he reviewed those themes in his 1979 Convocation Address, citing specific evidence that progress was being made and that a sense of community was emerging:

1. *The Commitment to the Idea of a University and to being a Residential College Community.* More precisely, Ping homed in on the heart of the university's function. "The goals reaffirm teaching as the primary role of the university. The intellectual and personal development of the individual student is our reason for being," he said.
2. *Commitment to Quality and to the Making of Judgments.* Eschewing growth for growth's sake, Ping emphasized that expansion in size would occur "only when consistent with demands of high standards." He also underscored the need for change in a changing world, a given that would force the university "constantly to critique and revise what we do." Making judgments, what he called "hard decisions," and developing instruments for assessing performance would in turn "enhance public and private confidence and support."
3. *The Commitment to Intellectual Community, to the Interaction and Integration of Knowledge.* Lamenting the process of learning by "bits and pieces" that opposes the capacity to synthesize, Ping decried the fragmentation that academic departmentalization can generate and called for courses that embraced more than one traditional discipline. Recognizing the traditional reward structure as an impediment to interaction, he also suggested a review of fac-

ulty evaluations to encourage the development of concrete activities on campus aimed at integrating separate disciplines and the faculty within them, not in mergers, but in efforts supplemental to routines.

4. *The Commitment to International Community, to Education for Interdependence.* Two events on campus threw a spotlight on international education in 1978–79—the visit by a delegation of educators from China and the hosting of the World Communications Conference. Though the president spoke with pride of Ohio University's role in these headline-making events, he emphasized that "the day-to-day work to open our eyes and the eyes of our students to the literal shrinking of this planet" was more important. Ping cited the fact that 900 students from eighty nations were studying at Ohio University in fall 1979. Add travel and study abroad by faculty and the yield was a community that reflected Earth's diversity.

5. *The Commitment to Lifelong Learning and to the Creation of a Broad Community of Learners.* Describing Ohio University as an alternative approach to the urban university in serving older students, Ping praised the institution's move toward new delivery systems for instruction in addition to expanded offerings at its branch campuses. The experimentation in content and delivery not only served the region, he said, but also positioned Ohio as a leader in "a new era of a learning society, where education becomes increasingly part of all life."

6. *The Commitment to Educational Justice, to being a Just and Socially Responsive Community.* Pledging to improve Ohio University's record in educating women and minorities, Ping called recent efforts only a beginning. "We are an educational institution. The best that we can provide is educational opportunity," he said, in order to "open doors closed by prejudice or practice." He praised initiatives in the College of Osteopathic Medicine, the Affirmative Action office (as it was then called), and faculty-staff recruitment as good first steps to redress imbalance in educational opportunity.

Throughout his summation of the six themes, Ping supplied examples of individuals whose singular efforts, when added together, yielded a total "greater than the sum of the parts." "The sum is Ohio University," Ping said, "a community of many individuals, who have come to love the University and who have been willing to invest years of their lives as students, as teachers, as deans, as counselors, as plumbers, or as presidents."

Committing to Educational Justice

One hundred years after John Newton Templeton became the first African American to graduate from college in the Northwest Territory, an auditorium was built at his alma mater that would one day bear his name. In 1928, finishing touches were completed for the January dedication of the new $300,000 auditorium on the College Green, paid for by alumni contributions. For the next sixty-five years it was known as Alumni Memorial Auditorium, or MemAud for short. In 1993, in Ping's last year as president, it was renamed the Templeton/Blackburn Alumni Memorial Auditorium, to honor the first male and female African Americans to graduate from Ohio University: Templeton, Class of 1828, and Martha Jane Hunley Blackburn, Class of 1916. In his 1979 Convocation Address, Ping reminded the audience of the university's history of striving for educational justice. "We take pride in that history," he said, then reported on efforts to continue the legacy.

When Ping had established his advisory University Council in 1975, the first topic it wanted to address was salary inequities for women and minorities, a grievance reified by the all-male cast at the University Council table (even the two students). The *Post* attacked. Women wrote angry letters. Rather than merely issuing a statement to the press, Ping waited until the next Faculty Senate meeting, a few days after the *Post*'s charge. "It is incredible that I was as insensitive as I was," he said at the public gathering of his peers. He promised to change the makeup of the council through attrition, but he didn't wait for the turnover. Within days he added two women to the council: ombudsman Carol Harter and Gwen Coleman, director of the Black Resource Center. The *Post* recanted its earlier rebuke in an editorial that praised the rare spectacle of "a public figure to admit openly and simply that he is wrong." The next nineteen years were marked by Ping's sensitivity to the role of public higher education in equalizing opportunities for women and minorities—a role society expected of its universities, he said on many occasions.

In 1978, Ping hired a new Affirmative Action director, William Y. Smith. (The name of the office changed to Institutional Equity in 1996 after Affirmative Action policies came under fire in courts and legislatures in certain states.) The position had been upgraded to Executive Assistant to the President to signify that Ping meant to be proactive in removing the barriers to academic success posed by inadequate preparation for higher education. Simply complying with equal opportunity laws would not be enough. Smith wrote an Affirmative Action plan in his first year and implemented several innovations. By 1979, Ping reported in his Convocation Address on several actions taken to prepare disadvantaged minority students for college. One was an early introduction to campus for minority students who had an interest in medical careers. Another program Smith's office sponsored in the summer was called minority introduction to college. "High school students, more than half of whom were women, were brought to campus for two weeks in an intensive program of study in math, computers, communications and composition. All were able students recommended by their high schools. Our hope was to broaden perspective on opportunities for minority men and women and to encourage them to think of Ohio University," Ping explained. Other plans included hosting students from Tuskegee Institute in Alabama, funding for salary supplements in recruiting, and a pilot program for development of faculty and staff already employed at the university who were women or minorities.

By 1981, Ping reported progress. In the Convocation Address that year he again emphasized that the university's aim was to bolster the numbers of women and minorities "in the professions and programs that historically have been characterized by limited access—medicine, business and engineering." Following the prescription of the Affirmative Action Plan, the university offered administrative internships for women and minorities, established a salary pool to make the university more competitive in recruiting, and created minority faculty fellowships. The summer program for talented high school students continued under the direction of Smith, who was then calling it MITCO (Minority Introduction to College). More specific programs were designed to address the shortage of minorities in engineering and in medicine, the latter of which developed into a national model to prepare disadvantaged students for admission to osteopathic medical schools. Recruitment efforts at the graduate level had begun to pay off in larger numbers of women and minorities. To insure that the historical hurdle of economic disadvantage was cleared, more scholarships were earmarked for women and minorities in business, engineering, and communication. Ping said the efforts via staff appointments and programs to advance the cause of educational justice were part of the university's mission. "This is where we can make our greatest contribution to social change," he said.

By 1987, universities across the nation were competing for the same pool of minority faculty and administrators, and the university's forward motion on adding African American faculty had stalled. Smith and Provost Bruning had already tried a visiting faculty idea for recruiting and a plan to install minority faculty in units that anticipated retirements. But the method that rejuvenated the process was the creation of seven tenure-track positions for African American faculty or upper-level administrators. Departments that filled one of the seven positions would receive a bonus of $5,000 for the unit's general funds. The bonus rose to $20,000 for units that filled a vacancy in an existing faculty line with an African American. To redress the drop nationally in the number of African Americans enrolling in graduate school, the Smith-Bruning plan also added $1,000 bonuses to the stipends of African American graduate students with financial need. "We have to be aggressive in getting people into the pipeline," Smith said. The results in one year helped to make up lost ground: eight new African American faculty had been hired, a ninth visiting professor had chosen to stay, and a tenth had committed to come the next year. Eight of the ten faculty hired under the Smith-Bruning incentive program were still teaching at Ohio University five years later. Similar successes were achieved in administrative recruiting. Five African Americans moved into new administrative positions, while five others filled existing posts. By 1989 Smith reported that the total number of African American faculty had increased from 53 to 80, or from 8 to 11 percent.

The university's record for hiring, retaining, and advancing women was mixed, despite the expenditure of effort, attention, and money. In 1980 Smith began collecting data for a decade-long longitudinal study on the status of women faculty and administrators. During that decade, the number of female undergraduate students had increased to 52 percent of the student body. A Women's Studies Program had been developed, similar to those at dozens of other universities. The incidences of sexual harassment and salary inequity, though diminished, still existed. Most troublesome was the lag in the number of women faculty and administrators. The hiring of women for tenure-track positions had increased 50 percent in the decade of Smith's study, but women made up only 21 percent of the total faculty by 1990. The percentage was not at all deviant from national data, Smith pointed out, despite the figures on earned doctorates. The National

Research Council reported that 35 percent of the earned doctorates in 1987–88 were awarded to women, but few universities had women faculty in numbers to match that percentage, at least not by 1990.

The reason for Ohio University's inability to attract more of the female Ph.D.s to Athens seemed to pivot on the phenomenon of dual-career marriage, combined with the location of the university. Newly minted Ph.D. women turned down offers when it became clear that there were few opportunities for their equally well-educated spouses at the university or elsewhere in Athens. Provost Bruning again used financial incentives to help solve the problem. For the departments of mathematics, chemistry, physics, and engineering (i.e., fields in which the applicant pool of women was particularly small), Bruning set aside a recruitment fund. Still, encouragement and pressure were two tools that had always complemented money in recruiting. Bruning credited Smith with "a special talent" for knowing when and where to use those supplemental skills.

One Ohio University alumna waged a one-woman campaign to attract women to the sciences. Jeanette Grasselli Brown was chair of the board of trustees in 1990–91, the year the report of Smith's study was released. A former director of research and development for Standard Oil of Ohio and later British Petroleum, Grasselli Brown was dismayed at the decline in the number of women who studied hard sciences. She provided funds to bring one or two internationally prominent scientists to Athens each year in a program called the Frontiers in Science Lectures. Grasselli Brown also funded a Cleveland-based Cutler Scholarship and research awards for students in math and sciences. Further, she pledged a deferred endowment for a faculty position in the sciences, with preference to be given to women candidates. A chemistry major in the Class of 1950, Grasselli Brown directed the university's research enhancement efforts before being named to the Ohio Board of Regents.

Three years later, new data emerged that showed improved status for women faculty. Though their percentage of the faculty was not equal to their percentage of the population, women were being promoted faster than men at Ohio University. According to Institutional Research figures for the period 1988–93, women moved up in all ranks in less time, Smith reported.

Perhaps the best evidence of Ping's personal commitment to changing the landscape at the university was the hiring of his own administrators. Dean of Students Carol Harter was the first woman to sit at the round table; three other deans appointed during his tenure as president were African American women—Dora Wilson of the College of Fine Arts,

Hilda Richards of the College of Health and Human Services, and Barbara Ross-Lee of the College of Osteopathic Medicine. Other female deans were Patricia Richard, University College; Margaret Cohn, Honors Tutorial College; and Barbara Chapman, Health and Human Services. When Ping retired, in fact, four of the ten deans on campus were women. Two other women served as vice presidents—Carol Harter, Administration; and Martha Turnage, University Relations.

Making Judgments—UPAC

Formulating goals was one thing; implementing them was another. The ten-year Educational Plan needed a process for keeping expenditures synchronized with the design drafted by all segments of the university community. As the entire process was predicated on the premise that "we must constantly critique and revise what we do," it would have to be continuous. First, the university was categorized into nineteen planning units, some academic, others service, the remainder administrative. (Over the next decade, the number of units expanded to twenty-three.) The units would submit plans listing objectives and priorities, in rank order, to cover a three-year time frame. The units' documents were then updated, adjusted, or revamped annually, depending on changing circumstances. For example, an academic unit that faced unexpected faculty departures in a sequence emphasized by the goals of the Educational Plan might be forced to shift priorities for a year or two until such gaps were closed. Most important, every objective and every priority had to be justified by showing how each conformed to the goals. Stripped of political wants and whims, the monetary needs of each unit were thus packaged as the means to advance the ends of the Educational Plan.

The structure created to make judgments about the merit of each unit's plan was called UPAC, the University Planning Advisory Committee. Though introduced in Athens in fall 1978, the planning process had been studied two years earlier by a team from Ohio University (Ping, Bucklew, Peebles, Harter, Vice Provost James Perotti, and Lyle McGeoch, vice chairman of Faculty Senate). Ohio had been one of a handful of universities invited to participate in a three-day seminar sponsored by the Kellogg Foundation in New Orleans in 1976 for the purpose of exploring methods and precepts of the planning process.

The first UPAC consisted of sixteen members, eight of them faculty, five of whom were Faculty Senate's Executive Committee. The eight non-faculty members included three members of the Deans Council, three administrators, and two students. One-third of the members would be replaced each year in order to balance continuity with fresh perspectives and, in Ping's words, "to insure the involvement of more people." Over the years, UPAC membership fluctuated from sixteen to as many as twenty-two, depending on a host of variables.

The task of UPAC was to advise the provost and the president on budget allocations. Initially there were three separate pools of money to allocate: one designated as a catch-up fund for needs described as "critical and pressing," a second to deflate inflationary distortions, and a third to boost the quality or viability of programs whose priorities matched the goals in the Educational Plan. The first reports by planning units were presented to UPAC in February 1978 for the 1978–79 academic year, along with each unit's tentative proposals for the next two years. Eventually there was only one allocation pool comprising 1 percent of the projected budget, give or take a few hundredths of a percent in some years. This 1 percent was subtracted from the budget and became the amount the units vied for each year.

UPAC decision making was easier the second year thanks to a codifying job completed by Vice Provost for Planning James Bruning (who became acting provost in 1981 and then provost after Neil Bucklew accepted a position at the University of Montana). Bruning had asked Provost Bucklew to meet him in Cutler Hall the Friday after Thanksgiving for the painstaking task of putting the entire UPAC process into writing. Bruning's Rules of Order included step-by-step instructions patterned after National Science Foundation proposals. Beginning with staff planning, the process moved to budget projections, which in turn permitted staffing projections. Proposals for awards from UPAC were submitted on a form Bruning devised, and they were judged according to evaluation criteria he listed. Bruning's standardization streamlined the annual UPAC process in three ways. It reduced the time and mental energy devoted to the packaging of proposals; it eased comparisons among proposals, as each followed the same format; and it precluded political fustian, since veering from the goals of the Educational Plan was not allowed.

After it had been used to expedite Ohio's budget and enrollment turnaround in the late 1970s, the planning process stood its real test in the 1980 recession, when red ink returned to the state and syncopated subsidies returned to its universities. Like a house battened down for a storm, Ohio

University was ready. The cuts that year were as follows: a 3 percent reduction from the prior year, a midyear 3 percent rescission, then another 1 percent rescinded—for a total 7 percent cut from the amount in the fiscal 1979–80 budget. In dollars this amounted to $2.2 million; this cut was compounded by the Legislature's failure to fund the actual enrollment for the year, resulting in a mammoth hole of nearly $6 million in the university's budget. Even though the university scrambled to make ends meet when revenues vanished, the UPAC set-aside kept innovation alive.

As the state's funding to universities became less and less predictable in the 1980s, UPAC countered with a range of funding analyses based on the potential high and low funding levels in order to cope with any eventuality. The process worked. Beyond its operational definition, the success of the planning process also gave a much-needed boost to the university's image, as those outside the community became aware of the turnaround at Ohio University.

One such notice came on May 27, 1981. Ping was in New York to attend a meeting of the American Council of Life Insurance as a member of an advisory board of university presidents. He picked up a *Wall Street Journal* and read the front-page headline: "Ohio University Finds Participatory Planning Ends Financial Chaos." Accustomed to daily scrutiny in the *Post* and the *Athens Messenger*, Ping paused at the headline, then read the thirty-eight-column-inch story by John A. Prestbo.

"While some colleges and universities across the country are in such financial straits that they are lopping off whole courses of study, firing faculty members and otherwise yanking their belts painfully tight, Ohio University, while also pinching pennies, is doing so in carefully planned rather than panicky ways," Prestbo wrote. The article held up Ohio University's planning process as the model and credited Ping, Provost Neil Bucklew, and their UPAC structure for devising a method of "shared responsibility for decision-making."

One example of a specific decision cited in the article was the top proposal of 1980, which granted a 9 percent increase in funding for graduate student stipends. The next year, the three projects ranked highest for funding by UPAC were (1) increasing teaching capability in math and computer science, (2) library acquisitions, and (3) an additional central computer processor. Low on the list was a request for a new bulldozer for shuttling coal, the university's cost-efficient energy source. Joel Rudy, from the Dean of Students Office, the chief proponent on UPAC of the machine proposal, later shrugged off the bulldozer's low ranking by UPAC. "We've been educated to think institutionally," Rudy said to the reporter.

"It was a coincidence that I was in New York when the article ran," Ping said years later, "but colleagues from the business world, most of whom pore over the *Journal*, were quick to congratulate me and engage in discussion about our planning process." The story had been pitched to the *Journal* by Wayne Kurlinski, Ohio's vice president for university relations. Though suggesting newsworthy items to the media is standard practice at universities, the news outlets themselves decide which ideas to pursue. Still, front-page coverage in the *Wall Street Journal* seemed like a coup. Kurlinksi, however, demurred, saying he was just doing his job and the *Journal* was doing its.

Several faculty and administrators were quoted, but the summary benefit was that UPAC "looked at the University as a whole and made decisions based on what would most benefit the entire institution," Prestbo wrote. Dealing with the $1.8 million reduction in state aid in 1980 did not provoke the haphazard response that the 1974 cuts had drawn, chiefly because of a planning process built on systematic decision making with widespread participation.

The *Wall Street Journal* article engendered more than cheers in Athens when the news spread. Among the administrators invited to address national forums were Ping, Acting Provost James Bruning, and Director of the Statistical Information Office (later called Institutional Research) Charles Harrington. The Ohio model also earned respect within the state. By 1982 UPAC became "a kind of trademark for Ohio University," in Bruning's words. "The chancellor of the Board of Regents, as well as OBR staff members, began telling other universities, 'Go down to Athens and see how they're doing it.' Several universities contacted us," Bruning said. By that time he was using the term *strategic* planning to describe his approach to planning, while Ping continued to use the term *holistic* planning. Using the different terms to explain how their approaches complemented each other as UPAC matured, Bruning said, "Charlie thought in big terms, the big picture. He would put all the parts in a box and move the box. My approach was to put together *strategies* to make the parts work."

By 1985 one outright imitation of the Ohio planning model had been adopted—for implementing the state incentive programs called Selective Excellence challenges. (The entire program, which had been drafted by the Ohio Board of Regents and passed by the General Assembly, is detailed in the chapter "Pioneering Knowledge.") The Academic Excellence program borrowed Ohio University's formula by earmarking 1 percent of the state subsidies for higher education as a set-aside for programs good enough to be boosted into national centers of excellence. The similarity between OBR's Challenges and UPAC was not a coincidence. Ping himself had lobbied Gov. Richard Celeste and testified in detail before the General Assembly about his model for planning.

There was other evidence to suggest that the Ohio method was working—gifts to the endowment went from $2.1 million in 1975 to $23.2 million by 1981. Only a strict constructionist would call the largesse a mere correlate of the planning process rather than a direct effect.

Though the original idea of submitting plans to UPAC had called for a long-range forecast as well as immediate plans by units, the year-to-year struggle of making recommendations in a climate of uncertain state financing had obscured attention to the three-year plans. A correction was made in the flush year of 1984–85 that was dubbed the UPAC Action Plan, a process aimed at planning three to five years into the future. Study groups had categorized goals into four themes to guide decisions: academic excellence, faculty research and scholarly activities, high recruitment standards for both students and faculty, and ways to keep up with technological change. The four themes also served as transitional goals, as implementation of the first Educational Plan segued into the drafting of the second. In the short term, units were required to address the "four agendas" in their annual plans to UPAC until the more expanded version was finalized by the Third Century Colloquium.

Assessing Quality—Institutional Impact

Though analysis of predictive variables played a central role in the planning process, merely looking ahead was not sufficient for making claims that Ohio University was making progress toward its goals. *Post hoc* measures of outcomes were necessary as well. As Ping said in his 1980 Convocation Address, "A commitment to quality is reflected in the temper of life that again and again repeats this expectation of measuring." Of all the various yardsticks held up as evidence of quality, the most difficult to read, in Ping's view, was institutional impact, or how well a university affected the intellectual and personal development of individuals—a theory called *value added*, which was borrowed from economics. Difficulty aside, the effort was essential as state and national bodies "subject to political life" took up the topic, he warned in his address. A systematic program of self-assessment was in order. Named to chair a task force to develop impact measures was Gary Schumacher, chair of the psychology department. The

Schumacher committee ultimately defined four categories of outcomes that contributed to the value added by a college degree: (1) cognitive learning, (2) emotional and moral development, (3) practical competence, and (4) direct satisfaction. The task force used a combination of measuring instruments, some nationally established and some locally produced, to capture such elusive constructs as "how much a student has learned" or "how satisfied a graduate is with his or her life."

In order to take a snapshot of changes in students' development, measures were taken during freshman and senior year, then after graduation. The longitudinal data provided (1) insights on trends in student characteristics, (2) knowledge about the impact of the university's internal efforts, and (3) information on how Ohio compared to other universities. The committee settled on six instruments initially: (1) the COMP/ACT exam (College Outcomes Measurement Project of American College Testing), a set of nationally normed instruments to assess cognitive learning; (2) the Student Involvement Questionnaire, to shed some light on satisfaction; (3) the Placement Survey, to tap alumni opinions on the utility of their Ohio degrees; (4) the Alumni Survey, to measure both practicality and satisfaction with Ohio degrees; (5) Educational Testing Service Reports, to view aggregate benchmarks of cognitive learning by Ohio students; and (6) the California Psychological Inventory, to tackle the most difficult dependent variable: emotional and moral development.

As Ping had warned, the call for such data did indeed come, first in the guise of the all-purpose term "accountability," and years later in the state's insistence on specific performance reviews. Again, Ohio was ready. What was distinctive about Ohio University's response was that faculty, exercising their governance powers, participated from start to finish.

At the turn of the century, the freshman/senior/career/alumni questionnaires were still being administered and the data were still being compiled. Beyond their face value for assessing past performance, however, the data are scrutinized by dozens of faculty and administrators to improve quality in the future. In planning program upgrades, devising strategies in recruiting, or making judgments about improvements in student services, the assessments put in place by the Institutional Impact task force have proven multifunctional. Ping had suggested precisely that in the 1980 address when he said, "The key issue is whether we can use the process of defining and examining to enhance quality. Usefulness ultimately becomes the measure for adequacy of both definition and the act of measuring."

Critiquing and Revising—Toward the Third Century

The first Educational Plan had been written with an expiration date—1987. In keeping with his philosophy of planning ahead, Ping had convened a group of faculty and administrators in 1985 to begin discussing the sequel. The goal of the Third Century Colloquium, as the three-year process was called, was to examine conditions that would affect the university in the future and to draft institutional priorities for resource allocations. In keeping with Ping's philosophy of widespread participation, the draft was written by a seventeen-member committee and was presented at a series of campus forums before it was logged onto a board of trustees agenda and adopted in January 1988.

One of the signature ideas aired at the forums was that the university would make even tougher decisions in the future as it balanced ideals with realities. The introduction of the report stated that "it is neither possible nor desirable to recreate the institution every ten years" in explaining the relationship between the 1977 Educational Plan and the 1987 refinement titled *Toward the Third Century: Issues and Choices for Ohio University*. More a position paper than a map, the report did not list specific goals and rationales thereof; instead it functioned like an intellectual fulcrum between real-world changes and the university's response options. "Rather than a blueprint for specific decisions, the report represents an analysis of structural change together with an exploration of the consequences for university planning," read the introduction.

The analysis, or External Environment section of the report, summarized salient changes in the world beyond the campus in three categories—economic, social, and educational. The state of Ohio, jolted by shifts in the manufacturing sector that had ravaged jobs in the 1980s, was counting on new relationships with its institutions of higher education to incubate new employment opportunities, primarily via technological developments and their applications. The older model of a distinctive and strong economic sector with loose ties to higher education was giving way in the "age of discontinuity" to partnerships with universities that might help Ohio remove some of the rust from the region's belt. The economic realities spread to the social arena, where increasing numbers of older students were pushed into lifelong learning by necessity. The educational environment featured adjustment to the "new world-order of interaction and interdependence," marked by an insistence on assurances that public higher education stay true to its mission "to nurture an aristocracy of talent, rather than wealth or privilege." And by the decade's end, more high school graduates were enrolling in colleges and universities to develop talents that might sustain them through a lifetime of career changes.

Against this backdrop, the members of the colloquium drafted guideposts for university planning in the four areas of the original Mission Statement: undergraduate education; graduate education; research, scholarship, and creative activity; and institutional support and services, the last a retitling of the original heading, Extended Community. The document did not stop at reaffirming the goals of the university, but broke new ground. By addressing the tensions created when traditional functions collided with challenges to their utility, the document elucidated new applications for academic traditions, giving them renewed value in a society that would need them more than ever.

In the realm of *Undergraduate Education*, the colloquium focused on nine areas:

1. *General Education.* Increased specialization in the workplace made the need for general education more essential than ever, the authors wrote. Rather than over-specialize, the successful person in the future would need a foundation of eternal verities that would not change each decade, but would actually aid adjustment to change. The prescription—a broad, liberal arts education.
2. *Disciplines and Professional Programs.* In a somewhat stern warning, the document called for limits on the development of new programs that would simply add to the breadth and diversity of offerings without contributing to the hallmark of quality. Instead, the report emphasized the need for interdisciplinary and multidisciplinary programs to expand on existing quality.
3. *Internationalization.* World interaction and interdependence would depend on a citizenry educated to think globally. Infusing the curriculum with more international content would not suffice, the report said. Students and faculty would benefit as well from more opportunities to live and work abroad for extended periods of time.
4. *Libraries.* The preface, "Education for an information age can never be a completed process," set the stage for the report's call not only for more and better materials, but also for education that recognized the importance of "information-seeking literacy for lifelong learning."

5. *Campus Life.* The report prescribed integration of residential life with educational goals, ideally via co-curricular activities centered in residence halls.
6. *Minority Access.* The university's commitment to educational justice compelled the report's authors to suggest ways to reverse the decline in the numbers of underrepresented groups at Ohio University: innovative recruitment, removal of economic barriers through financial aid, and compensatory education to insure retention.
7. *The Nontraditional Student.* The report noted that the university was positioned to reach students who combine work with study via its regional campuses, but there was more that could be done via correspondence courses and distance learning, especially as new technologies improved.
8. *Funding for Quality.* After lamenting the perpetual inadequacy of state support for attaining quality at the university, the report cautioned against using enrollment growth as an easy substitute for subsidies. Instead, the authors suggested, internal reallocations and private support were preferable strategies for generating new revenue.
9. *Values.* Going beyond a simple call for high academic standards and rigorous codes of conduct, this section of the report reiterated the necessity for continual measurement of program quality followed by judgments about program continuation. In addition, the authors articulated a quest for developing twin values in its students—a sense of purpose larger than the individual and a feeling of obligation to use one's talents and education.

In that quadrant of the Mission Statement titled *Graduate Education*, the *Toward the Third Century* report focused on seven topics:

1. *The Relation to Undergraduate Education.* After eschewing the option of sacrificing undergraduate quality for graduate program growth and arguing against the creation of a type of bicameral university with undergraduate and graduate divisions, the authors offered a solution. Getting undergraduate students involved in research would bridge the two domains, since research is the path to new knowledge and the hallmark of informed teaching at any level.

2. *Professional Training.* The report acknowledged the need for the university to offer programs for the professions, but the concept of balance was clearly spelled out in the caution to maintain "balance between training in specific skills and educating for scholarly inquiry."
3. *Medical Education.* The report pointed out the acute need for physicians in underserved areas like Southeast Ohio en route to recommending a better integration of medical curriculum with the premedical courses in the College of Arts and Sciences.
4. *Interdisciplinary Programs.* Twin practical reasons informed the call for more programs that crossed traditional discipline lines: saving money by pooling resources and avoiding needless duplication. The real benefit, however, would be to create new and attractive programs.
5. *International Connections.* Balancing a predicted surge in students and faculty coming and going abroad was the admission that certain forces might work against more internationalization of graduate programs. Cultural, financial, and political barriers notwithstanding, the statement argued that the university should not only maintain its international connections, but also defend them if need be.
6. *Faculty and Staff Renewal.* After recognizing that the rates of knowledge growth and knowledge obsolescence magnified the need for faculty renewal, the report emphasized the need for new funds that would give faculty release time to stay abreast or get ahead in their fields. One example of renewal lauded by the authors was the Tier III seminar experience, which created sustained interaction among faculty, a benefit in and of itself. Moreover, several faculty discovered that the interaction with colleagues from other disciplines opened up new intellectual directions to explore.
7. *Resources for Graduate Study and Research.* Concentrating on library holdings and access to equipment, this section promoted more sharing among cash-limited universities. Interdependence, recognized as an impetus for resource sharing in other arenas, also pertained to the building of collections of materials and the operation of major laboratories, the authors said. In the future, networks of institutions would all benefit from sharing both materials and facilities.

In the endeavors of *Research, Scholarship, and Creative Activity*, the *Third Century* report discussed four realities that affected the faculty role of contributing to new knowledge:

1. *Areas of Inquiry.* Interdisciplinary teams of faculty were held up as the ideal way for the university to be flexible and responsive when the future called for new research directions. Again, balance was proffered as the *modus operandi* in building the strength of research agendas that were already successful and standing ready to launch new ones.
2. *Support for Scholarly Inquiry.* The writers noted that grant money for research follows the big-ticket inquiries in science and technology because those are more likely to yield big payoffs. Admitting that such a scenario would not likely change soon, the report resigned the university to seek more grants and contracts for expensive but essential research in those fields. The state's Research Challenge grants were a start, but they were only seed money, the authors pointed out.
3. *Research and Society.* Because some support for research came with the price tag of demonstrating gains in economic development, the report recommended the pursuit of partnerships between the university and the state that might result in job creation.
4. *Research and University Values.* The report was frank in conceding that sponsored research might tip the balance between basic and applied investigations, as sponsors' grants could shape research questions and thereby alter the traditional role of academic scholars as directors of inquiry.

In the extended community, or *Institutional Support and Services*, the *Third Century* document touched on five topics:

1. *General Administration.* The central theme was that of flexibility and adaptability; the goal was for the university to be responsive to future changes.
2. *Academic Support.* Continued improvement of support units both major and minor was recommended in the report, ranging from physical facilities to faculty advising.
3. *Residential Life Programs and Services.* The report repeated the value of encouraging more involvement of faculty in residence

life and more integration of classroom content in residence activities.
4. *Student Services.* Warning against complacency in delivering student services, the report predicted an increase in student demand for a host of add-ons, particularly in career exploration and placement.
5. *University Relations and Development.* "Effective communication of the Ohio University story" might produce benefits more difficult to measure than dollars, but just as important in the university's quest for quality, the colloquium participants wrote. Thus the related efforts of university relations and development were cited as critical for building strong support for the university among all constituencies, private and public, alumni or not.

Though the *Third Century* report included an epilogue, the more contemplative summary appeared the following October in Ping's Convocation Address, titled "Challenge and Response: Opportunities for Excellence." Calling the colloquium document a "balancing act," Ping reminded the audience that goals are never realized, that the university was "on the right track but hadn't arrived." He condensed his summary to three challenges in the external environment that present the university with forced options: (1) balancing general education and professional education, (2) complementing teaching with research, and (3) offsetting constant comparisons in the name of quality with Ohio University's unique identity. The president then tackled two issues that would perpetually affect the university's planning: size, or rather, whether to achieve more of it; and resources, or how best to achieve more of them. His prescription was to limit size if increases in enrollment threatened to compromise quality, and to seek resources in two ways: via internal reallocations and by securing external grants and contracts.

Peering into the future and plotting responses to challenges was not the tone on which he ended the speech, however. Just as the colloquium participants had put in writing that their efforts filled them with a renewed sense of excitement about Ohio University's future, Ping articulated his assessment with restrained pride: "Are we as a university closer to being a community a decade later? I think so. There is a stronger, more widely shared sense of what we are and what we can be." The goals of the *Third Century* document were backed by more than praise from the president. Two months before the Convocation Address, Ping had approved the Foundation board's expenditure of up to 80 percent of the income from the 1804 Fund, the unrestricted endowment secured by the 1804 Campaign, for two overall goals—(1) strengthening of research activity on campus and (2) continuing analysis and reform of undergraduate education with a particular emphasis on the general education program.

Regarding Faculty

The major players in the effort to effect "intellectual and personal growth of the individual" are those who teach. Such mission centrality explains why Ping resisted the proposal to eliminate faculty positions in order to balance the budget in 1975. Beyond Ping's efforts to boost faculty salaries, three developments that affected faculty came to be viewed as improvements: early retirement, faculty leave, and tuition waivers for faculty dependents.

In the early 1970s, an extended budget crisis had caused the faculty at Ohio University to lose ground in faculty salary rankings among Ohio's universities and colleges. Before Ping arrived in Athens, a decision was made to forgo pay increases rather than solve the problem expediently by eliminating more faculty positions. Less than two months after the defeat of the faculty union, the board of trustees agreed with the new president that attention should be focused on improving faculty salaries. Ping called for an immediate raise pool of 10 percent for faculty compensation in the 1976–77 academic year and recommended that faculty salaries remain top priority in budgeting for the next two biennia. At its November meeting in 1976, the board passed a resolution supporting both proposals.

The facts that led to the salary recommendations derived from state and national rankings: In only two years, faculty salary rankings at Ohio had dropped from fourth (in 1973–74) to eighth (in 1975–76) among ten comparable state institutions. Nationally, the situation was worse. In the 1974–75 American Association of University Professors (AAUP) salary survey, compensation for Ohio University professors ranked in the bottom category in every faculty rank compared to similar universities. In contrast to the 10 percent recommended for faculty, the salary raise recommendation for administrators that year was only 6 percent. Again, national data informed the decision in numbers showing that Ohio University administrators ranked average in pay nationally.

Ping proved many times in his tenure as president that he was earnest about raising faculty salaries at Ohio to the top quartile of state rankings, only to see raises evaporate when subsidies due the university never materialized or when the legislature imposed last-minute cuts on politically expendable university budgets. Ping even coined a term for the state's budget recalcitrance—"Whoops! Now you see it, now you don't syndrome." When money did trickle down from Columbus, though, faculty got it. One example was the 1979–80 midyear 3 percent pay increase for faculty. Though Ping did not change the hearts and minds of those in Columbus who determined the budgets, he did win the respect of those he represented in Athens for lobbying governors and legislators again and again to reward universities with enough money to operate, to raise salaries consistently, and to move beyond a hand-to-mouth existence. Faculty pay did eventually rise in the rankings, to number three in the state in 1990.

One paradox in the effort to increase faculty salaries was the effect of retirement incentives on salary rankings of faculty at state universities and colleges. The Early Retirement Incentive Plan adopted by Ohio University in 1983 did more than act as a carrot to reduce the number of tenured faculty, its intended function. When replacements were hired, their entry-level pay was sometimes half that of the senior faculty who had retired.

"Savings generated by a reduction in staff will be used to make faculty and staff salaries more competitive with other institutions," Ping pledged to Faculty Senate. Though some viewed the plan suspiciously at first, more than fifty senior faculty signed up to retire early, thereby earning an additional five years' credit in the State Teachers Retirement System. With fifty or so top-end salaries freed up, the rest of the faculty enjoyed a 3 percent addition to base salary. The effect, though, of subtracting salaries in the upper range resulted in a lower mean salary at Ohio University, one of only two state universities that participated in the early retirement experiment at that point. Though real salary gains had been realized for continuing faculty, the perceived drop in salary rankings, considered apart from the effect of the early retirement program, made the gains seem illusory to some.

Senior faculty contemplating early retirement when it was first made available thought the gift of five years of retirement credit was too good to be true. Indeed, administrators of the state's retirement funds soon realized the perk was too expensive. By 1984 the credits in the State Retirement System had been reduced to exchanges. Faculty could forgo one year of part-time teaching for each year of free service credit in the retirement system. Eventually, retirement at the university boiled down to two options, both of which included benefits of life and medical insurance: (1) Teach full-time till age seventy. (2) Elect early retirement and teach one quarter per year till age seventy at one-third the nine-month salary. (Though employees are no longer required to retire at age seventy, taking the early option does necessitate retirement by seventy if a unit's policy so requires.)

Faculty at Ohio saw a threatened perquisite preserved when the board of trustees approved a method to replace the traditional year-long sabbatical leave, which the state had decided it could not, or would not, subsidize. Long an advocate of renewal in scholarly life, Ping urged the board of trustees to approve a faculty leave process in 1977 "for research and productive scholarship," for which faculty could apply once every seven years. Though the replacement version wasn't as generous as sabbaticals, leaves did offer a scale of pay in inverse proportion to time off. For one quarter off, faculty would earn full pay; for two quarters of leave, 75 percent; for three quarters, 67 percent—if approved through proper channels.

Ping himself took advantage of the leave "to return to Harvard to read, think and write" for three months in the winter of 1983. A regular lecturer in the Institute for Educational Management in the Graduate School of Business Administration every summer, Ping had not had time for his own scholarship since 1975, the year he took a sabbatical from Central Michigan University. In addition, it was Ping's push for internationalization of programs at Ohio that enabled another set of faculty to enjoy teaching abroad in various exchanges around the globe. Though clearly not the same as a paid leave to conduct research, the renewal derived from travel around the world changed or intensified the research focus of several faculty while bringing the world closer to Athens, Ohio.

Salary wasn't the only issue that concerned faculty during the Ping years. How to handle the status of graduate faculty in the late 1980s divided the members of Faculty Senate as it debated whether to maintain the stricture on who could teach a graduate-level course. Senate eventually voted against the graduate faculty policy. One factor that may have been pivotal in arguing to eliminate the distinction was distribution of a list of universities that did not draw a line between graduate and undergraduate faculty. Since most of the top research institutions didn't make the distinction, Ohio University faculty decided that spending time and effort to confer such status on teachers was not a criterion of excellence. The distinction was eliminated.

A more serious challenge was the workload standard imposed by the state legislature in 1993, by which faculty were to work 10 percent more hours. Following media attention on a rash of anti-professorial best-selling books, the legislature was determined to correct what it perceived as overemphasis on research and graduate instruction at its public universities. According to data collected by the lawmakers, faculty members were working 10 percent fewer hours in undergraduate classes. Luckily for Ohio University, James Bruning, who had retired as provost, was available to head the Ohio Board of Regents committee charged with devising policy on the workload increase. Also significant in the process was a study by Ohio University faculty documenting an increase, not a decrease, in time faculty spent in credit-generating courses and projects with undergraduates. The regents conceded that Ohio University was the exception to the workload decrease, but forged ahead with its new policy anyway as one thrust in a broader push for "management efficiency and cost containment" by state institutions of higher learning. The Bruning committee made "individual university circumstances" the parry of its response, resulting in workload implementation that took differences in undergraduate and graduate commitments into account—to the benefit of faculty at Ohio.

Last and most difficult to measure under the rubric of faculty conditions was the climate created by UPAC. After all, the 1981 UPAC top rank—"creating more teaching capability in math and computer science"—did beat the bulldozer. The process had proven itself as a viable method to avoid the very exigency, with its specter of layoffs, feared most by the faculty. In the words of Provost Bruning, "The UPAC formula took politics out of sensitive personnel decisions." While the advisory council did not determine pay raises, the collegial process of judging worth according to faculty-authored standards by a faculty-dominated body gave integrity to the decision making on faculty positions that money couldn't buy.

CHAPTER TWO

DEVELOPING HISTORY

Resolving the Residence Hall Crisis

Ohio University is off the beaten path, as people familiar with it well know. Coming from the north on U.S. Route 33, a driver's first view of the campus is dominated by buildings of uniform architectural design and color, made of red bricks from Athens County clay, marshaled along the Hocking. The buildings end and the golf course begins, spanning the river valley and giving space and light to the campus's southern border. The bike path, which follows the Hocking's curves, helps to frame a scene that is pretty and memorable in both its natural and its manmade aspects. The town above the campus, so closely contiguous that visitors cannot tell where campus ends and town begins, presents a picture of serenity and security with its backdrop of ancient hills. "The trees and hills are part of our richness," Ping said in his first address to the university community. "They force you to see and to respond."

Long before Charles Ping was sworn in as president, he realized that the physical distinctiveness of Ohio University is as much a part of its identity as the research grants landed by its eminent scholars. But behind the bricks loomed debilitating debts. In addition to solving an immediate debt service crisis, the university also faced the need to develop a space utilization plan. The charge was to show how the university planned to reduce the size of its physical plant. Ohio University was 25 percent "over-spaced," an Ohio Board of Regents' report decreed, a fair assessment given that the residence halls were only 60 percent full in 1975. Not only did empty space mitigate against the approval of new construction; it also meant that a disproportionate share of the budget was spent to heat, clean, and maintain space that was not being used. Classrooms and offices were likewise underutilized, according to the regents' report, and there would be no capital appropriations forthcoming until the problems were solved. The dorms, though, were intended to provide far more than merely a focal point in a vista. As Ping said in his 1979 Convocation Address, "We are a residential university. The housing of students on campus is not a matter of convenient sleeping and dining arrangements but reflects a determination to be a teaching-learning-living community." Beyond the obvious economies that would derive from debt reduction tactics was the imperative of preserving the residential character of the university and the charm of its campus, a historic showplace that upstart urban universities would always envy.

It was the handsome new residence halls, financed by bonds in the booming 1960s, that caused the upside-down finances of repaying indebtedness from non-dorm revenue. When the buildings opened for business, enrollment was ample enough (at nearly 20,000 students) and residence hall capacity large enough to earn plenty to pay back the annual interest on the bonds and to operate on a day-to-day basis. When enrollment crashed in 1974, there was inadequate revenue for both interest and operations, which meant that the first claim on all income, other than appropriations, was made by debt service on the bonds. The university even had to beg the state for handouts in order to pay debts. It was not a pretty picture.

The indebtedness on sixty-one residence halls in 1975 was $39 million. Add an additional $6 million for the annual rollover notes on the Convo, and the total jumps to $45 million in debt. The only way the university made ends meet for the biennium was through the special subsidy from the state. The university administration in 1975–76 responded to the crisis with a three-part strategy: slash operating costs for residence hall operation, remove excess buildings from the debt pool, and ask for more supplements. A spike in capacity of 500 additional students in fall 1976 helped, as did belt-tightening. Chief cincher was the new dean of students, Carol Harter, who eliminated free telephone service for students, insisted that the laundry service become self-sustaining, and implemented the sale of food items to area public schools to make a buck—anything to ratchet costs down. Dean Harter and Ping's newly appointed treasurer, William Kennard, implemented other money-saving ideas as well, measures that would have greater impact than trimming costs of operation.

The second strategy, removing buildings from the debt pool, entailed selling ten residence halls to the state for conversion to classrooms and research laboratories over the next eight years. One of the ten, Grosvenor Hall, built in 1962, was sold to the state, renovated, and reopened as a classroom building for the new College of Osteopathic Medicine as early as fall 1977. A capital appropriation that year for the renovation of Irvine Hall, built in 1965, meant that it too would soon leave the ranks of residence halls and join the medical school. Last to make the switch from residence hall to medical school was Parks Hall, built in 1962 and renovated in 1983. By the beginning of the 1979–80 school year, 138,000 square feet of space had been removed from university support and thus from debt obligations. The residence hall conversions reduced the annual debt-service payments by more than $500,000. Ping gave an analogy in his 1979 Convocation Address to help the audience visualize the magnitude of the space. "The eight buildings are greater in total size than the combined square feet in Morton Hall and Carnegie Hall [the public library that would later become E. W. Scripps Hall]."

The largest of all the residence halls on the West Green, Crook Hall, was the most difficult to renovate and convert because of the high-tech needs of its future resident—the College of Engineering and Technology. Formally dedicated in 1986, the building was named for its most generous benefactors, C. Paul Stocker and his wife, Beth. The planning and execution of the renovation had served as "the model of collaboration between those who design buildings and those who use them," in the words of campus planner Alan Geiger. "It was a project that conscientiously involved the 53 faculty members as well as Dean (Richard) Robe and two associate deans," Geiger said. Robe insisted on a design that would aid collaboration among disciplines and interaction among faculty. Architects from Trautwein and Associates were chosen for the Stocker project in part because of their willingness to respond to faculty wishes.

The lure of the endowments and the prospect of reengineering Crook Hall helped attract Richard Robe back to his hometown. He had graduated with honors in 1955 and had completed a master's degree before pursuing a doctorate at Stanford University. Ensconced for a decade at the University of Kentucky, Robe did not even apply for the Ohio deanship—he was nominated and courted. He got the offer but declined, then reconsidered, and finally accepted in 1980 after Ping applied his persuasive touches. In addition to money for research and a state-of-the-art facility, Robe also sought the best-prepared students. The College of Engineering and Technology was the first on campus to institute higher admissions standards.

As for more state help to alleviate the pain of empty residence halls, Ping went before a House Finance subcommittee in the spring of 1977 and recited a litany of improvements that had been made in just two years at Ohio University, along with plans for a healthy future. Then he asked for money: half a million dollars for each of the next two years, but after that, *decreasing* increments each year, as he assured the legislators that the residence hall system "would be self-supporting in operating costs and debt service" by the mid-1980s. He got the money.

Refinancing—Indebtedness Unbound

When one turns from U.S. Route 33 onto the Route 682 ramp bound for Ohio University, the largest building in the foreground, just past Peden Stadium, is the Convocation Center, built in 1968. "Its silhouette identifies Ohio University, particularly with the completion of the bypass highway which conveniently provides a new visual introduction to the University," the 1979 Space Utilization and Management Study reads. Though it looked, and still does, as imposing as the hills themselves, its shaky financing when Ping arrived belied its heft. Every year the Convo was financed to the tune of nearly $6 million with annual notes at a high interest rate. The solution, securing permanent financing at a better rate, was undertaken by Ping's new university treasurer, William Kennard, who spent eight months planning bond sales. Kennard's 1977 sale of long-term bonds on the Convo at only 6 percent saved the university colossal amounts of cash. And it was in the midst of the Convo game plan that he saw another use for the strategy.

Kennard longed to convert other of the university's high-interest bonds to lower rates, too. In particular he wanted to unload a $15 million series of high-interest bonds that had been sold in 1974 at 8.25 percent to finance residence halls. Kennard hoped to use some of the proceeds from the sale of dorms to the state to reduce the overall debt and put the university in a better position for favorable refinancing—if it were legal. For the next year he floated his idea, finally attracting the interest of a Cleveland investment-banking establishment that confirmed the legality and feasibility of Kennard's plan and underwrote the new bonds. The sale of seven dorms to the state had produced $5.7 million in capital funds, which

Kennard used to buy out high-interest 1974 bonds. The lowered debt helped the university secure better ratings from both Moody's and Standard and Poor's in January. The tourniquet of new long-term bonds on the residence halls at 6 percent interest lowered the debt by $2.6 million, and in good time, for interest rates soon headed upward. The immediate impact, though, was cash-flow relief—no longer would operational funds be threatened by debt service.

Trading Present Space for Future Capital

When Ping was negotiating for the job of president of Ohio University, he thought that the campus, though a classic beauty, was shabby—an opinion he did not admit to the search committee. Years of deferred maintenance had taken a toll on many of the older buildings. The remedy, in Ping's view, should include a plan that incorporated criteria for decision making appropriate to the task. In much the same way that the Educational Plan listed goals for academic decisions, a building and facilities plan would guide management of the university's physical assets. Demonstrating good stewardship, in turn, might aid the university in its quests for future capital funding from the state. The resulting plan, the first Space Utilization and Management Study (SUMS), weighed such variables as projected enrollments and age and condition of buildings in making decisions about demolition, remodeling, maintenance, and the sequencing thereof.

A SUMS first draft hit the campus in spring 1978. Prepared by Richard Fleischman Architects of Columbus, the SUMS draft plan had few champions on campus. Critics decried its insensitivity to the historic value of Ohio University's buildings, its neglect of architectural merits that should be preserved, and its silence on programmatic issues. Ping told the trustees in May, "Much of the criticism has substance and needs to be incorporated into the final draft of the plan." Two university committees, one advisory and one the Planning Review Committee, worked on drafts of SUMS while representatives of Fleischman met with individuals and groups from town and campus to discuss suggestions.

The university's campus planner, Alan Geiger, said the compromise plan addressed many of the criticisms of the first draft in formulating a sequence for prioritizing renovation and maintenance projects. "The sequence supported instructional space needed, and plans for programs that needed to be relocated," he said, noting that adhering to the planning timeline insured smoother relocations of programs while their home bases were being renovated. Geiger, who also doubled as a lobbyist for capital funding in Columbus, said he especially appreciated the longer-term understandings so that "decisions on capital requests did not depend on political jockeying every two years." Though the state, in its political fashion, caused some delays in capital funding, the university stuck to its SUMS script. "We were consistent, and that developed trust," Geiger said of the first SUMS, a document intended to chart space decisions for fourteen years.

Ping explained in his September 1978 Convocation Address that the regents' criteria on space utilization "call for little or no new construction and the concentration of resources on the replacement of obsolete facilities and funding for renovation." However, he learned that shifting ownership of buildings to comply with space reduction demands was easier than signing execution orders for demolition of "obsolete facilities."

Three landmarks on the central campus were razed during Ping's years—Howard Hall at the corner of Union and College; Ewing Hall, south of Chubb on College Green; and Super Hall, at the site of the new Bentley annex on Richland at President Street. The warrant was also signed for the old Natatorium, which was so compromised by neglect that the campus health and safety officer had threatened to close it in 1980. The new Aquatic Center that replaced the Natatorium was completed in 1984, while the old pool building came down in 1996 (after Ping had retired) in order to make way for the expansion and renovation of Gordy Hall. One footnote to the demolitions that followed Ping all his days as president of Ohio University was the timing of the takedown of residential Howard Hall—*before* it was sold in the package of ten back to the state. "Vern Riffe [Speaker of the Ohio House of Representatives for twenty years] never let me forget that," Ping said. Since deferred maintenance had caused so many of the space headaches Ping inherited, requesting capital funds for renovation became a high priority in his administration. With Alan Geiger as lobbyist in Columbus, funds were secured for the renovation of Clippinger, McGuffey, Kantner, the old Engineering Building, and the mysterious steam tunnels that traverse the campus, in addition to the renovations already described.

Like Ping's educational plans, a second SUMS was drafted in 1992 to plan space needs for the next fifteen years. The consulting firm of Bohm-NBBJ of Columbus worked with advisory committees from Athens and regional campuses to compile a list of buildings that needed makeovers. The classroom halls to be renovated were Bentley, Copeland, Ellis, Gordy,

Lindley, Putnam, Porter, Seigfred, and Tupper. Also recommended for renovation were non-classroom buildings: Baker Center, Bird Arena, Chubb Hall, Cutler, Grover Center, Hudson Health Center, the Industrial Technology Building (renamed the Research and Technology Building), the Innovation Center, and Memorial Auditorium.

In his very first address to the university community Ping had included his opinions on the campus. "There is a richness in the feel of the past here, a precious and rare asset for a Midwestern campus. As you walk across the College Green, you know that this University has been here for a long time and will be here long after you and I are gone from the scene." Ping had also pledged to incorporate "aesthetic and historic values" in the SUMS plan. Therefore, when a student came to the President's House on her graduation day in 1978 with tears in her eyes, Ping was forced to see and to respond when she said, "You cannot tear down Lindley Hall. It belongs to me and it belongs to others." With its exterior staircases highlighted by balustrades, its oversized windows, and the hardwood wainscoting in its wide hallways, the 1917 Greek revival landmark on South Court was spared.

Weathering Cold, Coal, and Conflict

There was more to withstand than enrollment plunges, chilly interest rates, and SUMS drafts in Ping's early years at Ohio. The literal weather blew in a whole new constellation of crises.

As one drives up Richland Avenue to the Convo, a left turn onto South Shafer Street leads to the new Lausche Heating Plant just beyond the point where Shafer turns north. The first-time visitor is struck by the mountain of coal in the shed beside the building, built in 1967, which contains the boilers to produce steam for heat and hot water for campus buildings. The coal kept the university less dependent on scarce natural gas in the brutal winter of 1977, but the decimation of the coal mountain by a strike in 1978 brought the university to the brink of closure.

As the temperatures in January 1977 bottomed out, utility prices skyrocketed along with demands for more natural gas and electricity. The university had to spend 17 percent more for utilities, but it had ample coal stockpiled to produce steam to heat the majority of campus buildings. Despite the declaration of a state of emergency in the state of Ohio by then-President Jimmy Carter, Ohio University remained open, but at a price that sent vexed administrators looking for solutions other than turning down thermostats.

One fix was to reduce the number of cold days that students would be on campus. Fall Quarter 1977 marked the beginning of an experimental university calendar designed to save on energy bills. Since there was not enough cold weather in September to generate demand for heat in buildings, the board of trustees approved an earlier beginning to the school year, right after Labor Day. The ten-week quarter would end before Thanksgiving, rather than in mid-December, in order to empty the residence halls of occupants for at least five cold weeks. Nonetheless, January and February 1977 sported temperatures that spiked costs at the university. Still, an ample supply of coal kept the boilers bubbling at Lausche.

The winter of 1978 was a different story. A repeat performance of disappearing mercury in thermometers was accompanied by one major snowfall after another. Ohio was one of the hardest hit states. Then on January 26 the blizzard that became the weather-history touchstone for an entire generation bore down from Siberia. Travel came to a standstill. The best example of dislocations came from Ohio's own basketball team, which had played at Bowling Green that night. On the drive back to Athens, the Bobcat bus was stranded for nine hours on a snowy road before being towed to a refuge center. There the team sat for four days.

Meanwhile, back on campus, the coal pile was melting the way everyone wished the snow would. On December 5, United Mine Workers throughout the nation had gone out on strike. Negotiations continued as winter worsened. The day before the January 26 blizzard, news media reported that miners were growing increasingly bitter. As is typical in national strikes, non-union mines were picketed by UMW strikers, making it difficult for non-union coal to reach markets.

In an effort to hang onto enough coal to make it through quarter's end on March 17, university officials ordered thermostats set at 60 degrees in all buildings except residence halls. Other measures to save electricity were implemented, and consumption was reduced by 25 percent. Among the eeriest tactics were the darkened streets of Athens, where the local electricity supplier deactivated street lights at Governor Rhodes's request.

On February 1, after telling the trustees that "our situation grows graver by the day," Ping reported that coal usage varied from 75 to 120 tons per day—depending on the degree of cold. If the weather cooperated, the university might have enough coal to last till the end of February. Ending the quarter early was actually discussed—an action taken only once before in the twentieth century, in May 1970 following the shootings at Kent State University. In early February, some help came from an unlikely source—Miami University. The cross-state rival, Ohio's second oldest public university, sold 300 tons of coal, less than a week's worth, to Ohio's oldest university. It helped provide the margin of difference that kept Ohio open, but the more significant cause was State Highway Patrol escorts of non-union coal in unmarked trucks that rattled through picket lines. By the end of February, with no end to the strike in sight, the UMW agreed, reluctantly, to permit some shipments to the university. Ping then told the trustees the coal supply should last till the end of March. It was hard to avoid speculating what an additional three weeks of cold under the old calendar might have wrought. In fact, it was in that cold and dark February of 1978 that Ping announced that the experimental calendar would continue for another year. The UMW strike did end, on March 10, a week before the end of the quarter, but not before the striking mood had spread.

Back before he was sworn in as president, Ping had implored the trustees not to let any faculty go in efforts to cut costs. Fired instead were union employees, who let the administration know what they thought of that action by staging six wildcat strikes in Ping's first year as president. It would be three years before formal bargaining took place.

The members of the American Federation of State, County, and Municipal Employees (AFSCME) had presented a list of demands to the university early in 1978. The wish-list pertained to fringe benefits, work week definition, job description of supervisors, contracting or subcontracting under Ohio law, automatic advances in job classification based on seniority, and payments into the union welfare fund. Negotiations failed to produce a new contract, and a threatened strike loomed when the contract extension expired March 1. On that date Ping told the trustees that emergency plans for critical areas were in place.

> Heating plant—we will operate with staff and faculty; food service—we will operate only one day into the strike then initiate a system of daily refunds for food; security—since the uniformed security force is part of the bargaining unit, we may be reduced to staffing by the director, his sergeants and a few others; cleaning, supplies and mail—we will be heavily dependent on volunteer help.

The next day, 750 workers went out on strike. For the next fourteen days, with picket lines set up at classroom and office buildings on campus, small contingents of staff, faculty, and students volunteered to help skeleton crews keep up essential services. "We were able to operate because many people worked very hard," Ping reported to the trustees on April 3. He detailed how students used daily refund checks to buy meals at restaurants in town, how faculty and administrators picked up trash, how those who crossed picket lines were abused. The bitterness did not end when the strike did, for the AFSCME unit had tried to include clerical workers in the bargaining, in effect to expand the union in mid-negotiation. But it was the strike *per se* as a tactic and its damage to the sense of community that bothered Ping the most. "There must be a better way to resolve differences and conflict," he told the trustees. "This is particularly true in public employee bargaining for a campus or city where the coercive pressure is not the economic pressure of industrial bargaining but inconvenience. The principal victims of the inconvenience are not the participants in the negotiations."

The 1978 strike lurked in the back of the mind of everyone who participated in subsequent labor negotiations at the university. There were no further strikes during Ping's tenure as president, but talks were not always cordial. The 1981 talks went down to the wire, but ended with no strike. A new state collective bargaining law met its first test in 1985 at Ohio University, where the AFSCME local was the first in the state to negotiate under its rules, though hammering out the three-year contract took an entire year. As soon as the ink was dry, Vice President for Administration Carol Harter announced that the new manager of labor relations for the university would be Fred Haynes, who had headed talks on the union side of the table for many years until his resignation from the union post in December 1984. The following year, the long-festering issue of bargaining for clerical workers reemerged, but it was rejected in a formal vote in spring 1986. The official position of the university was worded in a resolution passed by the board of trustees "to compensate non-bargaining unit civil service employees in a way comparable to that negotiated for union members."

By 1988, labor relations had improved to the point that both sides were making glowing comments about each other in the press. Ping's take was that the wage settlement that year reflected "fiscal restraint and met the tests of fairness, market comparisons and inflationary pressure." The official organ of the union, the *AFSCME News*, called the new three-year contract "the best agreement ever" and "a landmark settlement" that had helped close pay gaps between university employees. Even though tensions remained, official relations between management and labor had lost the edgy tone.

In 1990 a new vice president for administration was hired whose credentials and experience with labor unions made him the candidate of choice for a job whose description included oversight of bargaining. Gary North, who had handled labor contracts on an annual basis at the University of Illinois and earlier at Michigan State, spent a year learning the job at Ohio before the 1991 negotiations for the next three-year contract of 580 AFSCME workers in maintenance, housekeeping, and food services. Son of a United Mine Workers regional president, North knew the viewpoints from both sides of the bargaining table. Though a strike had been predicted in 1991, North's philosophy of keeping statements reasonable and free of invective paid off. Not only was a contract ratified, it was done so without public rancor.

Promoting Aesthetic and Historic Values

Most tours of Ohio University begin or end (or both) at the Class Gate, the one that frames Cutler Hall from Union Street in most of the signature portraits of the College Green. It bears the famous inscription from the Ordinance of 1787 attributed to Manasseh Cutler himself: "Religion, morality, and knowledge, being necessary to good government and the happiness of mankind, schools and the means of education shall forever be encouraged." The unique and extended history of the university is as much a part of its sense of place as the hills that surround it. Two years of financial crisis overlapped by two years of disastrous winters might have overwhelmed one of the new urban universities in Ohio, but Ohio University had weathered decades of difficulties. Indeed, it was preparing to celebrate its 175th anniversary. Third was not the charm in February 1979, however, where wretched winter weather was concerned. However, heavy snow did not ruin the birthday party.

175 Years

Back in 1804, the one-year-old Ohio General Assembly passed the act establishing its university on February 18. Highlights of the three-day celebration in mid-February 1979 included the 1804 Ball on Saturday night; the Founders Day Convocation on Sunday afternoon, featuring U.S. Commissioner of Education Ernest L. Boyer as keynote speaker; and a conference on higher education on Monday that brought back one of the university's more famous sons, Lt. Gov. George Voinovich. Historic snowfall on Sunday morning reduced attendance at the Sunday and Monday events, as travelers en route to Athens turned back and those already in Athens bolted for home. The snow diminished attendance but not spirits, as Ping later reported to the trustees. "The 1804 Ball was good fun. The Convocation was truly impressive. The reception marking the return to public display in Cutler Hall of the presidential portraits was a great success," he said. Four of those whose likenesses were unveiled attended the 175th anniversary—John C. Baker, Vernon R. Alden, Claude R. Sowle, and Harry B. Crewson.

In addition to the restoration of the presidential portraits after their tenure in storage, other memorable events debuted at the celebration but outlived the three-day revelry. In the Convo, a slide show on the university's history included a visit and monologue by university founder Cutler, a.k.a. Bob Winters, director of the School of Theater, who reprised the role numerous times in the years thereafter. An original composition written for the celebration by Richard Wetzel from the School of Music has enjoyed countless performances since February 1979. One notable effect of the polished pageantry was media coverage, favorable for a change, about the role of Ohio University in the lives of young Ohioans for one and three-fourths centuries. Vice President for University Relations Wayne Kurlinski, along with Elise Sanford, project assistant, planned the entire celebration. Kurlinski regretted that reduced attendance due to snow might have reduced column inches in the media as well. He was even overheard saying more than once, "I wish Cutler and Putnam had waited until summer to found their university."

Three distinguished visitors came to campus later in the year as part of the 175th anniversary of the university's founding. Henry Steele Commager, prolific author on American history, spoke on campus as a Kennedy Lecturer. Carr Liggett, advertising executive and Ohio University alumnus, personally presented to the library an illuminated thirteenth-century Bible as its official one millionth volume. Alden returned for Liggett's presentation and was honored at a meeting of the newly established Friends of Alden Library.

A historical marker of a different kind arrived during the university's 175th year. A gift from Chubu University added a new flavor to the native flora of the campus while also serving as a reminder that Ohio University's sequestered setting disguises its place in the world. In early September 1979, 175 Japanese cherry trees were dedicated in a ceremony along the Hocking River. Stretching a half mile along the curve of Shafer Street across from the Convo, the trees line the north bank of the river. The redolent blooms in mid-April every year are as much a regional draw as their cousins arcing the Potomac Basin in Washington, D.C. More importantly, the cherry trees commemorate a significant chapter in Ohio University's history. The first international graduate of Ohio University, a student from Japan, received his diploma under the elms of the College Green in 1895. In the decades that followed, Ohio University brought the world into its history via students from dozens of nations, a curriculum that incorporated the reality of globalization, and faculty who studied in distant lands and returned with learned perspectives to the hills of little Athens.

Historical accuracy was the centerpiece of a dinner that closed the 175th anniversary celebration. Dubbed the First Ohio Dinner, the event hosted by the Massachusetts alumni chapter took guests back to the Cutler era via food and symbols. Part of the menu of a meal served to Cutler by President Thomas Jefferson was served at the Kennedy Presidential Library in Boston that November night to Ping and company. In fact, the First Ohio Dinner was the first public event held in the new library. Lt. Gov. Thomas O'Neill III, on hand to represent Ohio's state government, was presented a plaque of reclaimed wood significant to the history of Ohio University's founding: American elm from the campus's legendary McGuffey elms combined with pieces from a plank of a circa-1787 building in Boston, birthplace of the university's parent, the Ohio Company.

Northwest Territory Bicentennial

Another birthday celebration in 1987, this time to mark the 200th anniversary of the passage of the Northwest Ordinance, showcased the university's role not only in the state but also in the nation. In fact, no event is more central to the founding of Ohio University than the document guided through the U.S. Congress by Cutler. The most recent updating of the story was told by the late Robert Daniel, Ohio University professor emeritus of history, in his 1997 book *Athens, Ohio: The Village Years*. Cutler's private land venture with Rufus Putnam and others, called the Ohio Company, included a clause in its contract with Congress mandating the creation of a university in the lands the Ordinance opened for official settlement. In 1802, Cutler himself drafted the first charter, patterned after his alma mater, Yale, and named his institution the American Western University. But politics in Chillicothe kept territorial leaders focused on other matters, and the experiment in frontier higher education languished until after Ohio attained statehood in 1803, when those who had prevailed in the political arena renamed Cutler's school for the new state.

Helping to plan activities for the state were Ping and Vice President for University Relations Martha Turnage, whom Gov. Celeste had named to the Ohio Northwest Ordinance and U.S. Constitution Bicentennial Commission. Events on campus to mark the 200th birthday of the Ordinance were scheduled throughout the year. Speakers included historian Daniel J. Boorstin, Librarian of Congress, and theologian Martin Marty, who weighed the contrasting views on the role of religion in public schools. As event organizers noted, most Ohioans knew more about the 1789 Bill of Rights than about its 1787 precursor, which included a proviso on religious freedom. Another original music composition was commissioned. Music professor Robert Newell's tribute to Cutler premiered Homecoming weekend at the Bicentennial Convocation in Memorial Auditorium. A special guest was Gov. Richard Celeste, who stayed for several days afterward to get acquainted with the state's First University.

Easily the most salient contribution of the Ordinance Bicentennial was the effort, sometimes against odds as formidable as any the wilderness had presented, to salvage the home of Athens pioneer Silas Bingham and relocate it on campus as the Visitors Center. Nestled among trees that echo its origin, the two-story log cabin is not even discernable from the bypass. But once a driver travels north or south on Richland Avenue, a surprise awaits. On the western side of the thoroughfare stands the rough-hewn home of one of the founders of the village of Athens, a man who had been recruited by Rufus Putnam to roust out the squatters from the college lands in order to establish a permanent settlement in 1797.

In the first decade of the nineteenth century, Bingham built his home on College Avenue, where it earned a history of its own as the first house in Athens built on a permanent foundation. A veritable Who's Who of Athenians lived in the house, including the third university president, Robert G. Wilson, and Ohio's first African American graduate, John Newton Templeton of the Class of 1828. The Bingham house was later moved to East State Street, where it suffered fire, the elements, and myriad indignities before hearty twentieth-century Athenians rescued it. The house was dismantled and moved to its campus location 184 years after its construction and dedicated July 4, 1987. There it remains, in architectural and functional counterpoint to the Convo that shadows it, a single lighted candle in each of its windows. It will be there "long after you and I are gone from the scene" as the quintessential reminder of Ohio University's aesthetic and historic value.

One newcomer who saw the buildings as priceless legacies had barely unpacked her belongings before delving into preservation projects in Athens and the university. Claire Ping, wife of the eighteenth president, may have seemed preoccupied with entertaining and adjustment, but she was quietly researching, inquiring, and planning a number of projects. One involved the buildings at the heart of the campus. Though more elegant than the Bingham cabin, the early nineteenth-century "wings of the College Edifice," as Wilson Hall (1837) and McGuffey Hall (1839) were first called, are only slightly younger. By Mrs. Ping's second year in Athens, the trustees authorized her and campus planner Geiger to seek a place on the National Register of Historic Places for the College Green and its coterie of classic buildings—all the buildings on the Green as well as those facing the Green. (Cutler Hall, or the College Edifice, had earned the distinction of National Historic *Landmark* in its own right in 1966. The sole Landmark in Athens and contiguous counties, Cutler Hall joined the elite ranks of edifices that "possess exceptional value or quality in illustrating or interpreting the heritage of the United States," in the words of the National Park Service definition of a Landmark.) The National Register application was approved, and the entire core of the campus was granted the honorific, which confers certain protections and benefits under the aegis of the National Park Service.

Regaining Alumni Confidence

From the Class Gate, a drive east around the College Green takes visitors past Konneker Alumni Center next door to the Episcopal Church of the Good Shepherd on University Terrace. One hundred and seventy-seven years after its founding, the university would have a building dedicated to alumni relations, and one with the architecture and grace to match the role. The Ohio University Fund bought the brick Georgian Revival house, known as the Grosvenor-Leete home, from the Episcopal Church for $200,000 in April 1980. The chairman of the 1804 Campaign, Wilfred Konneker, had also been charged with locating a site for an alumni center. He found a site all right, and even gave the university the money to buy it, but it needed more than a makeover. Enter the team of Claire Ping, Ann Lee Konneker, and Ann Grover, who delved into the task of converting the former church rental to an alumni center that would reflect the era of the university's founding. Behind the house stood a sturdy building, the former carriage house, a brick two-story charmer with outsized potential as a guesthouse, in Claire Ping's vision. The university also acquired the little carriage house, formerly owned by Rose Rutherford, with its secluded setting on campus yet removed from the daily hubbub. The rose garden beside the carriage house commemorates the lives of Rose and her husband, Dwight Rutherford, who served the University Fund as a board member for nearly thirty years. In appreciation of her many contributions to the university, the trustees renamed the carriage house the Claire Oates Ping Cottage when Dr. Ping retired in 1994. With Claire Cottage and the Konneker Alumni Center, Ohio offered historically correct accommodations for distinguished alumni and visitors who travel so far off the beaten path to visit the university.

If there were no room in the Konneker Alumni Center or adjacent cottage, there would be in the Inn. In 1986 the Ohio University Foundation Board (the name was changed from Fund to Foundation in the mid-1980s) authorized the purchase of the Ohio University Inn on Richland Avenue. Built by alumnus John W. Galbreath, the Inn had changed owners and management for three decades. With university ownership came more assurance that there would be additional accommodations for official guests. An independent management firm would operate the Inn.

The Konneker Alumni Center and Claire Cottage were among the physical manifestations of Ping's years of hard work to improve alumni relations. He had taken the time in his first year at Ohio to meet with alumni at home and beyond, despite conditions in 1975 that can only be described as crises on nearly every front. In mid-December after the students had gone home for the holidays, President and Mrs. Ping spent a week in Florida greeting Ohio degree-holders and speaking at alumni chapter meetings. Participating right away in this pre-Christmas tradition for alumni in the Sunshine State set the tone for Ping's determination to convince the graduates that the university would define a future for itself more illustrious than its past. He knew alumni sentiment, thanks in part to one particularly loyal and attentive alumnus, Frank L. Bowers, a 1957 journalism graduate who read about his alma mater from New York City, where he published magazines. Bowers gave Ping a rare and creative volume—a book of clippings about

Ohio University from numerous newspapers. He named his compilation after a Clint Eastwood movie of the time, *The Good, the Bad, and the Ugly*. Bowers didn't quit with scissors and paste, though. Interspersed among articles were his prescriptions for restoring alumni faith in Ohio University. Ping listened, to Bowers and to many other alumni as well, having visited nearly every alumni chapter in the nation over three years. He learned that alumni links to the university had been forged through cognitions and sensibilities.

Sometimes he was accompanied by Professor of English Sam Crowl (another survivor from the 1974–75 dismissal list), whose enthusiasm for Ohio University equaled his love of Shakespeare. Crowl urged other faculty to travel with the president so that alumni would hear more substantive content about the university than the usual reports on athletics, current students, and changes in general. By 1978 Crowl had an idea for reconnecting with alumni that would emphasize the primacy of the educational function, which was rapidly becoming known as the hallmark of the Ping administration. A summer Alumni College, designed to bring graduates back to Athens for a weekend of study and fun, would give alumni a chance to relive the totality of their college experience. Unlike traditional events for alumni, Alumni College focused on academics, giving visitors entree to some of the most popular professors on campus. Reading about outstanding new teachers in alumni publications was one thing. Being their students for the weekend was something else. The curriculum was one that undergraduates were lining up for during regular quarters:

- Walter Tevis, English department creative writing teacher and author of *The Hustler*, talked about the adaptation of his book into the 1961 movie, nominated as Best Picture by the Academy of Motion Picture Arts and Sciences and starring former Ohio University student Paul Newman.
- Alan Booth, history department, showed a film (scenes of which were shot illegally) about racial injustice in South Africa that presaged the coming revolution.
- Jerome Rovner, zoologist from biological sciences, lectured on "Behavior of Man and Other Animals."
- Robert Trevas, an ethicist from the philosophy department, discussed "Moral Problems in Modern Medicine."
- Edward Quattrocki, English department scholar turned com-

modities trader, did a formal presentation on Sir Thomas More, whose life and death were portrayed in the 1966 Oscar-winning Best Picture, *A Man for All Seasons.*

Other weekend events included golf and tennis, a production of the Ohio Valley Summer Theater, and informal cookouts, anchored by overnights in a residence hall, like the good old days. Just as current students talk up popular courses, the thirty-four alumni who attended the inaugural college helped spread the word about its intellectual and social value. Enrollment tripled in subsequent years, accommodations were expanded to include the whole family, and the college lengthened to a week-long summer highlight that had alumni scrambling to be the first to return their applications. Ping was especially pleased about Alumni College's success, not only for its tacit statement about the role of education at Ohio, but also for the lesson it taught about the role of the university in the lives of its former students. "This is what the University really is," he said, "not an interlude but a continuing process, a part of our entire lives." Crowl, who eventually earned two University Professor Awards conferred by students, was a hit with the alumni, too. They bestowed the title Dean of Alumni College on the professor whose confidence in the university was infectious.

Raising Funds—Two Campaigns, $155 Million

1804 Campaign, 1979

After three years of listening and responding to alumni, Ping asked his development director, Jack Ellis, to take a second look at a feasibility study for a fund-raising campaign, which the Ohio University Fund board had directed Ellis to conduct in the mid-1970s. Because an enrollment and fiscal abyss was not the best posture from which to launch a fund-raising campaign, the study had been shelved to await a brighter future. The Fund board had authorized Ellis to conduct the study not only to explore ways to increase the university's endowment, but also because there had not been a formal campaign in more than twenty years, the last being the 1953–54 Sesquicentennial Campaign during the presidency of John C. Baker. Ongoing development appeals had continued as usual, increasing the endowment to nearly $15 million, but Ping was looking ahead to the day he had predicted, when state universities could not count on steady increases from public funds. Besides, Ping reasoned, a campaign would afford the university opportunities unlike any other to showcase improvements and future plans under the new administration.

A historic weekend retreat was scheduled in 1978 at Salt Fork Resort and Conference Center near Cambridge to discuss the campaign and its goal of $14 million. For the first time ever, the boards of Trustees, the Fund, and Alumni met together. On the negative side of the question about launching a campaign was the budget reality—there were insufficient funds to staff and manage such a venture. On the plus side was a pledge from alumnus and trustee C. Paul Stocker to remember the university in his will, though the administration had no idea what the amount would be at the time the campaign was being contemplated. Stocker did reveal, however, the size of an immediate gift—$75,000—designated for the operational costs of the campaign. Ellis recalled that Stocker's two actions clinched the decision to move forward with the campaign. Campaigns must have names, and the one chosen by Ping and Ellis suited everybody—the 1804 Campaign.

Ellis said the group approached J. Warren McClure to serve as chairman of the campaign, but McClure had to decline. "He gave the university a million dollars instead," Ellis said, noting that McClure was too involved in other matters to take on the leadership of such a time-consuming effort. Will Konneker agreed to chair the campaign. After a twenty-year hiatus from involvement with the university, Konneker had gone from a critic at a distance to one of the university's staunchest allies and supporters. Following his graduation from Ohio University as a chemistry and physics major, Konneker had ventured to St. Louis and founded Nuclear Consultants Corporation, which later merged with pharmaceuticals giant Mallinckrodt, Inc. He transformed the knowledge he had earned at Ohio into six other high-tech companies that market breakthroughs in life sciences and medical diagnostic equipment. Some have called him the father of the radiopharmaceutical industry. He was busily at work in his St. Louis office one day when Alumni Secretary Martin Hecht appeared. During a transaction that had Konneker purchasing a $100 life membership in the Alumni Association, Konneker asked Hecht about some of the misfortunes that had befallen the school. "If you don't like it," Hecht replied, "maybe you should come back and get involved and see what you can do." The gauntlet had been flung. A few years, several thousand dollars, hours of volunteer time, and "a great deal of fun" later, Will Konneker was named

Ohio University Alumnus of the Year in 1979. Subsequently he has been named trustee-for-life of the university's Foundation board, has served as president of the National Alumni Association Board of Directors, and has endowed four Cutler Scholarships.

One of the stalwarts of the campaign, Robert Axline, had maintained ties with the university since his graduation, including stints on both the Fund and Alumni boards. A 1957 graduate of the College of Business, Axline was serving as president and CEO of Plastic Card Systems, Inc. and remained active in the Massachusetts Alumni Chapter. Those who could not be actively involved in fund-raising pledged pace-setting amounts. First up was J. Warren McClure, a journalism alumnus who donated $1 million for an endowed chair in communication. Later McClure gifts, totaling more than $1 million, established the school that bears his name, the J. Warren McClure School of Communication Systems Management, a unique program in the College of Communication for the study of voice and data transmission networks. These and other first-year gifts were to be announced at a kickoff dinner in October 1978 for volunteers, on the night before the public announcement of the 1804 Campaign.

While the kickoff dinner and major gift announcements were being planned in August, the man who had inspired the other leaders to forge ahead with the campaign died. C. Paul Stocker, who had invented devices patented in twenty-six nations, bequeathed 200,000 shares of Reliance Electric Company, valued at $7.5 million at the time of his death. An electrical engineering wizard, Stocker had left Athens in 1926, degree in hand, to work for Bell Labs. When he was laid off during the Great Depression, he started his own company in 1936, Lorain Products, which eventually employed more than a thousand people and later merged with Reliance Electric. One of his inventions, the Sub Cycle static frequency converter, revolutionized telephony and was the longest continually manufactured part in the telephone industry. In a nutshell, the Sub Cycle enabled differential rings in phone lines that made party lines possible. Stocker and his wife, Beth, an alumna of Ohio University, had given time, talent, and treasure to the university. He had served on all three boards (Trustees, Alumni, and Fund) as well as advisory committees with which he shared his technological expertise.

The Stocker gift was announced before the kickoff dinner, along with his specifications for using the proceeds of the stock sale. Stocker had said to Ping, "I am not interested in providing an engineering building, but in providing for the research capability that the state could not be reasonably expected to fund." First, a sum was set aside for an endowed chair in electrical engineering. The remainder was divided in half, with one portion earmarked for the College of Engineering and Technology, the other half for the university's unrestricted endowment to benefit the university overall. The college's portion for research and equipment purchases was then split into equal portions, one half for the Department of Electrical Engineering, one half for other departments in the college. As if Stocker had willed perpetuity along with money, his bequest "to create the gift of educational opportunity" set the stage for excellence at Ohio University that weathered the ups and downs of traditional revenue sources in academia for years to come.

The actual announcement was set in Columbus and was co-hosted by two Ohio University alumni widely known in the metro area—John Galbreath, real estate developer and former trustee; and Dean Jeffers, chief executive officer of the Nationwide Insurance Group of Companies and current trustee. From the boardroom of the new Nationwide Plaza, Ping told the assembled press corps that Ohio University was embarking on a drive to raise $14 million—and that $13.7 had already been raised or pledged. He called the gifts "an unprecedented outpouring of love, affection and belief in the future of the university."

After another of year of seeking contributions from faculty, corporations, and the university's 80,000 alumni, Ping detailed results—nearly $22 million had poured into the University Fund's coffers to provide the wherewithal to ensure excellence in the face of budgetary variances. By the end of the campaign, the original Stocker gift had nearly doubled from the $7 million estimated value at the time of his death. After Exxon bought Reliance in the summer of 1980, the stock's value surged to $13.5 million. Furthermore, the development office continued to receive gifts and pledges past the formal end date of the campaign, nudging the official total to $22.6 million after the formal closing date at the end of 1980.

Galbreath, who had hosted the kickoff announcement function in Columbus, hosted the closing leadership recognition dinner as well, this time at his horse farm near Columbus, Darby Dan Farm. Though Konneker had served as chairman of the drive, honorary chairs were also applauded—Galbreath, Edwin L. Kennedy, and the late Paul Stocker—along with the man who had directed all the logistics from campus, Jack Ellis. Nearly a hundred people attended the 1804 Fund closing dinner, which Ping described as "a victory dinner. The alumni activity in various communities seems full of new vigor and commitment to Ohio University," he said.

One aspect of the campaign more than any other secured the future of the funds' ability to guarantee excellence: 98 percent of the campaign total had been designated for endowment. By definition, an endowed account must have a specified principal amount before interest may be spent, and *only* earnings may be spent from the endowment total. As Ping said, "None of these funds will disappear into budget bases," nor would they be spent on operating costs. The endowments would be designated as follows: $3 million for merit and achievement scholarships, endowments for four academic chairs, a library endowment, and $7.8 million for centers of excellence. Though about three-fourths of the gifts were restricted for particular uses by the donors, the use of $6 million was unrestricted. The administration decided to use some of it as seed money for new programs and projects.

"We will be looking at ideas, programs and projects that will have long-range impact on the university," Ping said of the search process for beneficiaries of the seed money. The next year earnings of $450,000 from the newly established 1804 Fund launched 20 special projects. One example was a grant to the physics department, which cloned its $40,000 seed into a matching federal grant for the accelerator laboratory. By 1983, the 1804 Fund had earned enough to allocate $2.4 million to 96 proposals and 14 special projects. At the turn of the university's third century, 1804 grants were still enabling faculty who won them to explore innovations in teaching and research.

A few comparative numbers underscore the "margin of difference" the 1804 Campaign provided for Ohio University's posterity. In 1977, annual giving to the university had been about $900,000 from about 6,000 donors (individual, foundation, and corporate). The endowment was about $2.5 million. Ten years later, annual giving was between $6 and 8 million from 22,000 donors. The endowment was more than $54 million.

Positive publicity was one by-product of the 1804 Campaign in stories about rankings that helped secure favorable perceptions of the university. Among nearly three thousand private and public institutions of higher education in the United States, Ohio University's $22.5 million endowment ranked seventy-sixth in 1980. The ranking was even higher for public universities—fourteenth in the nation. "And if the definition is further refined to single units as opposed to multi-campus systems like the University of California or the University of Wisconsin, [Ohio University] ranks fifth nationally," Ping detailed in his 1980 Convocation Address. Ellis gave much of the credit for the campaign's success to

Ping, "whose leadership was the ingredient needed, and he provided it."

Such measures and rankings may even have abetted future alumni giving, for Ping reported in 1982 that alumni giving was up 17 percent in amount and 8 percent in number of donors over the previous year—and that was at the midpoint of the academic year. In 1982, two years after the official end of the 1804 Campaign, five individual gifts made headlines. The most widely publicized amount was $1.5 million from the Scripps Howard Foundation for support of innovative journalism programs. The gift paid for the renovation of the former Carnegie Library building, renamed Scripps Hall, for classrooms and offices. The sixty-year-old journalism program was also renamed for Edward Wyllis Scripps, founder of the first newspaper chain in America and the eighth largest in audited circulation at the turn of the twenty-first century, though the family's holdings have expanded to include broadcasting stations, cable programming, and web journalism.

Meanwhile, the costly College of Engineering and Technology, which had been hit-listed for elimination in the dark days of the early 1970s, benefited from the generosity of another of its alumni, Fritz Russ, Class of 1942, and his wife, Dolores. Founder of Systems Research Laboratories in Dayton, Russ did not limit his assistance to formal campaigns. He served on the Foundation board and advised the College of Engineering and Technology for four decades. As a trustee of the university, he flew his own plane to Athens in order to maintain perfect attendance throughout the 1970s and early 1980s. While universities were contemplating interdisciplinary research, SRL practiced it, with success measured in millions of dollars. Russ became a talent scout for the collaborative model after selling SRL and launching Russ Venture Corporation, which assisted new high-tech companies. Though it was not the first largesse from the Russes, another major gift was announced early in the Third Century Campaign. The total amount, however, was withheld until the end of the campaign—$10 million, the largest single contribution in university history. In 1994 the College of Engineering and Technology was named for Fritz J. and Dolores H. Russ.

Cruse W. Moss, Class of 1948, was another engineering alumnus who gave back to his alma mater in both dollars and time. As chair of the fundraising team for the College of Engineering and Technology, he donated half a million dollars in the Third Century Campaign to endow a faculty chair honoring Dean Richard Robe.

Another gift large enough to have lasting impact was that of former President John Calhoun Baker and his wife Elizabeth Evans Baker to endow a

Peace Studies Program of senior-level courses to explore alternatives to war. An anonymous donor gave $140,000, earmarking $100,000 for library acquisitions. Another $100,000 to fund visiting lecturers in entrepreneurial marketing came from the Scott Fetzer Company, whose board chairman was Ohio alumnus Ralph Schey. In fact, the Ohio University Fund Board, under the chairmanship of Alan Riedel, decided that *fund* was too small a word to describe the size of an endowment that was accruing national rankings. Thus the Fund became the Ohio University Foundation.

Third Century Campaign, 1989

No one could deny that fund-raising in the first ten years of the Ping administration was extraordinarily successful. But it was not enough. The stark reality of future needs was captured in a fact Ping cited in the 1988 Convocation Address: state support for higher education was barely keeping pace with costs. There was not, nor would there ever be, enough from the state to insure quality, much less excellence, in programming, even though enrollment at the university had grown 25 percent. "State subsidy is tied directly to numbers and levels of student programs; private support is tied to loyalty and enthusiasm," Ping summarized for his audience. Then he announced that plans were underway to double the endowment in the next few years. "In addition," he said, "our goal is to see the number of alumni, friends, companies and foundations active in the support of Ohio University increase to over forty thousand." He wouldn't have said it if he hadn't been optimistic about the loyalty and enthusiasm half of the equation.

In fact, alumni had already been planning the next fund-raising effort. The person Ping credits with moving discussions to action was Edwin L. Kennedy, two-term trustee and "patriarch of the Foundation." Along with Kennedy, honorary chairs of the campaign were former Ohio University president John C. Baker and Beth Stocker, president of the Stocker Foundation. Konneker and Axline would co-chair, with Stephen Fuller, Alan Riedel, and John E. Reynolds III completing the top tier of the management team. Fuller and Riedel were also veterans of the 1804 Campaign. Fuller, an Athens native and 1941 graduate of the university, was sharing his experiences in the classroom in the College of Business as a management professor, having managed entities that are household names in America. His titles included Associate Dean of the Harvard University Business School, founding President of the Asian Institute of Management in Manila, Vice President of Human Resources for General Motors, and President of the World Book Corporation. Fuller would direct the drive for pace-setting leadership gifts.

Riedel, a 1952 graduate of the College of Arts and Sciences, had served as vice president of administration of Cooper Industries, which he had also served as general counsel. Founded in 1833 as an iron foundry in Mt. Vernon, Ohio, Cooper had grown into an international giant in the manufacture of electrical products, tools, and hardware. Riedel and his wife, Ruby, provided for a Manasseh Cutler Scholarship and the renovation of the terraced gardens behind Bryan Hall, where they had met as Ohio undergraduate students. As the chairman of the Ohio University Foundation at the time of the campaign, Riedel would solicit gifts from the Foundation board's membership.

Reynolds, a longtime friend of Axline, co-chaired the major gifts division with Riedel. An insurance wunderkind, Reynolds had been the youngest person to head the international division of the Metropolitan Life Insurance Company, which he had joined soon after graduation from Ohio in 1957, in between studies at the Wharton School of Business at the University of Pennsylvania. At the time of the Third Century Campaign, Reynolds was vice president for Western Operations of MetLife in San Francisco. (After the campaign, Reynolds returned to Ohio University as an executive-in-residence in the College of Business, where he had helped establish the Insurance Institute.)

Rounding out the leadership team were Donald Voelker, Class of 1952 and hydraulics magnate; Leona Hughes, Class of 1930 and president of Hughes-Burnett, Inc., of Sarasota, Florida; and Eric Wagner, chair of the Department of Sociology and Anthropology.

Preliminary planning included hiring a Chicago consulting firm, John Grenzebach and Associates, which conducted a national feasibility study. The consulting firm also advised the development office on staffing and information logistics for the campaign. Though the management team approved wholeheartedly of the Grenzebach suggestions, there was one point on which the university differed with its consultant—the Chicagoans suggested a goal of only $65 million. Ping and alumni leaders set the bar at $100 million. "That was $100 million in new money on top of the current endowment," said Ellis, who by that time had been promoted to vice president for development.

Founded on the principles established in the Toward the Third Century Colloquium, the campaign of the same name had already begun in fall 1989, even though the formal announcement of its kickoff was scheduled for October 1990. Following the pattern of the 1804 Campaign, Ping hoped to have half the goal in hand or pledged before asking the majority of alumni for gifts. The end date was set for December 1993. The multi-year drive began in earnest with its National Campaign Council, which convened in Athens in September 1989. Comprising nearly five hundred alumni and friends with a record of giving to the university, the corps of volunteer fund-raisers traveled to Athens at their own expense. They were immersed in Ohio University facts and in fundraising pointers in order to polish up their credentials as advocates for the university. They were also immersed in rain that weekend, as storms spawned by Hurricane Hugo rolled across the Appalachian Mountains, forcing the relocation of some of the festivities from the College Green to Memorial Auditorium.

When Ping stood before the council at the Saturday banquet in the Convo, he announced that $38 million in gifts had already been committed. The money, Ping said, would provide the means for realizing the vision of the Toward the Third Century Colloquium: "I believe Ohio University can, in its third century, offer a model for a new synthesis in American higher education, a university serious about research and dedicated to students." The undergraduate focus was on selective centers of excellence that were distinctive to Ohio University; the graduate emphasis was on sharing resources and collaborating across discipline lines. Specifically, about half of the goal amount would be designated for academic support: for professorial chairs, program and curriculum development, and library acquisitions. One quarter of the goal was earmarked for student aid: merit and talent scholarships, graduate fellowships, and other student assistance. Another 17 percent was set aside to spruce up the campus and to support athletic and recreational facilities and programs. The remainder of the money would bolster ongoing programs launched with earlier gifts to the Fund.

The Third Century Campaign surpassed the 1804 Campaign on several measures, the first being the number of large gifts announced before the October 5 kickoff. Edwin L. and Ruth E. Kennedy put their multimillion-dollar collection of Navajo weavings on permanent loan to the university. The Charles Kilburger Trust provided $2.25 million in scholarships for students in Fairfield County to attend the Lancaster campus for two years. Will and Ann Lee Konneker's $2.2 million supported the Edison Animal Biotechnology Center as well as a scholarship for a student from Konneker's alma mater, McClain High School in Greenfield. Another $2 million gift from Jeanette Grasselli Brown, chair of the board of trustees, would fund an endowed chair in arts and sciences, awards for teaching and for undergraduate research, and an annual science lectureship.

Million-dollar donors included John Klinder, Class of 1929; J. Warren McClure, Class of 1940; and Digital Equipment Corp. An anonymous donor also gave $1 million to match the library's National Endowment for the Humanities challenge and to support the Program to Aid Career Exploration (PACE), which places students in on-campus jobs related to their career choices. Half-million-dollar donors were the estate of Edna Parker Jacobsen, the estate of Dr. Arthur L. Harbarger, and Cooper Industries.

The Campaign kickoff in October 1990, called the Third Century Weekend, brought volunteers back to campus for more than training and updates on university programs. The weekend was a celebration, highlighted by a gala dinner at the Convo co-emceed by Miss America of 1971, Laurel Lea Schaefer from the Ohio University Class of 1971, and Bill McCutcheon, Class of 1948, who is known to most Americans as Uncle Wally on *Sesame Street*. The film produced to describe the campaign was introduced by Phillies baseball great Mike Schmidt, Class of 1972.

Three years of fund-raising later, the Convo was again the scene of a gala, this time to celebrate the end of the Third Century Campaign and its record-setting success. Since the original goal of $100 million had been reached fourteen months ahead of schedule, totals announced at the closing dinner in 1993 surpassed the expectations of even the most optimistic fans of the university. When Ping told the gathering that $128 million had been pledged or collected, everyone knew the figure was not the final one. Indeed, at the official close in late December, the mark exceeded $132 million, more than twice as much as the Grenzebach consultants had recommended as the goal. Eighty-one percent of Ohio University faculty and administrators had contributed, along with 63 percent of the classified staff, to raise about $3.9 million and nearly quadruple their goal. "I don't know of any other public university in the country where you have two-thirds of your staff contributing to a campaign," Ping said of the employee effort. Of all the volunteers nationwide, Ping said, "It's been a convincing show of faith in the future of the institution by those who know it best. With all its warts and all its problems, there is something that is viewed as being of great value here."

Another way to view the two campaigns in the Ping era is to consider the safety net provided by the total in the endowment at the end of the two campaigns—$100 million, not including all the pledges and estate commitments that had yet to come in. Given the rolling average of 6 to 9 percent in earnings each year, the endowment would generate somewhere between $6 and $9 million annually, enough to move forward with innovative programs. Perhaps more important in the long run was the number of people and corporations making contributions—63,835, almost triple the total number of contributors in the 1804 Campaign of 22,000 and well beyond Ping's goal of 40,000. But surely the most sanguine measure came from the Grenzebach official seated next to Leona Hughes at the victory dinner. When she reminded him of the original $65 million recommendation, he said, "It's one of the biggest mistakes we've ever made."

Here is what the money provided:

1. Twenty-six undergraduate and graduate student scholarship endowments at the $100,000 level, including preliminary endowments for the Manasseh Cutler Scholars Program patterned on the Rhodes Scholar Program of Oxford University. Half a million dollars from Raymond C. Cook was designated for scholarships for graduates of Athens High School or Nelsonville High School who enrolled at Ohio University, and an equivalent amount from the Kibble Foundation would aid students from Meigs County who attended the university.
2. More than $20.5 million in computer equipment and associated software, and other technologies, including half a million dollars from Ameritech of Ohio for distance learning that had been spearheaded by Douglas Fairbanks, Class of 1957.
3. Ten new endowed chairs with minimum contributions of $1 million.
4. Thirteen endowed professorships at $250,000 each. In time, an endowment made earlier by the Charles G. O'Bleness Foundation grew enough to fund six professorships in the College of Business. The son of Ridges builder Henry O'Bleness, banker Charles O'Bleness, Class of 1898, had lived and worked in his hometown until his death in 1969.
5. Half a million dollars to improve athletics, a gift from W. E. "Gene" Engle of McArthur, Ohio.

Capitalizing on The Ridges

The view of the original Athens campus from the ribbon-cutting ceremony at the Voinovich Center for Leadership and Public Affairs in May 2002 topped the one from the Highway 33 bypass by the height of an aged native sycamore tree. No other point in Athens County offered a better panorama of the 500-acre matriarch of Ohio higher education. The contrapuntal view from the cherry trees along the Hocking was a tableau of another mood. The twin-towered, Victorian main building high on the ridge resembled a scene from a Dickens novel. For more than a century the buildings on The Ridges had housed people who strove to learn lessons of a nature different from those of their neighbors across the Hocking. The name of the facility itself is a lesson in historical amelioration, improving over the years from Athens Lunatic Asylum through three other updates before bowing out as the Athens Mental Health Center and assuming its new eponymous title, The Ridges.

In 1934, 170 employees worked at the mental health center on behalf of 1,600 patients. At its peak in 1954, the facility housed about 1,750 patients. The complex once straddled more than 1,000 acres of uneven terrain that had been tamed from Appalachian prototype to professional landscaping designed to restore the soul. In addition to the buildings acquired by the university, the establishment once included the Dairy Barn (sold by the state in 1978), orchards, and a farm, in addition to ponds that some believe were modeled on the suits of a deck of playing cards. The same Athens County clay that had provided raw material for university bricks was used in construction at The Ridges, which once featured on-site brick kilns. Most of the buildings, which were built by local contractor Henry O'Bleness, illustrate styles typical of late-nineteenth-century and early-twentieth-century institutional architecture, which helped twenty of them to gain National Register of Historic Places status in 1980. The Athens community cherished the handsome grounds adjacent to the university, though the prettiest and most accessible of the landscaping was destroyed when the channel of the Hocking River was rerouted and Rt. 682 was extended in 1968.

Ohio University's trustees had explored the possibility of obtaining surplus Ridges property as early as 1972. As the residential functions of the Mental Health Center diminished throughout the 1970s and more of the buildings became vacant, more citizens began to fret about the fate of the unique retreat on the hilltop. The university was the logical successor to title, but it was having its own crisis in the mid-1970s. One nonprofit corporation even got Governor Celeste's nod as the steward of the abandoned buildings. Named the Athens County Community Urban Redevelopment Corporation, the group gallantly tried to be David to a Goliath of a challenge. It became increasingly evident that among regional entities only the university had the need for the space and the equally essential potential to secure renovation funding. Sixteen years passed before the first official transfer, by which title to 668 acres was granted to the university (at no cost) by the General Assembly in 1988. The enabling legislation required that an advisory committee be convened and charged with reviewing proposals for re-deploying the buildings and grounds. Next, professional counsel was commissioned. The comprehensive land and building description by the Columbus consulting firm of Bohm NBBJ in 1989 revealed the possibilities—as well as the limitations—of transforming the property. Bohm NBBJ was not in the use-recommendation business, but the firm did provide the advisory committee with a sort of Northwest Ordinance of advice for incorporating the acquired territory into the university.

The next phase was more difficult. The advisory committee, comprising members who represented a host of local constituencies, attempted to derive some university/community linkages for the property. Led by Vice President for University Relations Martha Turnage, the committee members patiently read one proposal after another, most of them undoable for monetary, practical, or geographic reasons. Among the ideas championed by various proponents were an outdoor education and cultural resource center, an equine park, a retirement center, botanical gardens, a golf course, a museum of natural history, and storage for various university units. Nostalgia endured. Charges were levied by those denied their wishes, despite the university's position of land-poor heir.

The kaleidoscope of proposals for preserving the halcyon memory of the nineteenth century was framed by the twentieth-century reality. Maintaining the grounds and roads alone would cost the university $200,000 per year. The first order of renovation would be replacing water lines, sanitary sewers, and storm sewers—all before the first chunk of plaster could be scheduled for mending. The future of Ridges construction was explained in part by its past development. Ninety-two percent of the developable land was already claimed by buildings in which the mortar was crumbling, the electrical wiring fraying, and the woodwork splintering. "There were days that I wanted to tear all the buildings down," Ping said, recounting many long walks he and Mrs. Ping took to survey firsthand the condition of the ghostly buildings. "Claire wanted to preserve it all." The pros and cons debated in the Ping household served as a microcosm of the community at large, where sides were taken over what to do with the abandoned buildings that were useless without abundant infusions of cash.

To sum up, the university had inherited almost 700 acres and 600,000 square feet of building space, but not a dime for renovation. Any and all funding would have to be leveraged from a state with a history of miserliness toward its universities, and for projects more essential than rescuing a corner of Athens.

By late 1989 the Turnage committee produced a plan for renovating thirty buildings. The estimated price tag was $22.5 million in 1989 dollars. The task of implementing the plan fell to Alan Geiger, campus planner and lobbyist, who was undaunted. Though he had said it would take three to five years to *begin* to develop The Ridges, Geiger delved into the first task before the year was over. The trustees had approved $750,000 to renovate the small auditorium at the top of North Ridge Drive, straight up from Route 682. The result was a charming venue for events that ranged from local club meetings to Athens International Film and Video Festival showings to Athens High School's prom. Geiger also kept alive the spirit of community linkage by negotiating a transfer of five to eight acres to the City of Athens. The land Geiger traded at the corner of Richland Avenue and Dairy Lane is now the popular Athens Parks and Recreation's Southside Park.

One year later, plans were announced for the next projects at The Ridges: space for ILGARD, the Innovation Center, the Edison Biotechnology Institute (all discussed in the chapter on programs, "Pioneering Knowledge"), and an art museum. The transfer of the last twenty-four acres and twenty buildings was completed in 1993 after the Mental Health Center moved into a new site downhill, on land the university had traded for the remainder of the mental health property uphill.

The Edwin L. and Ruth E. Kennedy Museum of Art

Earlier plans for an art museum in Haning Hall had fallen through because the site in campus center had scant space for either expansion or parking. Geiger then secured a state appropriation of $4 million and added $1.4 million from university sources to pay for conversion of the first floor of the central section of the original administration building at the Ridges. Former offices became galleries for the university's collections of contemporary prints, photography, and Southwest Native American lore.

"Henry Lin wanted the university to have a serious art museum," Ping said. "It was his dream. Therefore it was fitting and proper to re-name the site Lin Hall in his honor." Dean of the College of Fine Arts for twelve years, Lin was not satisfied with the exhibition space in Seigfred Hall. He secured the university's first exhibition space outside Seigfred Hall, Trisolini Gallery, when his famous daughter, Maya, was still a student at Athens High School. The museum building on West Union was dedicated in April 1974 to Anthony Trisolini, once a chairman of the Department of Comparative Arts. Built as a private residence, the house was purchased by the university in 1927 as the president's home. Lin collected contemporary American prints for the university, among many accomplishments. He died in 1989.

The museum inside Lin Hall was named the Edwin L. and Ruth E. Kennedy Museum of American Art for the donors of the university's star collection. ("American" was dropped from the original name as the collection expanded to include artists from beyond America's borders.) Alumni Edwin L. and Ruth E. Kennedy had begun collecting weavings and silver items in the American Southwest in 1954, eventually adding pieces to represent "every period, style, technique and source" of Southwest Native American culture, according to the experts who study the subject. The Kennedys' collection was called one of the finest ever assembled, particularly for its Navajo blankets, rugs, and wall hangings. The pieces in the Chant Weave series, which are fabric versions of sand paintings used in Navajo religious rituals, were once taboo to outsiders but were rescued from possible extinction by the Kennedys, who commissioned the tapestries in order to preserve the process. Equally significant in cultural preservation was the Kennedy collection of silver and turquoise jewelry and silver artifacts of both Navajo and Zuni Pueblo origin. Before the new museum opened in fall 1996, its collections had been lauded in outlets ranging from respected art magazines to the *New York Times*. Also before the new museum opened, its benefactor died. In February 1994, Galbreath Chapel was packed for a memorial service for one of Ohio University's most loyal and most generous alumni.

The art collections were not the first contribution Edwin and Ruth Kennedy had made to Ohio University. In fact, the first major endowment fund at Ohio University—the John C. Baker Fund in 1954—was established with a gift the Kennedys made to honor their friend. Though the Baker fund originally supported the Distinguished Professor Awards and the Baker Research Awards, the Kennedy Lecture Series was added in

1962 after another major gift by the couple. The one or two Kennedy Lecturers per year, who are nationally or internationally prominent commentators, address major issues of American life in talks free to the campus and community. By 1986, additional speakers, prominent in their respective fields, were brought to Athens by matching Kennedy Lecture funds with money from host departments. During his service as lecture series chair, Richard Vedder, Distinguished Professor of Economics, expanded the scope of the original program so that co-sponsored speakers would not only make formal addresses, but also visit classrooms.

Following his graduation from Ohio University in 1926, Edwin Kennedy studied at Ohio State and at Harvard Business School before joining the investment banking firm of Lehman Brothers, where he retired as senior partner and managing director. Ruth Zimmerman Kennedy, Class of 1930, served Ohio University as loyally as did her husband. Ruth Kennedy died in 1984, a decade before the museum bearing her name opened at The Ridges. Edwin Kennedy served his alma mater on its boards of trustees (1959–76), alumni, and fund (now Foundation). For his contributions to Ohio and to four other institutions of higher learning, Kennedy was named national Volunteer of the Year in 1984 by the Council for the Advancement and Support of Education (CASE). At the black-tie awards dinner in Washington, D.C., Ping described Edwin Kennedy's great spirit: "The unspoken assumption of his life is the conviction that from him to whom much is given, much is expected. And so it has been. Together we salute him with much gratitude and affection, a good and faithful steward of the gift of life."

Charles Jackson Ping in 1947 as a senior in high school

Claire Oates in 1949 as a senior in high school

"Claire and I." Against a backdrop of magnolias, Claire Oates and Charles Ping exchange wedding vows in the First Presbyterian Church of Kerrville, Tennessee, June 5, 1951, only hours after Charlie had graduated from Southwestern College at Memphis (now Rhodes University).

Elder and younger Pings at the conferral of Charlie's divinity degree from Louisville Theological Seminary in 1954. *Left to right:* Ping's mother Mary Marion Ping, "Little Charlie," Claire Oates Ping, and Ping's father, "Big Charlie," whose name was Cloudy Jackson Ping.

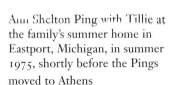

Ann Shelton Ping with Tillie at the family's summer home in Eastport, Michigan, in summer 1975, shortly before the Pings moved to Athens

Inauguration, March 6, 1976. On the dais as Ping spoke (*left to right*): Trustee John Galbreath, Trustee Kenner Bush, Faculty Senate Chair Richard Bald, C. William O'Neill Jr., Charles Ping, Charles Holzer, Trustee Donald Spencer, Trustee Fred H. Johnson.

Norm Cohn, Jim Barnes, Philip Handler, and Ping in 1976 at inauguration festivities

Distinguished leaders of Ohio University in 1976 at Ping's inauguration as president. *Left to right:* former president Vernon R. Alden, Marion Alden, Claire Ping, President Ping, Ruth Kennedy, Edwin Kennedy (Class of 1926), and former president John Calhoun Baker.

Ping helping Claire don her coat before the dinner celebrating his inauguration in 1976

President Ping in 1976 in a familiar spot—at the podium

Peking University President Chou Pei-yuan (*left*) with Ping at Ohio University during the campus visit of educators from the People's Republic of China to the United States (photo originally published in the *Chronicle of Higher Education*, October 30, 1978)

Ping planting the first Japanese cherry trees along the Hocking River with President Yamada of Chubu University in 1979 on the occasion of Ohio University's 175th anniversary

President Ping on campus with dignitaries from Malaysia in 1980. To Ping's immediate right is Dato Seri Dr. Mahathir bin Mohamad, who served as Malaysian prime minister until 2002. To the prime minister's right is Malaysian Ambassador to the United States Zain Azraai.

Left to right: Former president John Calhoun Baker, his daughter Jane, former president Vernon Alden, Beth Stocker, and Ping in 1983

President Ping at the antique table in the Office of the President, 1981

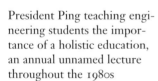

President Ping teaching engineering students the importance of a holistic education, an annual unnamed lecture throughout the 1980s

Wilfred R. and Ann Lee Konneker with the Pings at Alfredo alla Sarofa restaurant in Rome on one of their frequent trips together (Konneker family photo collection)

Ping, Robert Mahn, and Alan Geiger in front of the reading room in Alden that bears Mahn's name, 1984

Trusted assistant to the president Alan Geiger sharing a relaxed moment with Ping before a formal talk by the president in 1985

Geiger and Ping are joined by Provost James Bruning, 1985

Claire and Charlie in a 1985 portrait, a gift from the board of trustees on the occasion of Ping's tenth anniversary as president of Ohio University

Charles and Claire Ping opening a gift at the celebration commemorating Ping's tenth anniversary as president, 1985

Ping (*left*) and history professor John Gaddis (*right*) congratulating Sen. J. William Fulbright (*center*) on his honorary degree from Ohio University in 1985

Ping (*left*) and Speaker of the House Vernal Riffe congratulating Corwin M. Nixon (*center*), minority leader of the Ohio House of Representatives, on his honorary degree from Ohio University in 1985

A photograph that first appeared in *Outlook*, September 1986, with the caption: "Waiting for his part on the Freshman Class Day program last week, President Charles Ping may have had his mind on another freshman class many years down the road when grandson Sam Venable isn't a visitor but a dorm resident." That day came in September 2002.

The president dancing in 1987 with one of the university's staunchest alumnae, Leona Hughes (Class of 1930)

Office of the President staff in 1990 (*left to right*): Ping, Virginia Goodwin, Marie White, Ruth Phipps, and Alan Geiger

Claire Ping, Lt. Gov. George Voinovich, Janet Voinovich, and Charles Ping before the 1959 alumnus delivers the commencement address in 1991

CHAPTER THREE

STUDENTS BY THE SCORES

General Education Excellence

Freshman orientation at Ohio University, called Precollege, is a day-and-a-half summer whirlwind in which incoming freshmen are blitzed with information. Just when the student and parents think they can absorb no more, the student is handed a two-page document printed front and back in type the size of classified advertising. "This is your first DARS," a Precollege adviser announces.

"So this is a DARS," the student muses, gazing at the letter and number configurations that crowd the page like hieroglyphics. At the top of the page is the phrase that begot the acronym, Degree Auditing Reporting System. The quarterly, individualized snapshot of a student's progress toward his or her degree was first distributed to students at Ohio University in 1985. Once the first-timer reads through slowly, however, it begins to become clear. There, on page 1, begin the Tiers, the three components of General Education requirements that all Ohio University students must complete, no matter what major appears underneath the title Degree Audit Reporting System. Simply telling a freshman about the General Education requirements conjures up a blank stare at best, terror at worst, as the student tries to understand. But showing a freshman the DARS makes the Tiers clear.

Three courses constitute Tier I: freshman English composition, a math or quantitative skills course, and a junior-level English composition course. "That's all," the adviser explains, looking for the telltale sign of relief in the eyes of the one being oriented. "Let's skip to Tier III next, because it's only one course, and you have to have senior hours to take the synthesis course, so you needn't worry about it for a while. Tier II is the remainder, and it's carved into five categories, listed right here." The Tiers expert points out the Tier II requirements on page 2: applied science and technology, cross-cultural perspectives, humanities and fine arts, natural science and mathematics, and social sciences.

Ohio University's General Education component, so ordered by the document distributed to every student every quarter, did not emerge from faculty discussions as neatly as it appears on the DARS. Months of study, debate, and compromise (years in the case of Tier III) yielded a core curriculum that every student at Ohio University is required to complete. Only the students in Honors Tutorial College (HTC) are exempt, because much of the work would be redundant for them. Most of the students with the grades and test scores to gain admission to HTC have already completed these courses via Advanced Placement or in college courses taken concurrently with their high school requirements. The Tiers, then, are the common intellectual ground at Ohio, and DARS is the system that captures them in less than one page.

The story of the Tiers at Ohio University begins with Charles Ping, long an advocate of liberal education, who had himself been a student and a teacher in liberal arts colleges. His first encounter with a formal convention on liberal arts education was in the summer of 1967, when he attended the Danforth Summer Institute on Liberal Arts in Colorado Springs. Ping led a faculty team from Tusculum College, then another group from Central Michigan, to Colorado Springs for the annual faculty revival in liberal arts, now funded and named for its later benefactor, the Lilly Foundation. Despite the pressing problems facing Ping when he arrived to lead Ohio University, he was thinking ahead to the process of revamping the curriculum. He gave it high priority not only because he was committed to liberal studies as an ideal, but also because it was the surest way to restore Ohio University's image. The enrollment plunge at Ohio would be remedied by raising academic standards, not lowering them, and by strengthening the curriculum. Another advantage of discussing a general education curriculum would be the intellectual rejuvenation and morale boost the faculty would enjoy—especially important given the dark ages Ohio University had recently endured, and given Ping's intention to lead the stakeholders of the university toward a sense of community.

In his fourth year as president, Ping sent a team from Ohio to the summer 1978 Lilly Institute. Led by William Dorrill, dean of the College of

Arts and Sciences, the team also included Sam Crowl from the English department, Nick Dinos from the chemical engineering department, and Byron Scott from journalism. After returning to Athens, the team designated Crowl to serve as spokesman. A year earlier, it had been Crowl who had authored the section titled "Liberal and Fine Arts Education" in the Educational Plan of 1977. In fact, Goal #2 under that heading read: "The faculty should recommend the ways in which the university's general education curriculum can be reformed to provide students with a more rational, integrated and meaningful exposure to the liberal disciplines and the fine arts." Elaborating on the goal, Crowl wrote that the university's present system of "very broad distribution requirements" resulted in students who "shop quite randomly amongst course offerings without, or only rarely, having the opportunity to see how our various specialties or fields of inquiry merge or diverge from one another." He ended the rationale for the goal with the caveat: "Curricular changes which are not generated and supported by the faculty will not succeed." Three of the four members of the committee who drafted the first General Education proposal were, of course, faculty.

During the 1978 Convocation Address, Ping asked Crowl to explain the tiers, which would constitute about one-fourth of the hours required to graduate. Tier I would address basic learning skills—specifically, "the ability to use both words and numbers, an important step towards the mastery of clarity and elegance in thought and expression which distinguish an educated person," Crowl said. The second tier's five categories would include courses in "the major concerns of the liberally educated person: self, society, culture, heritage, nature and technology." The category of culture was especially important to updating the university's curriculum. Ping was committed to internationalizing the curriculum. The Lilly group was, too, and proposed that the common curriculum include courses designed to focus on the world's interconnectedness and interdependence. Thus one category of Tier II required some exposure to thinking outside the traditional Western framework that had shaped students' values. In addition, students would be encouraged to package Tier II courses into a cluster that built on logical connections across disciplines. Crowl had asked rhetorically in the text of the Educational Plan, "Is it legitimate to place the entire burden of the integration of knowledge on the student?" The answer was no, students should not be left to their own devices. Faculty mentors would work with freshmen and would explain the nature of the various Tier II course options.

Because the creation and designation of courses common to all students demanded an approval process, the Lilly group's proposal recommended the formation of a University Council on General Education. The body's tasks would be twofold: to designate which of the existing courses would satisfy Tier I and Tier II requirements and to recommend to the University Curriculum Council which of the new course proposals should be approved as Tier III. The third tier was conceptualized from the start as a capstone course in which the student would synthesize knowledge, skills, and values, to "enhance the student's capacity to integrate and absorb the diverse learning experience of the college years," Crowl said.

After Crowl sat down, Ping returned to the Convocation podium to emphasize that the process was as important as the product in working toward consensus on General Education. Though the curriculum already included courses that met the descriptions of the first two tiers, the third tier offered a greater challenge, that of creating new courses that would cut across discipline lines and faculty lines. "There are no right answers to questions raised by the report. There are many answers and workable compromises," Ping said. "Whatever the conclusion of this discussion, I believe we will be a more lively and effective community for having engaged in this study and debate."

As Ping predicted to the trustees, the General Education proposal stimulated campus-wide debate during fall 1978. The proposal authors had explained the details at three university-wide faculty meetings, at faculty meetings of eighteen individual departments, and at various committee meetings of Faculty Senate. Students even took notice, despite the fact that those on campus listening to the debate would graduate before the idea was fully implemented. The *Post* ran a three-part series on the proposal that Ping called "the most substantial analysis of an academic issue" he had seen in a student newspaper. The reporter was Scott Stevens, who later wrote for the *Cleveland Plain Dealer.*

The mood of the faculty on strengthening standards had already been evident the year before when the faculty approved the first university-wide requirement passed in nine years. Unless a student passed a writing competency test administered before the freshman year, the student would be required to take freshman composition. Again during the junior year, if the student did not pass muster, he or she would take an advanced composition course. The requirement took effect in 1978.

The arena that really counted in the General Education debate was Faculty Senate, which took up the topic in winter 1979. Senate's Educational Policy Committee (EPC), the body with the most clout to affect the outcome, had altered the original proposal of the Lilly Institute participants. The EPC pared down the five areas of Tier II to three areas, all in the traditional arts and sciences. The requirement to take a course in a non-Western tradition was gone. Tier III disappeared altogether. Faculty mentors were nowhere to be found in the EPC version.

Ping asked to attend the March meeting of Faculty Senate in order to champion the proposal. He admitted he might have done things differently had the proposal been his alone. But it was not his; it was the faculty's, and a faculty group had authored the proposal that had been diminished by a committee of Faculty Senate. Ping defended Tier III for its contribution to the development of critical thinking skills. "If we are to contribute to the preparation of men and women who can bring complex social and political issues into manageable focus, then the university must nurture the capacity to draw things together, to synthesize, to see steadily and as a whole." Bear in mind, he said, not every faculty member would want or need to become a Tier III teacher.

Likewise, not every faculty member could or should contribute to courses with an international focus, Ping said. He was adamant that a solid education in the late twentieth century was one that included an appreciation of the world's interdependence and its various cultures. A critical mass of teachers with credentials to teach about international topics would suffice. The entire faculty need not retool. At the April meeting of Senate, the EPC restored the two categories it had removed from Tier II, but Tier III was left on the back burner. The debate raged on.

In another month a vote was taken in Faculty Senate on the Tier I and Tier II components. Ping himself was surprised at the outcome, given the tensions, amendments, and rewrites that had preceded the election. The results were thirty in favor, two against. Earlier history on the topic had suggested continued politicization along college lines. Indeed, politics had sabotaged earlier attempts to restore distributive courses, which had been abandoned in 1969. In the era of scarce resources, colleges had viewed each other as rivals rather than as players on the same team. According to Crowl, it was Ping's appeal to a sense of community that helped the participants begin to view one another as allies instead of antagonists.

Tier II in its elected version comprised thirty hours from at least four of the five categories of applied science and technology, humanities and fine arts, natural science and mathematics, social sciences, and non-Western cultures, the last of which was later renamed cross-cultural perspectives.

Implementation of Tier III would wait until at least sixty sections of appropriate courses were available. Only the students in Honors Tutorial College (about 200 total) were exempt from the General Education that would be required of all Ohio University students beginning in fall 1980 with Tier I. Tier II would be required beginning in 1981.

There was still work to do on the ideal of faculty advising. An attempt to call the matter to a vote was tangled up in a review of University College *per se* by the Structural Review Committee. The chair of the Educational Policy Committee, Hal Arkes, resolved the predicament by asking Senate to vote only on the issue of whether or not faculty should be involved in advising students who had not decided on a major and to postpone action on reconstituting University College. Once the purview of University College alone, academic advising of undecided students officially shifted to "the faculty" in the 1980 proposal approved by Faculty Senate. Ping had lobbied for it, saying "We must tend to our faculty roles, not just as professors of a particular discipline, but as mentors and tutors to university life." Without the advising component, Ping said, the General Education curriculum would be "nothing more than a listing of courses and distributive requirements." Predictably, students endorsed the advising proposal, too. The question then remained, which faculty would advise? Vice Provost Bruning urged Provost Bucklew to back him in a plan to identify advisers in other colleges by hosting luncheons. The dessert would be explanations of the advising process and calls for volunteers. Only the faculty serious about advising would bite, and 138 did.

Five years later, Ping continued to endorse close contacts between faculty and students beyond the classroom. In his 1985 Convocation Address on excellence, he singled out mentoring of students by faculty as an important mission of the educational function. "I am convinced that intellectual values are much like measles. You have to get close to someone who has a contagious case to be infected. Such contagious contact is a mark of excellence in education," he said.

In the two years between adoption and implementation of Tiers I and II, the major task was to identify courses that met the category definitions. Tier I was easier, as nearly everyone agreed that English composition should be required. Just as important was the fact that the English department could handle the entire freshman class. The junior-level composition course that had been implemented in 1978 was likewise put under the Tier I heading. The math department, however, could not accommodate 3,000 freshmen per year. The compromise for the quantitative portion of Tier I was to permit students to take courses other than the purely mathematical, such as a statistics course in psychology or a logic course in philosophy.

Identifying Tier II courses was tougher. Throughout 1979–80, course after course ran the gauntlet through the General Education Council as colleges vied with one another for weighted-student-credit-hours futures. Some decisions were easy. Freshman-level history courses were beyond debate as providers of breadth of knowledge in the social sciences category, for example. Other choices were thornier. Permitting the survey course in mass communication to become a social sciences Tier II was less obvious and demanded discussion. In the end, every college owned a Tier II course, and University College would administer the entire package. Clustering of courses, however, was abandoned due to the realization that its configurations were infinite, given the number of courses approved as Tier II–worthy. The number itself, 582 courses approved in one year, is significant. While most university history is marked by dates on which great ideas are approved or implemented, the history of the General Education Curriculum centers on the faculty who gave the idea embodiment in hours and hours of reading, debating, and working toward consensus on course proposals. General Education Council chair Eric Wagner from sociology credited John Gaddis from the history department as the great compromiser in the process and Nick Dinos (the only Lilly participant on the Council) with keeping the group on task vis-à-vis breadth of knowledge.

By the time fall 1980 arrived, the 3,000 entering freshmen got their first exposure to Tiers I and II. Parents learned a bit, too, from none other than the president. Ping himself attended every session of Precollege to address parents, to explain the curriculum and to answer questions. "I always loved talking to the parents of freshmen," he said. "It's a good reminder of what our educational mission is all about."

Elsewhere at Precollege, freshmen took placement tests to determine which Tier I courses they could take. A failing grade would mean a student must take remedial courses before enrolling in writing or quantitative courses that satisfied the Tier I requirement. The results were skewed. Only nine percent of the freshmen failed the English proficiency test, but more than a third of the freshman class, 1,200 students, failed the math placement test, swelling the enrollment in remedial Math 101. Four years after the selective admissions policy was implemented, the number of students needing remedial math had dropped significantly. Only 10 percent of the freshmen were required to take Math 101 in 1989.

By the time the 1981–82 academic year rolled around, Tiers I and II, with advising, were part of the Ohio University landscape. But there was still no action on Tier III. Ping was determined the idea would stay alive. He had listed synthesis of knowledge as one of the six commitments of the university community in the 1977 Convocation Address, titling the topic "The Commitment to Intellectual Community, to the Interaction and Integration of Knowledge." Progress was being made, however. In the summer of 1981, a grant from the National Endowment for the Humanities (NEH) paid for a Faculty Curriculum Seminar, which was aimed primarily at developing course proposals that fit Tier III's interdisciplinary definition. Director of the NEH grant was philosophy professor Donald Borchert, who reported on the group's activities during Ping's 1981 Convocation Address. Five visiting distinguished scholars had come to Athens during the five-week seminar to jump-start the thinking of Ohio University faculty. Borchert called them "academic commandos who slipped into our campus and lobbed intellectual grenades into our seminar, thereby preventing us from dozing at the familiar sound of each other's voices." A second grant from the federal government's Fund for the Improvement of Secondary Education (FIPSE) would sustain the seminar through subsequent summers. The competitive FIPSE grant was viewed as a measure of accomplishment, as recognition that the General Education curriculum at Ohio had merit that was worth funding and continuing.

In February, with only 16 Tier III courses approved, the General Education Council recommended that the requirement be implemented the following year. That would give the faculty four and a half years to create and install the remaining 44 Tier III courses by the time the freshman of fall 1982 were seniors and eligible to take Tier III in the 1985–86 academic year. Crowl, still a General Education player in his new role as dean of University College, urged Faculty Senate to approve mandating language for the upcoming Undergraduate Catalog. Lots of senators had misgivings about the bravado of publishing a requirement with insufficient courses to meet it, as evidenced by the 20–16 vote on adding the Tier III requirement to the catalog in-press. The vote, close though it was, was the "go" signal for Tier III and would spur the faculty to develop a full complement of Tier III courses to meet the demand four years later. The nay-sayers continued to point out signs of trouble in the General Education curriculum and insisted that it couldn't be done.

Meanwhile, other faculty scored successes in new courses, new alliances, and new perspectives in the interdisciplinary arena. One of the new Tier III courses was offered as an elective in the 1981–82 academic year. Team-taught by Patricia Richard from political science and Ron Cappelletti from physics, the course explored the relationships among science, technology, and public policy. Among guest lecturers were two Ohio University professors who brought cutting-edge policy on science and technology to students enrolled in the course. Norman Cohn, a botany professor, had just returned to campus after a two-year stint at the National Science Foundation. Charles Overby, an industrial systems engineer, described his sabbatical in the Congressional Office of Technology Assessment. The Richard-Cappelletti course was one of eight that had been developed in Borchert's curriculum development seminar the previous summer.

The seniors of the Class of 1986 did indeed have sixty Tier III courses from which to choose by the time their Tier III clock chimed to enroll. Dean Crowl of University College and his assistant dean, Richard Harvey, designed advertisements to run in the *Post* to remind seniors to study the Tier III options and to plan ahead for second and third choices should a top choice be full. While there is no solid evidence on how the students viewed Tier III, the faculty who had participated in the ongoing summer seminars reported great satisfaction in interacting with colleagues from other disciplines. "The most important value of the seminars had been faculty development, not merely the courses developed, nor the basic effort at curricular reform," Ping said. The collegiality among the participants generated by the process did not reach everyone, however. In short, there was no incentive for a department to release a faculty member to teach Tier III because the unit received no compensation in its budget. Provost Bruning's solution was to compensate departments who released faculty for Tier III at the same rate given for teaching Honors Tutorial College seminars, thereby removing a potential barrier to future Tier III course development. The monetary side of the cross-departmental teaching assignments, however, would reappear in 1990 when changes to Tier II were proposed.

Measuring the excellence of the venture in advising was less anecdotal. In 1986, six years after 150 faculty members had volunteered to guide undecided students through the General Education curriculum, a Certificate of Merit was presented to Ohio University at the annual conference of the National Academic Advising Association. But the best award was yet to come. In 1990, Ohio University's General Education curriculum received a coveted Program Excellence Award from the Ohio Board of Regents, one of only ten awards given statewide and the first to a general-studies curriculum. With the accolade came money to fund future course development. Added to the earlier NEH and FIPSE grants, the new Program Excellence Award brought the total amount of money awarded to General Education to $600,000. With it also came laudatory comments about Ohio University's General Education from the reviewers, who came from Pennsylvania State University and the University of Rhode Island to judge curricula: "This is the best general education program we have ever seen in 35 years of collective experience in the field." The General Education program was also lauded by *Change* magazine, a national publication for and about higher education. The article described the Ohio University model as one of six in the nation with "reforms that are comprehensive and also penetrate deeply enough to make a difference with students." Ten years after its rocky beginnings, Ohio University's General Education was a nationally known star.

Ping had succeeded at his third university in leading the faculty to design, implement, and sustain a liberal arts curriculum. Yet he did not view the General Education core at Ohio University as an end, as meet and right for all time. As he said in the 1978 Convocation Address: "When you try to reconstruct the sense of mission of Ohio University from the designs given to the curriculum over the past one and three quarters centuries of this university's life, you get a varied sense of the self understanding of the university. In many ways we illustrate the history of American higher education. That history warns us not to be too convinced that we are right or that we are wrong. That history reminds us of the ongoing obligation to define and to examine our life as a university in terms of the basic educational design of our degrees."

That quote would have been the perfect introduction, twelve years after he uttered it, for his 1990 Convocation Address. Even though the Tiers of General Education had won widespread recognition, Ping said he thought the faculty should at least consider the possibility that there was room for improvement. In fact, he had asked nineteen faculty in 1988 to study the literature on general education and make recommendations to strengthen the current requirements. The study group reported in 1990 that Tier I and Tier III did not need fixing, but that Tier II was broken. The breadth of knowledge courses lacked intellectual focus and coherence, said the report, and had become mere distribution requirements. In its place the study group recommended a reconfiguring of Tier II into a year-long freshman core that would focus on the interrelationship of the ideas and approaches to knowledge that students would encounter in their college career. The group advocated summer reading as preparation for three of the core freshman courses to be taught by interdisciplinary teams.

In his Convocation Address, Ping endorsed discussion, but no particulars, of the report, opting only to emphasize the role of reforms in strengthening a community of learners. The ensuing discussion on campus was brief. Faculty Senate's Educational Policy Committee rejected it forthwith and opposed any pilots or trial versions. Some of the objections were philosophically based, some emanated from the Herculean work the change would demand, but most derived from the obstacle course faculty pictured in staffing and budgeting for the interdisciplinary courses. The silver lining to the exercise, in Ping's view, was its contribution to faculty development. Such exchanges among a cross-section of faculty helped "to counter the strong discipline-based focus of a university," he said, ever advocating a sense of community.

Quality over Quantity

Ping's devotion to raising academic standards led him to break a long-standing tradition at Ohio. During his second year, the president wanted to address Faculty Senate on the issues of the freshman grading policy and the composition requirements, but protocol kept the university's chief administrative officer from direct participation in formulating academic policies. He asked Senate's executive committee if he might speak to those issues. The response was yes, in language that read, "Senate would welcome such an exchange of views and ideas." Ping set the tone that day for the duration of his administration: "Academic standards, curriculum design and degree requirements, professional standards—the agenda of the Senate and reports pending before the Senate—focus on these central issues. Given a choice between such subjects and the topics sick leave, budget, politics in Columbus, my preference is clear. My comments will be as objective as I can make passionately held convictions." It was not the first time his priorities about the primacy of the educational function got a public hearing, nor would it be the last, but it was the first time his comments entered the record of Faculty Senate. Ping decried the erosion of academic standards during the past decade en route to espousing standards with "content, rigor and meaning." But he stopped short of recommending any specifics of implementation, since that was the purview of Faculty Senate. He had simply wanted to take a stand. It was viewed as such, and applauded by those in the room that day as the proper role of a former professor who had spent three decades as a champion of academic excellence. He made those points time and time again with hallmark consistency, but no time more emphatically than in his 1985 Convocation Address. "The hearts of all who love university life should be gladdened by this surging interest in the values of high performance. A university not committed to quality, to high performance, to quality at the level of excellence has lost its soul," he said.

Increasing Hours to Graduate

The General Education curriculum was the centerpiece of the strategy to raise academic standards during the Ping years, but it was not the only tactic, nor was he the only advocate of academic reform. During Ping's first year at Ohio, the Faculty Senate Educational Policy Committee (EPC) had voted to increase the number of hours to graduate from 180 to 192, as other quarter-system colleges in the state were doing. Ping readily agreed with the EPC and approved the increase, effective in the 1977–78 academic year. Thus the degrees of the Class of 1981 were the first to reflect the added value of 12 more hours. The increase to 192 hours not only put Ohio in the ranks of state schools that had raised the bar, but it also had a secondary benefit—an increase in state subsidy from the additional credit hours.

Freshman ABC Grading Scale

Another proposal EPC passed the next year eliminated the euphemistically titled ABC Grading Policy, a practice by which D and F grades were dropped from computation of grade-point averages (GPA) of freshman students. The ABC grading had not only contributed to grade inflation in general, but also prolonged failure for those students who were either unprepared or unmotivated to do college-level work. Numbers of students who do not stay in school past the freshman year are captured in a measure called the retention rate, which was another variable the state considered in assessing the quality of (and subsidy for) its various colleges and universities. The ABC grading scale may have helped the retention rate, but at an immoral price. A study on the effects of the six-year-long practice confirmed that the idealistic forgiveness of all D's and F's did not buy time for freshmen who might be late bloomers, but rather postponed their inevitable academic dismissal.

Also in 1976–77, EPC debated the requirement of two composition courses, one each at the freshman and junior level, which were later approved and set to take effect in 1978, as discussed in the section on General Education.

Selective Admissions

The next logical step in restoring the academic reputation of the university was to reform admissions criteria. In the same year that the freshman ABC grading policy was changed and a composition requirement approved, Director of Admissions Jim Walters promoted the idea of selective admissions. Before the beginning of classes in fall 1976, Walters reported to Faculty Senate that the number of applicants to Ohio had increased by 25 percent from in-state and by 12 percent from out-of-state since the mid-1970s slump. If the trend continued to 1980, the year that demographic models predicted a decline in the number of traditional applicants to college, Walters said he hoped the university would consider selective admissions. Despite a state mandate to be a "college of opportunity" and to admit any graduate of an accredited high school in the state without further testing, Ohio University should start being choosy, Walters said.

Improving the profile of students, as measured by test scores and high school grades, would become a sales strategy in its own right by increasing desirability. Cross-state rival Miami University, Walters's former employer till Ping stole him in 1975, was selective in its admissions, state law notwithstanding. Miami administrators justified their selectivity by arguing that theirs was a residential campus and that space was limited. By fall 1979, enrollment at Ohio was approaching the 1970–71 high point for the Athens campus—setting the stage for serious discussion of also using the "residential space limitation" argument as grounds for adopting selective admissions. Ohio University, however, would not turn its back on its role to provide opportunity and kept doors open for students at its regional campuses, for students from counties contiguous to Athens at its main campus, and for students from underrepresented groups.

When Ping hired Walters, the president told his admissions director that Ohio should market its strengths: its medium size and its residential character. In addition, Ping wanted Walters to emphasize the university's strongest academic programs, those recognized as leaders in UPAC funding. In 1980, the colleges of Business and Communication joined the

College of Engineering in admissions selectivity, though Walters recommended that the two colleges new to selectivity begin modestly en route to pushing the admissions bar higher.

"The more people you turn down, the more desirable the place becomes," Walters had said. Numbers soon proved him correct. By the 1984–85 recruiting season, half the colleges at the university had some form of selectivity in their admissions process, stoking an unprecedented 33 percent increase in the number of applications, 7,000 total, for places in the fall 1985 entering class. The evidence was sufficient for the board of trustees, which approved a new university-wide selective admissions policy to take effect in the 1985–86 recruiting year. In essence, under the new admissions procedure, the university would offer immediate admission only to outstanding students. The rest would have to wait. Periodically, admissions counselors would review the accumulated applications again, selecting only the best qualified to admit. The target enrollment was 3,000 freshmen. Because any more than that would not be subsidized by the state anyway, the administration agreed it was counterproductive to exceed that mark.

Selectivity worked. Each year the average scores of the entering freshman class on the American College Test and the Scholastic Aptitude Test rose higher. By the end of Ping's term as president, the average scores of the 1993 freshmen on the entrance exams stood 20 percent higher than those in 1986, the first year of selective admissions. Even though the ACT had been renormed in the 1980s and scores crept up about half a percentage point nationally, the 20 percent gain at Ohio was significant by anyone's standards. The initially modest selectivity in Engineering, Business, and Communication had reached unprecedented heights: requirements to enter the College of Engineering (with the exception of Industrial Technology and Aviation) included an ACT score of 24, or SAT of 1100, with four units of high school mathematics, one of chemistry, and one of physics. To be admitted to the College of Business, applicants had to show scores in the upper one-third and high school grades in the top 20 percent of their class. The E. W. Scripps School of Journalism published a minimum ACT requirement of 25 (SAT 1140), and sought the upper 15 percent of high school seniors.

Walters, however, took no credit. "More than anything, Ping's leadership was responsible for the turnaround in academic quality and enrollment. Ohio University is a great case study of the difference a leader can make," Walters reflected in 1995 after he had moved to the University of

North Carolina at Chapel Hill. (Walters's replacement as director of admissions in 1991 was Norman "Kip" Howard, who was hired from Muskingum College.) Other reasons cited for the surge in applications were the retention efforts in the residence halls, faculty advising, widespread perception that Ohio's academic programs were of high quality, and creative recruitment materials. A more difficult task was to determine the effect on enrollment trends of the shifting economic base in Ohio from industry to service and technology. Even though the number of high school graduates in Ohio was declining, more eighteen-year-olds were applying for college than demographic models had predicted, and the Bobcats were getting the lion's share in the state. In fact, by the early 1990s, Ohio University was Number 1 in admissions, boasting the highest ratio of applicants to available slots in the freshman class among the state's public institutions of higher education.

At least one set of data did single out the university's academic programs as the chief variable in explaining the enrollment increase. A fall 1985 questionnaire administered to students who had been freshmen in fall 1984 showed that "academic programs" was the reason cited most often, by 47 percent of respondents, for applying to Ohio. Three years earlier in the annual survey by Gary Moden of the Office of Institutional Research only 33 percent had named academic programs as the chief reason for applying.

Later measures also validated the fact that the selective admissions experiment was well worth the risk. In the year after the university-wide admissions policy on higher test scores and high school grades was enacted, freshman enrollment rose by 150 to 3,150, though the target had been 3,000. The university had admitted the requisite number to achieve its target, but the number of admitted students who actually enrolled, termed the *yield rate*, was rising along with the number of applicants. In admissions data, the yield rate is considered a more valid measure of an institution's ability to attract students than is mere number of applicants.

The new policy was driving the retention rate upward as well, as evidenced by internal data. Furthermore, a study by American College Testing released in 1986 showed that Ohio University's 72 percent retention rate from the freshman to sophomore year was 5 percent above the national average. By 1990, the university's retention rate was 85 percent, while the national average stood at 50 percent. By the time Ping retired, it was 87 percent, 20 points higher than in 1977, the first year in which records were kept. Retention rates were viewed not only as evidence that Ohio was doing things that mattered, but also as a source of additional funds, as state subsidy formulas remitted more money for advanced students. Occupancy in the residence halls, an embarrassment a decade earlier at 60 percent, soared to the ideal level of 97 percent of capacity in 1986 and 99 percent in 1989. And happily for the budget, coffers finally filled with over-earnings in state subsidy in 1985–86 as enrollments shot past the mark the board of regents had allocated in support for the university, even though the enrollment projections had anticipated some increase. In addition, news media took note of the university's selective admissions policy, publicity that surely helped spread the word and the desire for a spot at Ohio.

Transfer applications were also up at Ohio, thanks in part to a statewide effort to improve articulation, the term that describes comparing and equating courses at one institution to those at another. In a process that pivoted on reviewing catalog descriptions and syllabi to determine if one course were the equivalent of another, the board of regents hoped to ease much of the difficult decision making for transfer students by tabulating information. The Transfer Guides at the university were the time-consuming project of Bill Jones, assistant dean in the College of Arts and Sciences, who later became registrar. Provost Bruning had secured a grant from Chancellor William Coulter of the board of regents, who wanted a pioneer to develop transfer models that other schools might emulate. In short, the guide should make it easier for students at two-year colleges, for example, to figure out precisely how their coursework would count toward a degree if they transferred to a four-year college. By 1985, transfer guides had been completed for ten of the twenty-four two-year technical and community colleges in the state. The obvious measure for judging the effectiveness of the guides was the increase in transfer enrollments from those ten to Ohio University. It was up 30 percent over pre-guide years.

One of the best measures of the effect of the improvements at the university likely did double duty as a causal agent to generate even more applications. It came in the form of "best buys," a designation conferred by several magazines in the business of ranking colleges for quality, value for the money, or both. Fiske's *Guide*, Barron's *Profiles of American Colleges*, the annual *101 of the Best Values in America's Colleges and Universities*, *U.S. News & World Report*'s best colleges lists, *Money Magazine*, *Peterson's Competitive Colleges*, and *The 100 Best Colleges for African-American Students* all placed Ohio University high in national rankings. The first accolade, the Fiske guide in 1985, was compiled by Edward B. Fiske, education editor of the

New York Times. It listed the university's best programs, lauded the General Education requirement, and captured the sense of place. "And it is hard to think of another public university where you can stroll to class on brick walkways and never get lost in the crowd. Socrates would have loved it," read the copy. Other kudos appeared in 1988 with the publication of a new guide book, *How to Get an Ivy League Education at a State University*, which listed Ohio University among the 115 best four-year public schools in the nation and gave it a seven-page profile.

Honors Convocation

The efforts to improve the quality of the student body called for better recognition of how much the university valued its top students. One ceremony that spotlighted achievement was the Honors Convocation, initiated in 1977 and continued as an annual ceremony to applaud scholarship students. In 1978, HTC Dean Margaret Cohn and Registrar John O'Neal changed the format and moved the date to Saturday morning of Parents Weekend in October. More than 2,000 people in attendance—scholarship winners, their parents, scholarship donors, and faculty in full regalia—heard Distinguished Professor Hollis Summers of the English department praise the university's improvements in general and its emphasis on academic excellence in particular. The Distinguished Professors at the university sat on stage to honor the newest addition to their rank, who would be the featured speaker at the next year's assembly. (The title Distinguished Professor originated in 1959 with accompanying monetary awards funded by Edwin L. Kennedy.) The Honors Convocation's formal celebration of scholarship by both students and faculty continued throughout the Ping years to fill Memorial Auditorium.

Commencement

By the end of the 1985–86 academic year, it was time to alter the structure of another ceremony in order to communicate how much the university valued its hard-working students—in this case, those who completed their degrees. Following a decade of commencements in which students did not receive individual recognition, the university returned to a more personal approach. As each senior walked to the stage to receive congratulations from his or her respective dean, the student's name reverberated through the Convocation Center public address system. Parents and friends cheered, reversing a decade of impersonality wrought by mass conferral of degrees by colleges. The attention on the individual bestowed by the new format may also have contributed to the increased dignity in students' decorum. The 1984 commencement, for example, had been marred by rowdiness fueled by champagne smuggled into the ceremony in the roomy robes. Perhaps the prospect of walking a telltale line to the stage gave the tipplers pause. Graduate degrees, with their more time-consuming hooding formalities, were conferred on Friday, undergraduate degrees on Saturday. Attendance at commencement increased immediately, with more than a third of the graduates donning robes and marching into the Convo for the return to individual handshakes in 1986. By the time Ping retired, the proportion of graduates who participated in commencement surpassed 50 percent. In 1994, it is hard to determine whether they marched to hear their name called or to listen to the commencement address, which was delivered by the eighteenth president of their alma mater in his last year as president.

Ping empathized with the young people sweating on hard seats who were listening to sedate speakers striving to be memorable. He admitted that he couldn't remember much about the speaker at his own commencement in 1951 at Rhodes College in Memphis, Tennessee. "Claire and I were scheduled to be married that night in Kerrville, Tennessee, and I fidgeted all during the commencement address. There were bags to pack, a car to get ready, things to do. The speaker droned on and on. Forty years later, I have no idea who the speaker was or what he said, but he was memorable. I very clearly remember thinking that he would *never* shut up."

Ping's final commencement address began with a story that never saw newsprint or videotape, about a policeman in pursuit of a streaker on campus. He shared vignettes memorable to him, then took the audience on an imaginary walking tour of campus. Along the way he stopped at points and recounted hallmarks of university history as well as high points of his nineteen years as president. For some in the audience, the information was news, not history. One example was the explanation of the purposes of the inscriptions, front and back, on the Alumni Gate. A gift from the Class of 1915, the gate commemorated the 100th anniversary of Ohio University's first graduating class, which was also the first college graduation in the Northwest Territory. The brick structure at Court and Union played a role as students entered the university through it at Freshman Convocation and exited it at commencement as alumni. The freshman side reads: "So enter that thou mayest grow in knowledge, wisdom and love." The senior side reads: "So depart that daily thou mayest better serve thy fellowmen, thy country and thy God." It was a lesson the students ought to remember, though he did not charge them to, whether they remembered the speaker or not.

After sheepskins were mailed in 1994, the total number of degrees awarded during the Ping years topped 73,000. When he retired, after nineteen years as president, 56 percent of the 137,000 living degree-holders from the university owned diplomas with the signature of Charles J. Ping.

The Court Street Scuffle

Though the university was basking in the improved cognitive measurements of its students, the behavioral yardstick applied found some still wanting. The attitudes of the students who took over Court Street had improved by the late 1970s over the combat on Court at the end of the Vietnam War era, but the street was nonetheless hostage to occasional mobs of students. The dates and circumstances changed, but the result was always the same—negative publicity in state media outlets that found little else to cover in a region that was otherwise pacific and, bluntly, not newsworthy. Inebriated students out of control make good copy, and better video. They also make administrators and law enforcement personnel nervous about the possibility of injuries and property damage after hundreds of students have shuffled from one bar to another from North Lancaster to West Union. Such was the case in spring 1978 when students took over Court Street the Saturday before final exams. It was the third year in a row that students had chosen this particular anniversary to conquer little Athens, and three years constituted hallowed tradition in the memories of students who spent only four years in the cocoon of college. The spring 1978 disturbance, however, was exacerbated by rock fusillades thrown by students at the police who had come to clear the street. Police volleyed back with wooden kneeknocker bullets and arrests. A student from Indonesia, standing at the edge of the crowd, lost an eye when police fired blanks to disperse the crowd of about 1,200. Ping swore that students who instigated such melees would face consequences in both campus and off-campus judicial proceedings.

The next spring a campaign was being mounted against the annual headliner hooliganism, but the perpetrators launched a surprise attack two weeks early, on May 21. Twenty-eight students from the mob of five hundred were arrested after a gratuitous blocking of Court Street when the bars closed both Friday and Saturday nights. Ping ordered suspensions for three of the ringleaders; two were later expelled. Most students were appalled by the misbehavior in the street. The *Post* editorialized on page 1 against the bad apples whose misbehavior spoiled the image of the university. When the anniversary for battle rolled around two weeks later, would-be rowdies were met by police in riot gear, a sight that thinned the ranks of the antagonists to about two hundred. The strategy was repeated in spring 1980, when a force of sixty officers from Athens and neighboring towns took positions on Court Street and prevented hostilities for the first time in five years. The spring peace lasted throughout the remainder of Ping's tenure as president.

Less pugnacious crowds swarmed Court Street the weekend closest to Halloween in spontaneous partying that erupted on Court Street in the mid-1970s. About five hundred happy students in costumes had frolicked into the street in numbers large enough to prevent traffic from moving. Police blocked off the street for four hours, but hostilities did not break out. The students were bent on fun, not war. In fall 1976, Dean of Students Carol Harter and Associate Dean Joel Rudy advocated control by sanction. We're the party hosts, the university and city said in effect. Rather than wait for crowds to make Court Street impassable, the city closed the street early in the evening. The university provided a stage for entertainment by local bands, served cake, and even judged costumes. It was one big happy street party in 1976.

Word spread, however, and the next year students from other schools in Ohio flocked to Athens for the party, swelling the numbers on Court Street to a monstrous 12,000. The size of the 1977 Halloween crowd forced the university to rethink its posture. The specter of personal injury with no access for emergency vehicles and the danger of major property damage or fire gave university and city officials nightmares. The dean of students' staff scheduled diversionary events on campus that were well attended, but the revelers gravitated to Court Street late each evening anyway.

The next year the university limited the number of guests in the residence halls during Halloween weekend to one per resident in an attempt to discourage out-of-towners. University staff and faculty began volunteering each year to assist the legions of professional law enforcement personnel from campus, city, and county to keep the masses from careening out of control. What was as disconcerting as the size of the crowds was the damage the outsiders did to the image of the university. Year after year, police blotters bore out what Ohio students had claimed—most of the drunk and disorderly ghouls were not even Ohio University students. They beamed into town for the weekend, crashed the party, and left the hosts to pay damage and clean-up costs, police overtime, and liability insurance, and to make excuses to reporters who buried the arrest statistics at the bottom of news stories. Numbers from 1982 were typical. From a Saturday night crowd estimated at more than 10,000, there were 159 arrests; only 22 of them lived in the Athens area. By 1991 the Saturday night arrest statistics showed only 11 Ohio University students among the 90 arrested. Halloween raved on. Crowds reached a staggering 30,000 by the 1990s. When Ping retired in 1994, he singled out All Hallow's Eve tensions and the spring quarter student disturbances of the late 1970s as the events that had caused him the most anguish in his nineteen years as president. Spring spillovers into the street had been extinguished, but not the late October horrors.

Learning outside the Classroom

Code of Conduct

A mass of students misbehaving in the streets could be corrected by means external to academia, but such off-campus controls had no bearing on individuals whose moral compasses needed calibration on campus. Irresponsible antics in residence halls and classrooms likewise demanded that the university teach its charges more than who founded Rome. The vacuum created by the demise of *in loco parentis* in American universities was being filled in the 1970s by a host of attempts to adjudicate and correct misbehavior. The earlier models of campus judiciaries evolved into troughs for hungry lawyers, who came to campuses to represent students before the judiciary bodies. When Residence Life Director Joel Rudy became Associate Dean of Students in 1978, he was charged with developing a new student code of conduct that would make students accountable for their actions—and rid the proceedings of lawyers. During the 1978–79 academic year, Rudy met weekly with a group of student leaders and administrators to draft a code. Six months later the document was approved by the trustees, and it was implemented in fall 1979, one of the first of its kind in the nation. In the words of its purpose statement, it "set forth those acts that constitute unacceptable conduct for graduate and undergraduate students of the University while on University-owned or controlled property." And furthermore, "the University will make an effort to educate the student through a sanction." A new era of teachable moments had arrived.

Sanctions ranged from statements of concern, to reprimands, to probation, to suspension, to the ultimate punishment—expulsion, along with a category for customizing sanctions to the offense, such as restrictions and restitution. The procedure was not unlike the justice system outside the university, except that neither prosecutor (the university) nor defendant (the student) relied on lawyers. Referrals—by residence hall staffers, faculty, or administrators—were the counterpart of arrests. Hearings and appeals before judiciary administrators or boards followed guidelines that derived from the categorized offenses, complete with wherefores and what-ifs. The code divided misbehaviors into two categories: Code A offenses paralleled felonies, and Code B offenses resembled misdemeanors. Actions that might be differentiated as criminal or civil in legal codes were blended in the judiciary code. Most important, the wrongs and corrections were codified *per se*, and the entire process was communicated at Precollege to students, along with details on General Education and meal plans. The process was designed to be quick and fair. While it did not altogether replace action in the judicial system beyond campus, most cases ended in satisfactory outcomes for both parties: students learned without suffering a criminal record; and the university treated its students like adults in a process that fit its educational function.

Residence Life

The vast majority of students at Ohio never have brushes with Judiciaries. They do, however, live in residence halls until they complete ninety hours of coursework. Ping was determined to capitalize on the educational opportunities afforded by the residential nature of the university. One of his first actions, in fact, was to move responsibility for the dorms from the auxiliaries function to the dean of students. Ping wanted to see informational programs and dorm activities that expanded teaching beyond the classroom buildings.

In addition to financial problems detailed in the chapter "Developing History," the residence halls featured an environment that no one could describe as conducive to learning, as some residents brought their street behaviors home with them. Soon after his arrival in 1976, Rudy met with the directors of the four residence greens to review the situation and to make recommendations for improvements. One of the suggestions was accepted by Ping immediately—increasing residence hall staff. Two years later the staff had doubled to achieve a 19-to-1 student-staff ratio. In fact, one of the hallmarks of Rudy's era as director of residence life was staff development. For example, so that staff might be imbued with the primacy of the educational function, Rudy encouraged them to teach a University College course, UC 115, on a volunteer basis. Titled "The University Experience," the course was designed to help students adapt to the demands of university life, academic and social, and to develop skills for success. It was the perfect bridge for staffers whose focus in the residence halls was on first-year students' adjustment to college.

Among the programs Rudy and company implemented for students were cross-cultural experiences, leadership development, and volunteer opportunities. Beyond the overtly educational activities, another reform in the residence halls was a student security program, which 1970s students preferred to police patrols.

While campus Greek-letter organizations had long required their members to log time in volunteer activities in the community, it was harder to devise structures within residence halls (and harder still for students off campus) that might encourage and reward student involvement in the larger community. Ping had advocated volunteerism, not only for its face value of benefiting the community, but also for its efficacy as a learning and leadership tool. The goal was aided at the national level by a program called Campus Compact, which had been created by a group of college presidents who hoped to encourage service learning. Ping, a member of the consortium's executive board, sent four faculty members and Director of Student Activities Terry Hogan to a Campus Compact summer institute at Brown University in 1992. Its title, "Integrating Service with Academic Study," aptly described what Ping hoped to achieve at Ohio for students who were service oriented.

The very next year the effort to link volunteers with community service agencies was formalized in the Volunteer Center, operated under the aegis of the Student Affairs Division of the Dean of Students. It was a start, but the locus in Student Affairs perhaps explained the dearth of faculty involvement. A summer workshop in University College, however, began to incorporate the academic half of the equation into service learning, as faculty explored ways to build service projects into coursework. In addition to the University College workshops, Dean Patricia Richard experimented with learning communities for freshmen in which their first assignment was summer reading on environmental issues. Once the participants arrived on campus in the fall, the agenda called for group discussions as well as future service projects related to environmental improvement.

An annual awards ceremony that recognized student leadership in a variety of categories showcased the work Rudy's staff had done in making the residence halls more than bed-and-breakfast sites. One example of a student leadership venture was convening the presidents of the 120 student organizations on campus for consultation on student programs and activities. Called the Presidents Council, it provided a chance for student leaders to meet each other and to share ideas. When student government was reactivated in 1981, Rudy also consulted that body for advice and ideas on programming. After six years of accomplishments at Ohio, Joel Rudy was named to succeed Carol Harter as dean of students in July 1982, a post he held until 1996.

Student Governance

Interest in national politics on campus in 1980 seemed to rejuvenate interest in student governance. In the early 1970s, Ohio University students had voted the student government out of existence, a pattern repeated on campuses across the nation. Ping wanted it to return. As he told the trustees in 1981, "The acceptance of responsibility for the good health of the university community on the part of the students is an important part of the educational program and life of the university." In Ping's first year as president, an ad hoc committee was formed to consider reviving Student Senate. It produced a constitution with an article requiring 25 percent participation in a ratification vote. With anything less than 25 percent, the students reasoned, there was little point in going through the motions of electing and operating a governing body that would have little impact on students. It was an overly ambitious percentage, as participation in student government elections had always fallen short of 25 percent, even at the height of the student-power movement during the presidency of Vernon Alden in the late 1960s. The vote was close enough in 1976 that Ping decided to let the students proceed for a trial period with the understanding that the senators would have to submit the constitution to another student vote.

Three years later as an election date neared, it was apparent to everybody that Student Senate leaders would not muster the requisite 25 percent. The senators requested a lower minimum voter turnout. Ping agreed to their 18 percent minimum. A scant decade after the height of the student-power movement on American campuses, the 1981 ratification vote at Ohio failed to achieve 18 percent participation, falling short by 78 votes. Dismayed senate proponents asked the president for a second reprieve and got it, prompting the *Post* to editorialize that Ping had "accomplished what 78 more votes would have." Though student voting levels during the Ping years never reached the proportion of the electorate that bona fide elections reached in the real political arena, budding student leaders nonetheless got the chance to help shape the community.

Despite the dismal participation level of students in campus elections, a vocal statewide group had been clamoring throughout the decade for student representation on university boards. The Legislature enacted a compromise—student representation with no vote—in 1988. The next year Gov. Richard Celeste appointed two students to each board of trustees of the state-supported colleges and universities. Ohio's first student trustees were Damon Scott, a senior legal communication major, appointed for a one-year term, and David Blackburn, a sophomore finance major, appointed for a two-year term. Subsequent student trustees would serve two-year terms. Scott and Blackburn had been chosen by Governor Celeste from a list of five names submitted by Ping. The five were among those selected by a committee in a procedure approved by the board of trustees. Selection committee members were from both Athens and regional campuses and included undergraduate, graduate, and medical school students.

Ping was as opposed to students on the board of trustees as he was in favor of representative student government on campus. He had approved student members on university committees as well. His stance was not a paradox, because he viewed student participation in its own senate and on university committees as good learning experiences, and, moreover, proper application of the concept of vested interests. A board of trustees, however, was not intended to be a representative form of governance. Ping had testified against the legislation to install student trustees. "The genius of the distinctly American idea of a university board of trustees was that members did not represent different university constituencies—faculty, administration, students, alumni—but the people of the state." Indeed, the compromise bill that passed—naming student trustees but not permitting them a vote—got a favorable assessment from Ping years later. He was pleased that student trustees had behaved like members of the community. "They brought the student perspective to board discussions without seeing themselves as spokespersons for student interests," he said.

Education for Leadership—The Cutler Scholars

When the Cutler Scholar Program was announced, some people viewed it as a way to attract talented students away from the Harvards and Yales of academia to Ohio University. Indeed, "Harvard on the Hocking" had long been a nickname for Ohio University, in part because presidents nos. 14 and 15, John C. Baker and Vernon R. Alden, had been recruited from Harvard University. The 1988 book *How to Get an Ivy League Education at a State University* had helped to reinforce the Harvard image of Ohio University. Ping, too, had spent numerous summers and professional leave periods at Harvard learning and teaching. But it was not the intent of any of these presidents to recreate America's oldest university in Athens, Ohio. "We are not a Wellesley; we are not even a Harvard on the Hocking," Ping said in his last Convocation Address. "Nor should we try to be as much like any of these institutions as possible." The point of the Cutler Scholars was to add a level of education that was the proper role of public higher education, not to mimic a private university with only one stratum of students.

First announced at the victory dinner at the end of the Third Century Campaign, the plan rendered the expression "full ride" inadequate. The four-year awards would cover tuition and fees, room and board, plus travel and living expenses for summer enrichment, for all four summers of a college career. Named for Ohio University founder Manasseh Cutler, the program was patterned after the Rhodes Fellowships at Oxford University and the Morehead Scholarships at the University of North Carolina. "Education for leadership in democratic societies and education to an ethic of service and civic responsibility are the high goals of the Manasseh Cutler Scholars Program," Ping wrote in the introduction of the program's literature. Students selected would meet the highest standards in academics, integrity, breadth of involvement and achievement, physical stamina, and leadership ability.

The idea for the scholarships had originated early in the Third Century Campaign when Will Konneker shared plans with Ping, Jack Ellis, and Robert Axline for scholarships he was establishing for students from his hometown, Greenfield, Ohio. Konneker said he thought the university should have renewable scholarships to cover tuition and living costs not just for athletes, as was the case at the time, but also for academically talented students. In their subsequent discussions during the campaign, the four men ironed out details for a plan to raise $40 million to fund two hundred Cutler Scholars, fifty per class year. Several scholarships were pledged before the end of the campaign, which made Ping's formal announcement even more dramatic. The earliest pledges for scholarships had guidelines that based selection on geography (such as the inaugural scholarships for students from Greenfield), but the program was soon expanded to include scholarships earmarked for discipline-based scholars and organization-based scholars, the latter chosen from children of employees at participating companies.

Though Ping designed the admissions process and the program requirements, he consulted a host of people who had held leadership positions themselves at Ohio University and beyond. He described the ideal candidates as "transformational leaders, those who can envision an ideal and energize those around them to achieve it." Potential Cutlers cannot apply for the scholarship, but must be nominated, Ping determined. Specific nominating bodies approved in the process were personnel at eligible secondary schools, colleges for academically based awards, or members of any active Ohio University alumni chapter. In the first round, applications are reviewed by regional, national, or international selection committees, which comprise alumni and friends of the university. Each selection committee identifies two finalists, who then advance to interviews on the Athens campus by the Cutler Scholars Selection Committee, the group that makes final decisions about who will be selected. The campus committee is composed primarily of faculty.

The first six Cutler Scholars matriculated in 1996, after Ping had retired as president, but he continued to serve as co-director (with Herman "Butch" Hill from the Department of Electrical and Computer Engineering). The program is an immersion in study and contemplation. In addition to the scholars' regular academic courses, they are expected to gain understanding of knowledge bases pivotal to leadership (e.g., technologies); to hone their powers of discernment with balance and foresight; and, like the measles of Dr. Ping's intellectual contagion, to infect others with the desire to get involved. To achieve these ends, the scholars work year round. During the school year they meet weekly in Colloquia to delve into "issues and choices encountered by societies and institutions." One such example of a theme for the year was the presidential electoral process. During the summers, the scholars engage in individual pursuits that fit certain parameters. Before the freshman year the goal is self-discovery in an outdoor leadership program (e.g., Outward Bound). The second summer requires a community or public service experience (e.g., Habitat for Humanity). Summer number three features a private-sector internship, ideally one related to the scholar's career goals (e.g., work in a law office for the prospective lawyer). Before the senior year, Cutler Scholars cap their summer experiential learning with travel or study abroad.

The four founders had pledged to continue raising funds even after their official retirements. At this writing they are still working to raise funds for more Cutler Scholar Awards.

CHAPTER FOUR

PIONEERING KNOWLEDGE

Educating Physicians—The College of Osteopathic Medicine

It took the Ohio General Assembly 152 years to act on the board of trustees' vote in 1823 to establish a medical school in Athens. But when the General Assembly voted to start a College of Osteopathic Medicine, Ohio University was given a deadline of ten months to find a venue, hire staff, design curriculum, admit students, and open the doors. Charles J. Ping, president emeritus, recounted that history at the College of Osteopathic Medicine commencement in 2001, the year the college celebrated its twenty-fifth anniversary. "The commonly accepted rule is that it takes five to six years of planning to start a new medical school," he explained, recalling that many had said it couldn't be done (some even hoped it couldn't be done) in ten months.

One story Ping told was about Sen. Robert T. Secrest from Cambridge, Ohio, in the 20th District, during the Senate debate on whether to approve establishment of the medical college. Senator Secrest pointed to his hometown on a map, then drew a circle with a radius of forty miles around the town. If the bill to create a new medical college resulted in only two doctors to serve this economically depressed area, the senator said, it would be worth the cost. The Senate applauded Secrest before passing the bill by a wide margin in August 1975. The House had passed its version in March 1975, after an amendment had been added naming Ohio University in Athens as the location of the college.

A national study in 1972 had listed Ohio as a state with a severe shortage of physicians, particularly family practice doctors in underserved areas. In response, Rep. Tom Fries introduced a bill to create a college of osteopathic medicine, which was endorsed by House minority leader Corwin Nixon. The Ohio Osteopathic Association (OOA) and its governmental relations director, George Dunigan, had lobbied for three years for an educational structure for training new physicians. In June 1975, between the House and Senate votes, the OOA approved an annual $250 assessment per member for six years to support the new college. The funding, viewed as more than tacit approval of the new medical facility, may even have warded off the mounting opposition in the Senate. In the closing days of his one-year interim presidency, Harry Crewson lobbied hard for the bill at its critical moment, assured that his successor would minister to the newborn college should it emerge. Then Secrest drew his prescriptive circle, and the rest is history in a hurry.

The complaints of those opposed to the medical college pivoted on cost and the unknown of osteopathy as a medical field. Ohio was already supporting six medical schools in 1975. Indeed, when Ping addressed the medical graduates in 2001, he cited the figure of $15,872,688 invested over four years to educate the graduating class of nearly one hundred. That total was operating subsidy only and did not include the cost of buildings and equipment, nor the approximately 20 percent of the costs borne by the students themselves. But each of the graduates was required to serve the people of Ohio for at least five years, a return on the investment that is as hard to calculate as it is easy to value. In addition, it was gratifying to contemplate in 1975 the timely plug the medical college would put on the residence hall debt drain after Grosvenor, Irvine, and Parks Halls were converted to medical college use.

When the bill passed, there were only nine other osteopathic colleges in the nation. Osteopathy, though 100 years old in 1975, was little known and widely misunderstood. The "total patient" approach to health care, spelled out in the college's current literature, is predicated on four principles: (1) the body is a single unit, (2) the body has intrinsic self-regulatory and healing mechanisms, (3) the body's structure and function are interrelated, and (4) disease is an effect and not a cause. Osteopathy emphasizes the prominent role of the musculo-skeletal system in human wellness in the quest for a greater role for prevention that might reduce the prevalence of treatments. In his twenty-fifth anniversary address, Ping said, "It was a difficult and sometimes bitter battle in generations past" to gain respect for the osteopathic degree, and Ping charged the graduates of 2001 "to encourage and help students who come after you as they are inducted into the practice of osteopathic medicine."

Among reasons to champion the new college was one Ping cited often. In addition to the face value of putting more physicians in more circles, the medical college would add value to the sciences and related health fields on campus. It was also apparent that the Ping approach to blending the medical facilities into the West Green residence halls would help build the sense of community that was his prescription for the university's lasting health.

Following the Senate vote, the antagonism surrounding the creation of the medical college spread from the legislature to the academic arena. Gerald Faverman arrived in Athens in November 1975 with a cadre of administrators who swung into action like a SWAT team. Though Faverman had succeeded in steering the Michigan State University College of Osteopathic Medicine into existence, his status and style rankled some at Ohio University who took to heart Ping's insistence that the medical school be integrated into the university. Science faculty would hold dual appointments in the medical college and the College of Arts and Sciences—but not the dean, who was not a physician and who held no academic position at all. Faverman's non-faculty status aside, Faculty Senate was accustomed to participating in academic decisions, not reading or hearing about them in the news media. Faverman's publicity apparatus matched his network in osteopathy, with news releases announcing affiliations he had arranged with hospitals for students' training. All the details of the fall 1976 launch of the medical college blitzed across the pages of newspapers: appointments of physicians to staff training sites, appointments to admissions and scholarship committees, decisions on curriculum, assurance of provisional accreditation, faculty hires, equipment purchases, and the renovation of Grosvenor Hall.

The mission impossible was completed on schedule, if one overlooked the crews whose tools were hammers and saws rather than stethoscopes and thermometers when the inaugural class of 24 students entered Grosvenor on opening day in September 1976. The 8 women and 16 men had been chosen from a pool of 250 applicants. When the building was formally dedicated, the two most powerful men in the state stood together on West Green: Senate President Pro-Tem Oliver Ocasek and Speaker of the

House Vernal Riffe, along with other politicians and physicians who had helped create the state's newest medical institution. The trustees of 1823 would have loved it.

Before the renovation dust had cleared in Grosvenor, a search was begun for a dean who would have the doctor of osteopathy degree. Frank W. Myers, associate dean of the college during its first year, was named dean in October 1977. Myers's tenure of sixteen years would set a record for longevity and stability among medical college deans in Ohio. (When Myers retired in 1993, Barbara Ross-Lee, D.O., was named dean.)

Enrollment in the second class was 36, an incremental increase on target toward the eventual goal of 100 new students per year. By the end of the year, though, the man who had beaten the deadline to establish the medical college left the university. Faverman, who had remained in his post as vice provost of planning after Myers became dean of the medical college, left amid charges of conflict of interest in the admission of a medical student. As Ping told the trustees, "He is a talented and able man. I felt compelled to call for his resignation, but I did so with anguish and sorrow." Faverman left Ohio to take a position in medical research, but he returned in 1992 to accept the Phillips Medal of Public Service for his work in taking the medical college from a piece of paper in the General Assembly to a functioning college in record time.

The Phillips Medal had been created in the college's inaugural year, 1976, to honor J. Wallace Phillips and his wife, Jody Galbreath Phillips. Phillips had been an attorney for his father-in-law's real estate business, John W. Galbreath and Co. in Columbus. Galbreath, Class of 1920, and his daughter Jody, Class of 1946, were among Ohio University's most loyal alumni. She served as trustee of Ohio University from 1970 to 1979, and chaired the search committee when Ping was hired. The Phillips Medal rewards service in three categories: osteopathic medical practice, osteopathic hospital administration, and "public policy leadership exemplifying the best traditions of democratic concern for the public good and the public welfare." In the latter category, the medal was bestowed on such Ohio luminaries as Gov. James A. Rhodes, in 1976; U.S. Sen. John Glenn, in 1979; and Charles J. Ping, in 1985.

News that arrived in 1978 about the achievement of the inaugural class in the College of Osteopathic Medicine compensated for all the strain of the rapid creation. More than 90 percent of the students in the first class scored better than the national average on Part I of the National Board Examination administered in spring 1978. The class average was near the

70th percentile for the exam taken by 1,050 osteopathic medical students nationwide. "No official rankings of colleges are released," Ping told the trustees. "However, unofficially it appears that Ohio's students placed first in the nation among students taking the exam this year. This was the first opportunity for students in our college to take this examination, which is recognized by most states as part of the licensure process."

By 1980 the college enrolled 202 students and expanded into Irvine Hall, the second former residence hall converted to classroom use for the medical college. Frank Myers was in his third year as dean. In 1983 he began a fourteen-year stint as the voice of *Family Health*, a two-and-a-half-minute radio program of advice on various wellness issues. Produced by the Telecommunications Center at the university, *Family Health* grew into a network of 250 radio stations with an estimated audience potential of 10 million listeners by the turn of the century. The radio show was the first, but by no means the only, contribution the medical college made in service to the region outside its clinics.

The medical college got a scare in 1983 when the Ohio Board of Regents used the state's expensive medical education institutions for cost-cutting target practice (in one of many tight-budget years). Either reduce enrollments or lose three medical schools, the regents summarized in a report to the higher education establishment in Ohio. As the youngest medical program in the state, Ohio University's College of Osteopathic Medicine suffered anxiety, but no ultimate damage to its health. In fact, by 1987, data in Grosvenor Hall admissions began to mirror the numbers in Chubb Hall for undergraduates. While applications to medical schools were down nationally, demand for places was up 10 percent at Ohio University. Ping also pointed out in a letter to the trustees that the class entering in 1987 was 14 percent minority and 29 percent women, numbers that confirmed the college's commitment to reflect the demographics in American society. Applications for the one hundred places grew each year and reached two thousand by 1992.

Another distinction for the college came in 1990 with accreditation by the Association for Ambulatory Health Care (AAHC). Considered by many in medicine to be the premier accrediting agency of medical facilities in the nation, the AAHC gave its seal of approval to three hundred ambulatory medical centers in the United States and only fifteen in Ohio. Ohio's college had already earned accreditation from the OOA, but the AAHC process included more than osteopathic facilities and was national in scope. Placement data a decade after the first class had graduated showed that a high percentage of graduates of the medical college continued to practice in underserved areas, particularly rural and small communities. By 1992, 70 percent of the graduates were working in Ohio, a fourth of those in communities with less than 10,000 population. Sixty-one percent of the graduates were engaged in primary care rather than in ancillary duties removed from direct contact with patients.

During Ping's last year as president, the College of Osteopathic Medicine was well enough established to offer new services to the region in addition to those in its five clinics. (In addition to the main clinic in Parks Hall, satellite clinics had been added in Coolville and Nelsonville.) The state funded an immunization program in 1994 that became the first such clinic operated by a university anywhere in the nation. Using a mobile unit, medical college associates would travel to public schools, shopping centers, and community centers in order to immunize children, free of charge, in twenty-one counties in southeastern Ohio. Medical students would now get early opportunities to practice primary care in rural areas while medical faculty would get opportunities for clinical research. Poor families would get life-saving protection for their children at no cost, not even for the gasoline for a trip to the county health department. A second outreach program that began in 1994 served underinsured and uninsured women in ten area counties. Mammograms and pap smears for breast and cervical cancer screenings were provided free of charge in the mobile unit, funded in part by AmeriCorps.

What happens inside the clinics, however, is central to the college's service, and the numbers underscore the benefits to the community provided by the College of Osteopathic Medicine. More than three hundred patients are seen each day by more than forty physicians in Parks Hall alone, a hub of medical expertise that serves nearly a fourth of the state. Other osteopathic physicians affiliated with Ohio University practice at nearby O'Bleness Memorial Hospital. Students learn medicine, citizens get wellness information and treatment, research is conducted, and new physicians remain in Ohio to give back to the larger community in a symbiosis that would have made Sen. Secrest applaud.

A New Home for Health and Human Services

With a medical college being integrated into the academic complex of the university, the time had arrived to discuss reconfiguration of health-related programs. The Educational Plan of 1977 was explicit about the possibility of consolidating such offerings into a single administrative framework. Under the rubric Health and Human Services, Goal #1 read: "To establish a sound structure that assures appropriate identification, coordination and development of those programs directly involved in the education and training of health professionals." As a corollary, Goal #3 read: "Eventually to house all units identified as health and human services within a comprehensive health education complex." The goals of the plan, however, were statements of principle and did not offer any specifics.

In 1978 Provost Bucklew named a faculty task force to evaluate organizational options for such a college. Heading the study group was Sam Goldman, former dean of the College of Education, who was serving on the provost's staff at the time. The report the task force drafted, while acknowledging the logic of restructuring health and human services programs into one entity, stated that costs and lack of a broad enough program base argued against forming a new college anytime soon. Instead, they recommended, an existing college, Education, should be restructured to incorporate health programs. The suggestion did not surprise anyone, given that Education might lose the most programs to a new college.

Bucklew saw it differently. As he maintained to the trustees, the benefits of creating an entirely new college would include closer cooperation and sharing among programs that were already strong. The increased visibility of college status might also generate external support and stimulate student recruitment in programs expected to grow, in light of national trend data in health care and services provided by both the public and the private sector. Bucklew reported that dozens of faculty from affected programs had initiated meetings with him to express support for a new college. Since Bucklew had also received petitions and other written endorsements, he told the board of trustees at its June meeting that he wanted to act on forming the new college. Furthermore, the College of Education was embarking on a search for a new dean, the perfect juncture for self-study and restructuring as the tandem establishment of the new structure progressed. Bucklew pledged to put a proposal before the board in January. To that end, he named a council for the creation of the new college and charged it with completing a report in time to present, discuss, and amend before January's board meeting. The report that entered the faculty arena in November was attacked immediately and harshly.

Faculty Senate decried the proposal *per se*, the speed with which it was moving, the administrative costs, and the specter of existing colleges' losing units to the newcomer. The College of Arts and Sciences opposed the existence of another professional college on campus. Tension mounted about the process for choosing which units would constitute the new configuration as affected colleges braced for the losses to come.

Bucklew countered with facts and figures. The costs would be minimal. Decisions on which units to move would be based on maximum functionalism, not faculty perception of loss of turf. He continued to point out that a large group of faculty representing programs central to the mission of the new college had endorsed it from its first mention. Other units were taking a "wait and see" posture. In short, the proposal for a new College of Health and Human Services had both support and opposition. The support came from the core programs under the rubric Health and Human Services; the opposition emanated from units whose sphere of influence might shrink. Still, senators against the idea asked for a meeting with the president in January before the issue went to the board.

"There is no room for debate over territorial jurisdictions," Ping told Faculty Senate, insisting that program duplications, which would be more costly than the new configuration, were not an option. At the meeting with the president, the support of faculty most affected by the proposal was emphasized. Professor Donald Fucci presented a statement signed by forty faculty members asking Senate to support the creation of the new structure. Senate's Educational Policy Committee passed a resolution approving the proposal, but not without expressing "very serious reservations concerning the establishment of the college and the process by which that decision was made."

The trustees voted in favor of the new college on January 27, 1979. The tenth degree-granting college at Ohio University would include the following units:

- The School of Hearing and Speech Sciences (later named the School of Hearing, Speech, and Language Sciences),
- The School of Health, Physical Education, and Recreation (later split into the School of Recreation and Sport Sciences and the School of Health Sciences),
- The School of Home Economics (later named the School of Human and Consumer Sciences),
- The Nursery Child Care Center,

- The Center for Human Development, and
- The School of Nursing.

A search for a dean began. Then an announcement came weeks after the formal approval that served as an affirmation. The Appalachian Regional Commission announced a three-year grant in the amount of $257,000 for development of the College of Health and Human Services. In June 1980, Hilda Richards came to Athens from New York City to become the first dean of the college. She brought credentials ideal for both the academic and administrative challenges ahead—psychiatric nursing—and helped to yield a unique distinction in only three years. The National League of Nursing granted full accreditation for eight years to the new School of Nursing, even though the university's model did not fit existing patterns of accreditable nursing instruction. Most nursing programs either trained Registered Nurses or conferred the Bachelor of Science in Nursing degree. Both required clinical training. Ohio University's program conferred the BSN on RNs by taking the instruction to working nurses via the regional campuses. Ping himself accompanied nursing faculty to New York to explain to the league that RNs in southeastern Ohio needed opportunities for development and continuing education and had few options to get it. The university's contingent in New York convinced the league that the BSN program filled that niche in the sparsely populated, entirely non-urban region.

A new School of Physical Therapy, added to the college by the Ohio Board of Regents in 1983, featured state-of-the-art laboratory and clinic facilities in the Convocation Center and was funded by grants from the Appalachian Regional Commission.

Former Provost Bucklew, whose steadfast action had created the college, returned to speak at its tenth anniversary symposium in 1989, as did its first dean, Hilda Richards, who was provost at Indiana University of Pennsylvania at the time. It was more than a celebration of achievements. Acting Dean Michael Harter detailed the societal needs that would make the college's programs even more essential in the future: an aging U.S. population, the explosion of knowledge in health fields, the growth in interdisciplinary teamwork to meet health-related challenges, and a shift in focus from treatment to prevention of illnesses. The promotion of wellness and healthier life styles as a means to avoid health problems, which was the key trend for the future, was central to the mission of the College of Health and Human Services.

Educating Government—ILGARD

Serving local governments in the twenty-eight counties surrounding Athens with educational resources was the mission of a new entity created in 1981. The Institute for Local Government Administration and Rural Development, condensed so often to its acronym ILGARD that many do not know its full name, provided such services as assistance on surveys, statistical data-gathering, and workshops on financial management for a host of regional, county, and community governing bodies. As the mechanism for converting the university's expertise into assistance for the region (and later the state), ILGARD was created to provide "applied research and technical assistance to government and development organizations," according to the introduction in its literature. In the words of its own mission statement, ILGARD's goals are:

1. to improve the performance, innovation, and efficiency of government;
2. to serve as an applied research center for state, regional, and local policy issues;
3. to provide information and technology services for increased regional competitiveness; and
4. to involve undergraduate and graduate students in public service projects.

The last goal assured that ILGARD would serve as a learning laboratory for students in several academic disciplines while serving its nonacademic clients.

As federal grants for public works projects declined in the 1970s, rural areas were left with little assistance in formulating policies for investment and development. With tax bases that barely funded schools and roads, such areas had no money left over to consult experts on how to implement state-mandated standards on various functions, such as establishing solid waste districts. In response, the board of trustees approved ILGARD as a resource center to serve the region. Its director, Mark Weinberg of the political science department, would coordinate an interdisciplinary staff that included graduate students.

ILGARD received additional financial assistance from the state in 1985 that permitted expansion of services and an increase in clients. Ohio University's government outreach unit would serve as the coordinating institution of a three-university consortium called the Rural Universities Program (RUP), overseen by the board of regents. Other members are Bowling Green University and Miami University. Technical assistance and management training were added. One example was ILGARD's assistance in the computerization of budget planning and records to bring county governments in the region up to modern standards they could not afford to meet on their own. Another ILGARD service aided counties in complying with the state's directive to collect information on infrastructure in a systematic way. Through workshops on automated computer mapping, spreadsheet analysis, and capital improvement planning, county engineers learned they could park their pencils and paper and use computer screens and keyboards to compile information on bridges, roads, and culverts with greater accuracy and speed. Eventually, nonprofit/nongovernmental organizations too became clients for ILGARD's services.

Taking stock at its tenth anniversary, ILGARD counted nearly 500 completed projects, from nuts-and-bolts tasks like preparing grant applications to more strategic exercises such as planning for long-term economic development. The growth in personnel, though not as significant as the output, totaled seven people with a part-time group of ten graduate students and six faculty advisers, all overseen by a seventeen-member advisory committee. Key examples of ILGARD's accomplishments at the ten-year mark were economic and demographic analyses of three southeastern Ohio counties, which were made available to both public and private entities. Another milestone was reached, thanks to a grant from the W. K. Kellogg Foundation, in assisting municipal and township officials through additional workshops in environmental management, computer use, mapping, and financial management.

Meanwhile, students from geography, geology, and environmental studies were applying classroom lessons in hands-on activities at ILGARD, such as digitizing and editing maps that described soil types, geological features, and underground mines and lakes. Though such information was useful in determining where to locate a landfill, to cite one example, it also became crucial to later projects on watersheds and creek restoration efforts that made verifiable improvements to the environment of the region by the turn of the century. By its tenth anniversary ILGARD's list of services ranged from child and family program assistance (e.g., a needs assessment report for a potential Head Start launch) to Geographic Information Systems to welfare reform efforts. ILGARD is now one of five units that make up the Voinovich Center for Leadership and Public Affairs, formally dedicated in May 2002.

Learning for Life

The premise of the Lifelong Learning and Regional Higher Education category in the first Educational Plan was that a host of societal changes was generating the need for educational responses. The proliferation of new knowledge was creating the necessity for people to update their education throughout their lives. The number of eighteen- to twenty-four-year olds, the traditional age to enroll in college, was shrinking. Trends in the workplace also showed an increasing number of people making career changes more than once in a lifetime, especially since manufacturing jobs were disappearing. The concomitant effect in higher education of the changing demographics and diminishing opportunity in industry was a new appreciation for older students. Yet people outside the traditional mold of eighteen- to twenty-four-year-old, full-time students required different options for enrolling in classes, methods that would permit them to build education around work schedules. In addition, with new technology on the horizon that would expand the choices for nontraditional classroom learning, it was clear that an administrative structure to encompass all the nontraditional options would put the university in a better position to meet the demands of a new constellation of educational needs. Goal #1 in the category of Lifelong Learning and Regional Higher Education therefore read: "Establish a University office concerned with lifelong learning."

The goal was met when the new administrative unit called the Office of Lifelong Learning was approved in January 1980 after Faculty Senate had approved the proposal the preceding October. Vice Provost James Bryant, whose duties included the regional campuses and the Telecommunications Center, would oversee the new unit for the time being. A cafeteria of choices—some old, some new—was collected under the new title: adult learning services, correspondence courses, assessment of experiential learning for credit, course credit by examination, a program for the incarcerated, and campus continuing education, including workshops and conferences. On-line courses, a glimmer on the horizon, would also be included as the enabling technology advanced, with the Telecommunications Center providing the delivery. (The Telecommunications Center, however, would be moved to the College of Communication in 1997.) Though there was an attempt by Senate's Educational Policy Committee to delay implementation, the office proceeded with its mission under interim director Edward Mitchell until Joseph Tucker was named director of the Office of Lifelong Learning in late summer 1980.

The last photograph taken of former president John Calhoun Baker with Charles and Claire Ping, at Chatham, Massachusetts, August 1992

Fritz Russ (Class of 1942), founder of Systems Research Laboratories, with Ping in Dayton in 1993 (photo by Dick Robe, former dean of the Russ College of Engineering and Technology)

The first family during Ping's last year as president. *Front row, left to right:* Choung Ping with son Jackson in her lap, Sam Venable, Stephen Venable, Ann Shelton Ping Venable with daughter Katie in her lap. *Back row, left to right:* Andy Ping, Claire Ping, Charlie Ping, and Jim Venable.

A surrey with a green fringe on top carries Ohio fans in the 1994 Homecoming Parade. Katie Venable is seated in her grandmother Claire's lap and holds the parade marshal's hand. Samuel and Stephen Venable take the back seat.

Kenner Bush presenting the Outstanding Service Award on behalf of the Athens Chamber of Commerce to Charles and Claire Ping, 1994

Claire Oates Ping, 1994

Andy Ping on the beach with son Jackson in San Diego in 1995

Robert Axline (Class of 1957), Vice President for Development Jack Ellis, and Ping in 1996

Inaugural class of Cutler Scholars, 1996–97. *Front row, left to right:* Assistant Director Ruth Phipps, Amanda Sledz, Heather Baird, Co-director Butch Hill. *Back row, left to right:* Kevin Fritz, Co-director Charles J. Ping, Cary Bishop, Alanna Beatty. *Not pictured:* Marcie E. Barber.

At the presentation of the Baker Award to Ping in November 2002: "everyday citizen" Ping with Professor of English Sam Crowl and Ping's grandson Stephen Venable (Photo by Daniel Shao, Class of 1972)

One new feature of Lifelong Learning was its Adult Learning Services Office, which focused on adults returning to college or attending for the first time. Ping reported in the 1981 Convocation Address that the office had established a program, subsequently approved by the University Curriculum Council, to grant academic credit to adults for college-level learning acquired outside the classroom in real-world experiences. He also reported that independent study enrollments had increased by 25 percent over the past five years. Of the 250 faculty who taught correspondence courses or course-credit-by-examination, several had won national awards for the design of their courses.

"Over the past five years, the composition of the student population on our regional campuses has changed dramatically," Ping said in the address. In short, the university was serving more adults at its regional campuses, which were evolving into more than mere branches. Among the achievements Ping cited at the regional centers were the Executive Master of Business Administration program at the Lancaster campus, begun in 1976, and the Master in Liberal Studies, a discrete intellectual program of study independent of specific career goals. In addition, Ping praised the wide variety of educational, cultural, news, and public affairs programming produced and broadcast to the region via the university's public radio and television stations in the Telecommunications Center.

Transferring Knowledge to the Marketplace

The State of Ohio's traditional industrial economy was fast disappearing in the 1980s. As the state budget suffered, universities steeled themselves to be first in line again for budget cuts. A new idea, however, was gaining momentum—maybe universities held the keys to economic recovery. After all, many of the new technologies that were revolutionizing the surviving industries as well as creating entirely new businesses had emanated from thinkers in higher education. More fundamentally, universities were already think tanks by definition, and were the most likely sources of better mousetraps—or a better mouse, as the case would be. As the realization spread that the economy of the future would be knowledge based, another idea was spreading: that the real economic benefits of valuing higher education truly outweighed the political capital of merely saying so. Dick Campbell, editor of the *Columbus Citizen Journal* (and Ohio University trustee from 1985 to 1993), captured the spirit of the shift in his pithy sentence: "Maybe Ohio is going to start using its brains instead of its back." Terms such as *innovation, incubation, transfer,* even *park* were retooled to describe the process of harnessing intellectual talent as the engine of economic recovery. The newfound appreciation for universities' potential to aid economic recovery manifested itself in rewards and incentives that underscored state government's recognition that its higher education system, like the girl next door, had grown into something worthy of attention. At Ohio University, the trend was discernable in science, engineering, and business research, which had geared up without waiting for the state to offer incentives.

The first and best known of the university's transfer examples pivoted on the very term *transfer,* before the corporate world borrowed it to denote "transferring knowledge from the laboratory to the marketplace." Gene transfer—the technique of removing a gene from one species and transforming it into a genetic legacy in a different species—was born at Ohio University. The first successful gene transfer was accomplished by Thomas Wagner, biochemist, and Joseph Jollick, microbiologist, who transferred a rabbit gene into mice. Not only did the gene function as nature intended—manufacturing part of the hemoglobin in blood—but it also was inherited by the next generation of mice. Formerly the stuff of science fiction, genetic engineering had been hatched in an oven in Athens, Ohio. Quite literally—lacking a full complement of research equipment, the pair of researchers used Jollick's oven to incubate the first litter of transgenic mice.

Wagner had been working for eight years on the key variable of the timing of the DNA injection into mice egg cells. Some of the related experimentation had been conducted in collaboration with Jackson Laboratory in Bar Harbor, Maine, but Wagner and Jollick were Ohio University faculty who lived in Athens, Ohio, an address that may have influenced the treatment of their discovery by some in the scientific community.

Gene transfer theory was not new. Neither was tinkering with the variables that could be manipulated in transfer research. As in most experimentation on revolutionary theories, lots of other scientists were racing to achieve the same breakthrough. Wagner and Jollick's gene transfer, however, was the first (1) to work and (2) to appear in subsequent generations of laboratory animals. Appropriately, it was also scheduled to be the first in print in the scientific world's premier journal, the *Proceedings of the National Academy of Sciences,* in September 1981. Another story, however, one befitting a journal of media ethics, unfolded when a more prestigious laboratory tried to upstage the little university in Ohio.

The story goes that Wagner, who was senior author, contacted the academy to discuss coordinating the university's announcement to the daily press with the publication in the scholarly press. He had followed protocol in submitting his findings to the academy, waiting for peer review, then postponing announcements until the *Proceedings* issue appeared in print. Wagner was told to wait some more, that the Ohio University research had been bumped from the September issue to make room for similar findings from researchers affiliated with the other, better-known lab. Wagner and Jollick's paper would appear in October. Exacerbating the insult in the scholarly press was the news that the *New York Times* was preparing a story on the rival research to coincide with the academy's September journal issue.

An unhappy Wagner called Ping. An angry Ping called an old friend, Dr. Philip Handler, who was still serving as president of the National Academy of Science. Ping reported the saga of the journal postponement of the findings by Wagner *et al.* and some additional twists to the story that more than called into question the ethics of the recognition raiders. An outraged Handler contacted Walter Cohn of the *Washington Post*. Science writers in the mainstream media, steeped in the journalistic tradition of conflict, hurried to prepare their competing stories. A second race was on.

The Pings' relationship with Handler could avert a serious slight to the Ohio University researchers. (Handler had been the Kennedy Lecturer five and a half years earlier during the weekend of Ping's inauguration as president. Claire Ping had been Handler's administrative assistant when he served as chairman of the Biochemistry Department at Duke when Ping was working toward the Ph.D. in philosophy.) A native New Yorker, Handler was actually gleeful, by Ping's description, at the prospect of a rumble in the politics of science. "Let me take care of it," he said to Ping on the phone. And justice did prevail, but the story behind the story has never been circulated until now.

Cohn's September 8 story about the Wagner-Jollick research was first to the front page. A host of media outlets, print and broadcast, that subscribed to the *Washington Post/Los Angeles Times* news service then picked up the story. Cohn's scoop called the Ohio University achievement "a historic first that can be expected to speed the already swift progress of genetic engineering." Cohn explained the potential human applications of the gene transfer process, which might become the ultimate weapon in conquering disease. The drama played well in television news, too, which featured a news conference in Irvine Hall. Though lights glared and cameras whirred,

Wagner and Jollick explained their research as if they were in a routine class, only the whole world was enrolled that day. Follow-up stories generated more than six hundred news clippings in publicity for the university, including political cartoons, which—though amusing—had very serious consequences. Ping said the national visibility played a role in attracting research grants as well as awards from the state once it did formalize incentives.

In a later interview, Wagner credited the president of the university with inspiring a can-do atmosphere for the research team, which also included Peter Hoppe, Richard Hodinka, Janice Gault, and David Scholl. "Ping had welcomed the challenge of trying to compete with anyone in the world," Wagner said. Ping couched the achievement in his signature term of community. The achievements, the publicity, and the later grants "all fed each other to create a total greater than the sum of its parts," Ping said.

The state soon came up with concrete plans to aid cooperation among the players working to craft a new economy. An Ohio Board of Regents' plan in 1982, written by Deputy Chancellor William Coulter, formally advocated legislation to improve linkages among higher education, business, and industry in the form of university "research parks." The pooling of talent within the research structures might speed new ways to link new technologies to the marketplace and boost the economy thereby. Ping lost no time in charging a committee with investigating the feasibility of such a park in Athens. Chaired by Dean of Arts and Sciences William Dorrill, the committee comprised researchers who brought different talents to the table. In the area of product application were Robert L. Savage, Chemical Engineering, whose research specialty was removing sulfur from Southeast Ohio coal; Roger Finlay, Physics, whose expertise was using neutron beam irradiation in cancer treatment; and Jollick, Microbiology, whose skills in DNA hybridization went beyond basic gene transfer to creating probes to improve disease diagnosis. Other committee members were Ellsworth Holden, Management Information Systems; Ronald Barr, Associate Provost for Research; Thomas Shevlin, visiting Stocker Professor in Mechanical Engineering; and Thomas Porter, Ping's administrative intern.

The group studied models and visited sites of research collaboration structures sponsored by other universities and concluded that Ohio University would benefit from a research park. However, the committee recommended that the university first launch an innovation center that would provide "needed incubation space for small high-tech entrepreneurs." Rather than wait for space and resources for a full-fledged research park, the group advocated using space in old Morton Hall (later renamed the President Street Academic Center) as a temporary site for the innovation center. Ping was eyeing acreage at the newly acquired Ridges for a future home for the research park, but the former chemistry classroom building, following a partial makeover, would suffice for now. Companies born in the innovation center might move into a research park eventually, but the university need not wait till then to provide business founders with faculty consultation in science, engineering, and business, plus management services that would cut start-up costs for new companies. Attracting the amount of capital required for a *bona fide* research park would be difficult, given the limitations of the university's setting in transportation-poor Southeast Ohio, the committee cautioned. Another argument against moving forward on establishing a research park was the daunting success-rate statistic—half of all attempts to establish and maintain research parks failed.

The fortunes of the region and the university were married at the altar of business incubation, with science, engineering, and business as attendants. Thus when the report went to the trustees, it got an attentive hearing. Trustee Fritz Russ, whose credentials in transferring research at Dayton's Systems Research Laboratories into profitable technology were impeccable, taught the other trustees the basics of innovation center benefits. The board approved the proposal in October 1982 to establish a research park and companion innovation center. Early in the planning phase, none other than Will Konneker agreed to serve as director of the new Innovation Center, giving up time at his own technology businesses in St. Louis to oversee the new venture at his alma mater one week per month. Ohio University was in business.

The next tasks were to establish a governing authority and to write operational guidelines. Since the title Innovation Center and Research Park was cumbersome, the authority that emerged in January 1983 was called ICRP. Chaired by Ping, its other members were three people from the business sector and three academic deans, as follows: Will Konneker, the volunteer, part-time director; Kenner Bush, Athens newspaper publisher and trustee; Ralph Schey, president of Cleveland-based Scott Fetzer Corp. and trustee; William Dorrill, Arts and Sciences; John Stinson, Business; and Richard Robe, Engineering and Technology. Serving as associate director was university planner Alan Geiger, while Provost James Bruning sat as an ex-officio member.

Bruning's participation was crucial, as he allayed concerns of the faculty that the ICRP would drain resources from more traditional academic functions. He assured the community that the center made good use of some excess building space and would soon be self-supporting. The start-up money came from the Ohio University Fund, not the university's budget, and state economic development grants were pending. Later, rents paid by clients would ease the cash flow at the ICRP. Involvement by faculty either as consultants or as entrepreneurs would be handled in contracts that separated the accounting of faculty time and center time. The Innovation Center was itself innovative; only a dozen or so existed nationwide in early 1983.

In the language of its literature, the Innovation Center "creates a community of entrepreneurs by providing short-term, flexible leases, access to expert networks and entrepreneurial education and guidance." In addition, the center offers more specific services: access to computers, printers, copiers, and fax machines; expertise in web-page development; workshops and seminars; mentors in business practices; high-speed Internet access; free access to database subscriptions; mail services; and a conference room with audio-visual equipment for presentations. The ultimate goal of any business incubator is to see its hatchlings (the industry term is *graduates*) become self-sufficient in an average of three and a half years. Potential clients of the Ohio University version would be focused on new or emerging technology, service businesses, or light manufacturing enterprises, with access to capital or potential thereto. Statistics from the National Business Incubator Association (NBIA) cited on the Ohio University Innovation Center web site underscore the imperative of the venture: 87 percent of incubated companies remain in business, and 84 percent of these remain in the community in which they were incubated. Graduating these viable businesses into the community adds jobs and income, plus sales and property tax boosts, to the local economy. In 1984, the three-year-old NBIA, the fledgling trade organization that tracked incubators' progress, moved its headquarters from Carlisle, Pennsylvania, to Athens.

Konneker, at work in the classroom building where his own knowledge of chemistry had been incubated thirty years earlier, predicted the Innovation Center would have clients by summer, since he was quite sure there were "good commercial ideas floating around the research labs." He was right. Seven months after Konneker moved into his office on President Street, Ping told Faculty Senate about the center's first three clients, and revealed that a fourth was coming.

The fourth business, announced in 1983, tapped the ongoing research of university faculty in genetics. Diagnostic Hybrids, Inc. (DHI), founded in 1984 by Jollick and others, included Konneker as a partner, except that Konneker donated his shares of stock to the Ohio University Fund. Using the gene-splitting and recombinant genetic expertise of Ohio University scientists, DHI would produce diagnostic kits that identified infectious diseases in minutes instead of days. In the words of the company's literature, "DHI is engaged in the development, manufacture and marketing of innovative molecular diagnostic products for clinical and research use, employing gene cloning, DNA probe, advanced cell culture and transgenic technology." A license was later awarded for cells used in the detection of infectious herpes simplex viruses, among other organisms. However, the license had come some years after DHI had been beaten to the license and patent offices by rival researchers in other races typical of efforts to corner the profits from new knowledge. DHI did win one race when Konneker obtained an exclusive license to produce genetically engineered cells for virus identification. Profits from royalties poured in at last, followed by $666,000 in grants from the National Institutes of Health. By 1992 the director of research at DHI was David Scholl, who had been a graduate student working for Jollick and Wagner when their 1981 gene transfer showed up in the grand-mice of a rabbit. Also by 1992, the Innovation Center had graduated twenty companies from its business boarding house to their own places in the community.

A separate office was added to the mix in 1991 for the express purpose of assessing the marketability of Ohio University research ventures. It was becoming increasingly difficult for a faculty member immersed in basic research to devote equal time to potential applications of the new knowledge as profit-making businesses. The new configuration, called the Technology Transfer Office, was launched to manage technology-based intellectual property through assistance with patenting, licensing, and kindred research on pricing and marketing products. The end result was not necessarily a new business housed in the Innovation Center, but that would have been welcome.

Winning the Selective Excellence Sweepstakes

In fall 1983 the state debuted its incentives "to enhance excellence and bring national recognition to Ohio's higher education system." Ohio was not the only state in the race to link talent in higher education with economic development, but it was surely one of the better coordinated. Gov. Richard Celeste, the General Assembly, and the Ohio Board of Regents all agreed: money must be targeted to university ventures that would improve the economic position of the state. As such, selections would be based not on the perennial measures of number of students or cost of programs, but on the concept of quality, which had been historically elusive in state budgeting. As Ping said in his 1984 Convocation Address, the state had moved "beyond access, beyond equity, beyond continuation budgets to a state commitment to quality and to the making of judgments." When Celeste, both as candidate and as governor, consulted with experts on how best to package the incentives, he listened to Ohio University's president, who advised Governor Celeste to focus on rigorous academic programs combined with campus-based research. He told the governor that the universities' role should be "to carve out a niche for Ohio in a variety of emerging technologies." The approach Ping recommended became part of the Ohio brand of incentives to higher education called the Selective Excellence Program.

Ranked fortieth in the nation in the percentage of its population holding college degrees, the state of Ohio had its work cut out. The aim was to grow more of its own experts with the Selective Excellence money, who might then found, underwrite, or manage new economic ventures. In round 1, $7.5 million was allocated for two specific competitions—(1) Program Excellence awards, earmarked for undergraduate programs with a track record of quality, and (2) Eminent Scholars, allocated for world-class scholars. One of the most appealing features of the new incentives was that the money came with short strings attached. Programs and scholar winners would have wide latitude to spend the money as they saw fit. The board of regents would award twenty-two Program Excellence awards of up to $200,000 each and name nine Eminent Scholars with $1 million endowments. The state gave half a million for the professorships; the university winners were responsible for raising the other half.

At the sound of the bell in 1983, universities scrambled to craft proposals and compete for the prizes. At Ohio University, an internal screening committee selected seven program proposals, the regents' limit from any one institution, to forward to the board of regents for consideration. The finalists were dance, geography, geological sciences, journalism, telecommunications, visual communication, and a list of Honors Tutorial College specialties. In the category of Eminent Scholar, two proposals were forwarded: Cellular and Molecular Biology and coal research in Chemical Engineering. In the first winnowing of proposals in March, the state narrowed its program choices to thirty-nine. Five from Ohio University's original seven were still in competition. In the scholar selections, both of the university's proposals were still in the running for nine chairs statewide. At this finalist phase, only five universities in the state were still represented. In the two months before winners were chosen, external reviewers visited campuses to learn more about the proposals than paper applications could communicate.

Ohio University fared well in the first biennial Excellence awards tourney in May 1984. Governor Celeste himself came to Athens to announce the Ohio University recipients of the state's $7.5 million largesse. Telecommunications, visual communication, and the science and mathematics majors in Honors Tutorial College won three of the twenty-two distinctions conferred by the state in the Program Excellence category. Honors Tutorial College Dean Margaret Cohn used the $107,000 grant to equip a computer laboratory in Hoover House, the residence hall where freshman and sophomore HTC students lived. Remaining money was used to provide modems to HTC students who lived off campus. The School of Telecommunications, whose director was Drew McDaniel, spent its $120,000 to establish a center for computer applications in broadcasting. The largest amount, $169,000, enabled Chuck Scott and Terry Eiler of the nascent School of Visual Communication to modernize the third floor of Seigfred Hall (and thereby to collect its students from various points on campus into one site) and to purchase equipment.

Another university program garnered Program Excellence funding in the second round of competition in June 1985. The E. W. Scripps School of Journalism, recently renamed to honor the founder of the Scripps Howard media conglomerate, got the largest amount that year from the state, $152,000, which the school used to equip its in-house broadcasting laboratory and to update the video display system in its graphics laboratory.

The timing of journalism's grant punctuated the Scripps School's momentum with an exclamation mark. Though the program comprised nearly 1,000 majors—bachelor's, master's, and doctoral—and was the largest at Ohio University, its quality had been validated by external reviewers in both the academy and the profession. A longtime stalwart in earning and re-earning national accreditation for its six sequences, the journalism school was ranked among the top ten in the nation by the Associated Press Managing Editors. In January that year, the faculty cheerfully made a midyear move from Lasher Hall to E. W. Scripps Hall at the end of South Court Street. One month before the Program Excellence announcement, the School of Journalism had celebrated its renaming and its new facility with distinguished guests from the Scripps family and other members of the Scripps Howard Foundation from Cincinnati. The dedication of the former Carnegie Library as E. W. Scripps Hall, made possible by $1.75 million in gifts from the Scripps Howard Foundation, drew other founding families in journalism to campus that May. Among them were descendants of School founder George Starr Lasher, relatives of School Director Cortland Anderson (who had died in December), and kin of Gordon Bush, publisher of the *Athens Messenger*. A later Scripps Howard grant paid the salaries of Scripps Howard Visiting Professionals, journalists with international credentials hired to come to Athens for a year to teach students and to bring worldly perspectives to the Ohio University community.

The university's three early winners in the Program Excellence awards parlayed their success into additional recognition. Telecommunications, Visual Communication, and Journalism earned the distinction for a second time in 1990. The General Education curriculum also got a 1990 Program Excellence grant, the first such honor for a general studies program given by the board of regents.

The graduate program in molecular and cellular biology earned a coveted Eminent Scholar award in the first round in 1984—not a surprise given the program's standing in the world, but nonetheless gratifying in that it was honored in its own land as well. (Of the nine scholars, four were at Ohio State, four at the University of Cincinnati, and one each at Akron and Ohio.) Dr. Thomas Wagner, lead writer of the Eminent Scholar proposal, said the award would aid the university's effort to be "a world leader in mammalian embryology" and would help recruit additional scientists and graduate students. The state grant of half a million dollars was matched by Milton Goll, Class of 1935, and his son, Lawrence Goll, Class of 1966, for Ohio's first Eminent Scholar chair, which was named for the two alumni. The person hired with the first Eminent Scholar grant and its matching alumni gift was John Kopchick, a microbiologist with Merck Research Laboratories. He had originated genetically immunized chickens and experimented with bovine growth hormones, among other projects. Moreover, Kopchick's objectivity about basic versus applied research would help to bring Ohio University's research community into a more synergistic productivity.

A later round of Eminent Scholar Awards from the Selective Excellence competition resulted in another chair for the university in 1988, this time in Contemporary History, filled by Albert Eckes. The third Eminent Scholar, in the School of Film, was announced in 1990, and was eventually filled by Rajko Grlic from Croatia.

By the close of the biennium, three new incentives called Challenge grants—Academic, Research, and Productivity Improvement—were added to the Selective Excellence palladium by the state. Researched and written by William Coulter, Ohio Board of Regents Chancellor, the new infusions of cash for higher education enjoyed strong support from the governor as well as the legislature because of the strategy of insuring the advancement of programs that were already good, rather than trying to build from scratch. Among the experts to testify in behalf of the new incentives was Ohio University's President Ping.

Academic Challenge grants, which bore an uncanny resemblance to Ohio University's UPAC model, would help to build nationally prominent centers of excellence to serve the state's interests. One percent of each public university's basic instructional appropriation would be awarded as a supplement that each institution would then award to the programs of its choice. Only two stipulations governed the selection of program awardees: (1) grants must be at least 10 percent of the unit's base budget, and (2) funding must last six years. The latter condition was foreshortened by the biennial and political realities of the legislature's budgeting, but the university preserved the spirit of the law by increasing the base funding of Academic Challenge designees from university coffers.

The university added a premise of its own. Ping and Bruning agreed that the Academic Challenge awards should be large enough to make a significant difference. Rather than dilute the money across a large number of units, the academic officers decided to concentrate the money's power in naming only three programs as recipients. A committee appointed by the provost ranked proposals before the state distributed the award, which surpassed $1 million in the first one-percent-of-subsidy computation in 1986. The three grantees were the Department of Management Systems ($300,000), the School of Telecommunications ($150,000), and Molecular and Cellular Biology ($560,000). The Computer Systems in Business Program in the Department of Management Systems, designated as a center of excellence serving the state's interest, parlayed its grant into a match from the Xerox Corporation for $200,000. The combined amounts funded an office automation laboratory in Copeland Hall and a distributive processing system for data collection. The program began with three majors but quickly surpassed two hundred. Telecommunications used its money for activities that brought faculty and students into contact with industry professionals, primarily through a visiting professionals program. Four departments in the College of Arts and Sciences shared the interdisciplinary graduate program in Molecular and Cellular Biology—botany, chemistry, psychology, and zoology-microbiology—and would share instructional and research equipment purchased with Academic Challenge money. The bulk of the grant, however, would pay for two new faculty lines in microbiology.

In the next biennium, the programs chosen to receive Academic Challenge money—that is, those with the potential to become nationally recognized—were Condensed Matter and Surface Sciences ($489,000), Avionics ($278,000), Film ($185,000), and Creative Writing ($175,000), the last of which used its grant to fund the Spring Literary Festival.

Research Challenge grants, for either new or expanded projects, were percentages of the amount of external grant support already secured by an institution. The university received $780,000 from the state in May 1986 to award to researchers. Moreover, the grants were intended to function as seed money to attract funds from the federal government, business, or industry. At Ohio University, Research Challenge awards were designated for those whose applications were simultaneously submitted to external grantors. In the words of Ron Barr, Associate Provost for Research, Research Challenge money would be delivered to a principal investigator "the day a research proposal goes in the mail" to an external agency. In short, the research project could begin immediately, rather than wait for the external sponsor to say yea or nay.

The last of the Selective Excellence categories, the Productivity Improvement Challenge, was an attempt to reward efforts to move more Ohioans into post-secondary education, primarily at two-year institutions, whether for traditional academics or for job training. The definition bypassed most of the university's mission, but did fit some of the associate-degree programs at the regional campuses, which got $310,000 of the $4.4 million the state set aside for Productivity Improvement. For example, at the Belmont County campus (the previous name of the Eastern Campus), an $80,000 grant was used to recruit area high school students. A project coordinator forged a network of teachers, counselors, and parents to persuade young people to consider post-secondary study, especially since the area's declining stalwarts of coal and steel production offered fewer opportunities for sustainable careers.

Sponsoring Research

Seeking more external dollars for research was an agenda with widespread support at the university. As early as 1977 an Office of Graduate Studies and Research was established with the twin purposes of expanding graduate-level offerings and encouraging research. The first Educational Plan had emphasized research, and a strategy for attracting external research money was one of the major topics in the Toward the Third Century Colloquium. Key researchers agreed that the university should focus on "pockets of specialization" that did not duplicate work at other universities. That strategy eventually paid off in the following figures: for every dollar the university invested as seed money for research, $7 came back from external sources. The policy of using either internal funds or Research Challenge awards to entice external grants served the university well as it built a research reputation "at the same time" (Ping's emphasizing phrase) that it insisted on excellent teaching. External funds would also move the university toward its goal of earning Research University status from the Carnegie Foundation for the Advancement of Teaching.

By the 1988–89 academic year, external grants in all disciplines at the university were up 60 percent from five years earlier. Some of the amounts were large enough to generate mass media headlines as well as research findings for scientific journals. Easily the largest amount was a $6 million federal contract for the Aviation Engineering Center. Richard McFarland and Robert Lilley in Avionics would test a new microwave landing system (MLS), scheduled for use by the nation's 150 largest airports, for the U.S. Department of Transportation. Earlier grants to Avionics came from the National Aeronautics and Space Administration—$600,000 to test the revolutionary navigational device called Global Positioning System (GPS)—and $900,000 from the Federal Aviation Administration for earlier MLS testing. But the largest grant for Avionics was yet to come. In late 1989, the aviation experts on campus received $18 million in federal contracts to test aviation safety devices. Private research and development firms would be partners with the university in the four year experimentation on air traffic surveillance, navigation, and communication.

In the $1 million category was a 1987 grant from the National Heart, Lung, and Blood Institute to Thomas Creer and Harry Kotses of the Department of Psychology, who developed a program to teach adult asthma patients to take more responsibility for their own treatment. Another million arrived in 1988 from the National Institutes of Health to Lawrence

Bergman of the Department of Chemistry for genetic research on yeast and its role in human cell response to environmental stimuli.

A major grant in 1988 was $519,000 from the National Science Foundation to physics faculty Jacobo Rapaport and Roger Finlay for their research program on the interaction of nucleons with matter. In addition to using the university's accelerator laboratory, the physics team oversaw experimentation in the Los Alamos National Laboratory and the Indiana University Cyclotron Facility. By the early 1990s, the university's accelerator lab had been eclipsed by higher energy labs elsewhere for research in nuclear physics. The campus facility's future lay in ion beam technologies, "analyzing and characterizing exotic new materials to be used in everything from human hip joints to space shuttle engines," Finlay said. In an evolving collaboration for an evolving field, the physics faculty in both experimental and theoretical physics joined forces with the interdisciplinary Condensed Matter and Surface Sciences Program (CMSS) for research in a renovated and renamed facility. What was once the John E. Edwards Accelerator Laboratory became the Institute for Nuclear and Particle Physics in 1991. CMSS faculty then landed a $400,000 grant for new equipment, giving new life to the sole remaining accelerator in the state of Ohio as an incubator, of sorts, for "designer surfaces" for industrial needs. Accelerating ions to high velocity in the accelerator enabled them to penetrate the surface of materials. The results were new chemical and metallurgical structures formed when the charged particles became implanted in the existing materials. The twenty CMSS faculty who collaborated on such projects were housed in six different departments—chemistry, physics, and geology in Arts and Sciences and chemical, mechanical, and electrical-computer engineering from the Russ College of Engineering and Technology.

The Ohio Department of Development awarded $244,000 for additional research on "scrubbing smokestacks," the industry term for reducing sulfur dioxide emissions in the burning of coal, which was hypothesized to contribute to acid rain. Other research recognition at the university came in the form of national awards. Jon Ahlquist, whose research on the evolution of birds changed the traditional classification system of the entire class of *Aves*, was co-recipient of a named award from the National Academy of Sciences. John Zook, a neurobiologist, garnered a Research Career Development Award from the National Institutes of Health for his research on the auditory function of bats, the findings of which had eventual human application. Richard McFarland of the Avionics Engineering Center was presented the Distinguished Service Award by the Federal Aviation Administration for his contribution to aviation safety.

Ping's 1989 Convocation Address detailed additional developments in research, beyond a mere list of who obtained how much money in grants and who won what awards:

1. Shared research laboratories on two floors of the former engineering building, not only to reduce duplication costs, but also to foster collaborations.
2. A statewide Supercomputer Network used by the university.
3. A revolving fund of half a million dollars that the provost would use to recruit junior faculty and jump-start their research.
4. Announcement that the state's Research Challenge would provide $800,000 in seed money for research in the next biennium.
5. A progress report on the research enhancement project directed by alumna Jeanette Grasselli.
6. Citation of data from Vice Provost for Research and Graduate Programs Lloyd Chesnut on the university's continued growth in research grants for both individuals and projects.

Ping always maintained that the university could and should excel in both teaching and research. "We are the heirs of two distinct and venerable traditions which have shaped American higher education: the residential college and the research university," Ping said in the 1989 address. The residential background, which was American in origin, blended with the German legacy of "faculty immersed in research and the search for new knowledge." The university's accomplishments in research by 1989, added to its 184-year history as a residential campus, led Ping to conclude: "Ohio University is, I believe, well positioned to make unusual contributions to the lives of students and faculty by drawing together into one the two traditions which have shaped American colleges and universities over the past 300 years."

The amount of grant money continued to increase at the university even though there was more competition for those dollars and fewer sources, as federal support stagnated. At the state level, a new governor would retain the Research Challenge as the sole remaining component of the Selective Excellence bounty. When Ohio University's 1958–59 student body president moved into the governor's mansion in 1991, state coffers were so depleted that George Voinovich brought his desk chair from

Cleveland rather than spend state money on a duplicate. But he retained the Research Challenge awards as the piece most likely to help restore Ohio's economy.

There were other measures of research excellence as well, one quantifiable, one qualitative. Before Ping retired, the university he had shepherded for nineteen years attained the status of Research University, one of only 125 in the nation recognized by the Carnegie Foundation for the Advancement of Teaching. The Research University II classification meant that Ohio University was in the same league with institutions conferring at least fifty doctoral degrees per year and attracting between $15.5 and $40 million in federal grants and contracts annually. The 1993 university total was $29 million; the 1976 total had been $2.8 million. A minuscule 3.4 percent of 3,600 colleges and universities reviewed by the Carnegie Foundation in 1993 met the criteria for research stature. The successes in research attracted more than dollars and status to Ohio University, just as Ping had hoped. As Tom Wagner had pointed out years earlier, "There must be a critical mass of major players in a research area, so that an area of excellence is not dependent on one person." It did become easier to attract new faculty with research credentials once it became apparent that Ohio University intended to encourage pioneers of new knowledge. In the Ping perspective, the research community had become greater than the sum of its parts.

Uniting Research and Markets—the Edison Biotechnology Institute

Though Governor Celeste's Thomas Alva Edison Partnership Program was not under the Selective Excellence rubric, it stemmed from the same premise, that the state should encourage higher education and private industry to work together to revitalize the state's economy. With the Department of Development as matchmaker, the state offered dowry to technology development centers, most of them housed at universities, if they joined private businesses to advance research that had market potential. The contract required the business partner to provide half the money, while the state paid the university's half. Along with seed money for small business incubators, the program functioned as a mega-incubator for the State of Ohio that aimed to bring new jobs to Ohio's displaced factory workers.

The Ohio Board of Regents encouraged universities applying to become Edison Centers to link their proposals to the strengths of their academic infrastructure. Because the gene transfer accomplishments of Wagner had put the university on the biotechnology map of the world two years earlier, the proposal from Athens pivoted on genetic engineering. Wagner would head the venture. An animal biotechnology center, with the specific goal of improving livestock, would draw upon the expertise of faculty and doctoral students in the year-old graduate program in molecular and cellular biology. Gene-transfer technology, applied to cattle and swine, could produce animals that grew faster, used food more efficiently, and resisted diseases. Conventional breeding methods might take a decade to produce a beefier cow or a healthier pig, but biotechnology's shortcuts could generate profits more quickly for Ohio's farmers as well. One specific example was Wagner's work on growth hormones, illustrated in media reports with photographs of his big, fast-growing laboratory rats. Livestock that grew as fast would cut the time to market size and use less feed en route.

In addition to its partnership with the Ohio Farm Bureau Federation, which would serve as liaison to livestock farmers, the university's proposal included two other partners from higher education: the medical school at Case Western Reserve University and the Agricultural Research and Development Center at Wooster, administered by Ohio State University. The all-important business link, the company that would provide matching funds for the state's Edison grant, would be Athens's own Embryogen, Inc., co-founded by Will Konneker. The application for the center also emphasized that the university was submitting a bid for an Eminent Scholar in molecular and cellular biology. With its own Innovation Center taking shape and the potential for another scholar in the field, the university was well positioned to land an Edison Center in Athens.

At a press conference in Columbus in July 1984, Governor Celeste announced the first six Centers for Applied Technology Application through the Thomas Alva Edison Partnership Program. Both Ping and Konneker were present for the announcement that Ohio University had won the state's first biotechnology research center for the Athens campus. The state grant of $3.1 million, when added to Embryogen Inc.'s match, yielded $6.2 million for the next biennium. "This represents the largest single grant of funds for basic and applied research in the history of Ohio University," Ping said in the October Convocation Address. "In this project I am firmly convinced that we are riding the crest of the wave of the future as universities respond to the changing expectations of society."

In addition, Diagnostic Hybrids at the university's Innovation Center got an Edison seed grant of $250,000 to continue Jollick's genetic research applied to diagnostic probes. The company provided the required match through its own resources. Moreover, the Edison seed grants, unlike the money for the center itself, had to be repaid once the company's products were on the market. As such, the state's $250,000 functioned more like a loan or venture capital than an outright gift. Five years later, DHI got approval from the Food and Drug Administration to market its Herpes Probe Test, which was based on technology on which DHI held the patent, thereby securing DHI's profit-making stability.

The Edison Center, however, encountered an array of formidable challenges en route to equilibrium. Even though the center at Ohio University got a second Edison grant from the state for $2.5 million, Department of Development officials and legislators began to grumble about the paucity of profits and jobs generated by their gifts to the Athens center. Investors, including the state, wanted results and profits. Scientists in the academy, on the other hand, wanted to replicate basic research (which took time) rather than to market half-incubated ideas. While pure science enhanced the reputation of the university, filled scholarly journals, and spawned stories in the mass media, basic research did not generate immediate dollars or jobs. To complicate matters further, profits depended on licensing of practical applications of patented basic processes. Until the university mastered these commercial details, the Edison Center's partners would not be happy with the match. In short, it had been impossible at the beginning of the biotechnology age to certify the best mix of research-and-development and overt assistance to manufacturing, but the picture was becoming clearer. First, university partners would have to acquire more business savvy. (The Technology Transfer Office was created in 1991 to focus on the business arrangements.) Second, scientists in the academy would have to yield some basic research in favor of applied modes.

Not to be marginalized in the debate were critics in the general public who saw gene transfer as a violation of world order on either natural or religious grounds and lobbied their legislators accordingly. Though the Edison Center was never jeopardized by such opposition, it surely added weight to the state's charge to the university to "hurry up and produce results."

One turn of events in the story of the university's Edison Center illustrates how close the partners came to divorce over money matters. Konneker had to concede the license on the gene transfer technology to capitalists in New Jersey in exchange for their continued support of Embryogen, the university's original Edison partner. Embryogen had not attracted investors until 1990, despite Konneker's concerted efforts. The gene transfer field was too new, too risky, and too crowded with research trials to be considered a safe investment. The company even moved to New Jersey in 1990, to the chagrin of partners in Ohio government, and was renamed DNX. The relocated company agreed to retain a farm in Athens County just to mollify the Ohio Department of Development.

An additional paradox further illustrates the complexity of the situation. The license on which DNX was making money was based on a patent that was not granted until 1989, when it was finally awarded to Ohio University. It was Tom Wagner's 1981 gene transfer procedure using micro-injection, co-owned by Peter Hoppe, who had relocated to Jackson Laboratories in Bar Harbor, Maine. One science writer even recited a litany of scientific breakthroughs (some of them licensed) around the world that had been dependent on the 1981 discovery in Athens, all of them created in the eight years before the formal patent was awarded in 1989.

Yet another development affected the profit-making potential of the Edison Animal Biotechnology Center. The real money was not in animal research at all, but in human medical diagnosis. The reason was clear. Each successive generation of humans was a potential market. On the other hand, subsequent generations of transgenic livestock produced no royalties for underwriters, no sustainable business for the state, and no new jobs for politicians to tout. At the center, scientists were quietly making the shift from animal biotechnology to human medical applications. It was the right prescription for profits.

By 1990, one finding after another was converted to commercial application via licensing that would return money to the university. In addition to the original DNX (which had begun as Embryogen) and Diagnostic Hybrids, Inc., two other companies were built on headline-making research by Edison Center scientists. Progenitor, Inc. was poised to develop antiviral drugs from stem cell production, based on basic research by Wagner and colleagues. Sensus would manufacture drugs that would retard cell development in diseases. The creation by Kopchick and Wen Y. Chen of a growth hormone antagonist laid the foundation for a new class of drugs that Sensus would market. Money followed such sales potential, and the university announced major grants from Procter and Gamble and the National Institutes of Health to projects underway at the Edison Biotechnology Center.

By 1993, Ping told the trustees, "The annual budget of the University's Edison Center exceeds $2.5 million, with about 40 percent of the research funding derived from Ohio-based companies." One more modification in 1994 certified the change in direction from animal to human research. The local Edison Animal Biotechnology Center dropped the words Animal and Center from its name, added the word Institute and affiliated with the statewide Edison Biotechnology Center. There were reasons for what seemed confusing at the name level. The statewide Edison Biotechnology Center was a new and improved state network that had the business acumen to assist scientists in commercial details and the business connections to find commercial partners. The new name, new affiliation, and new research direction in human therapeutics had remedied a host of ills as the Edison Biotechnology Institute prepared to move into its new home at The Ridges. The year the move was completed, 1995, a survey by the Association of University Technology Managers ranked Ohio University seventh in the nation, and number 1 in the state of Ohio, in ratio of invention disclosures to sponsored research dollars. Productivity ratio aside, the data also showed that Ohio's innovations cost less per invention. Both measures served as diagnostic kits for the future health of biotechnology at Ohio University.

CHAPTER FIVE

ENLIGHTENING INTERDEPENDENCE

Circumnavigating a Holistic World

A popular graphic design hangs on the wall in various offices at Ohio University. Created by Catherine Steiner for the geography department's Cartographic Division in 1983, the illustration features a map of the world as its centerpiece. And the center of the world map is Athens, which is marked on the globe by a star proportionately larger than the town's actual dot on the map. Major landmarks at Ohio University and in the Athens community—Cutler Hall, City Hall, and the Convocation Center, to name only three of the eighteen—are positioned around the world. Edging the design in counterclockwise order are portraits of Ohio University's presidents, with Jacob Lindley on the left side of the Class Gate at the top center of the design, and Charles Ping on the right.

Words from Ping's 1977 Convocation Address had formed the axis for the illustration's meaning. When he introduced his six themes of the community, number four was *The Commitment to International Community, to Education for Interdependence*. "One of the unusual and significant characteristics of the present state and history of Ohio University," Ping said, "is the number of international students, the resources and programs in international education, and the movement of our faculty and students back and forth between this campus and the world." He then outlined how the movement between campus and the world was transpiring, beyond the obvious mode of travel itself: in curriculum content, research design and emphasis, library collections, training of practicing professionals, and delivery of professional services.

In 1979, the year the cherry trees were planted along the Hocking, more than nine hundred students from eighty different nations were enrolled at the university, a geometric increase from the lone Japanese man in 1895 who was the first international student to graduate from Ohio University. The international experience was more prominent among faculty than it was in the student tallies, as Ping pointed out in the Convocation Address in 1979: "The number of Ohio University faculty who have lived, taught and done research in other countries is surprisingly high. Their activity is not limited to countries that are so much a part of our common western heritage; rather it centers in Africa, Asia, the Middle East, South America."

Ping then described two events that lent drama and focused attention on the university's commitment to international education in the preceding year. One was the fall visit of a delegation from the People's Republic of China headed by the president of Peking University, who gave his first press interview in the United States on the Athens campus of Ohio University. The other event was the World Communications Conference in the spring, which made Athens the center of worldwide debate on the role of mass media in a changing world. The videotaped record of the conference was broadcast on more than two hundred Public Broadcasting Service stations nationwide. Ping emphasized, though, that discrete events such as these should not obscure the continuous task at hand. "What makes a difference is the day to day work to open our eyes and the eyes of our students to the literal shrinking of this planet, where instant communication and immediate economic impact make the earth a single interdependent community."

From the International Film Festival to the International Street Fair, reminders of Athens's friendships around the world kept interdependence salient to the community. The street fair, begun in 1982, grew each year as a Court Street showcase of food, dance, and culture of Asian, African, and Latin nations. One of its highlights was the colonnade of flags on either side of the walkway on College Green between the College Gate and Cutler Hall, one flag for every nation represented by a student at the university. By the 1984–85 academic year, international enrollments at the university had increased to 1,394 students, about half undergraduate and half graduate, from eighty-four nations, or 9 percent of the total fall enrollment. Once the students from around the world arrived in Athens, they were aided in their transition to study by the university's Ohio Program of Intensive English (OPIE). The university's international student services office and a community-based network called Athens Friends of International Students (AFIS) helped the students adapt to life in small-town America. OPIE teacher Mary Kaye Jordan spearheaded the founding of AFIS.

Agreements—research projects, contracts for service, exchanges, and staff development—between Ohio University and institutions beyond U.S. borders had grown from twenty-eight in 1982 to sixty in 1985. Added to such opportunities as the Peace Corps and Fulbright Hayes Scholarships, such agreements yielded a percentage that validated the star of Athens on the world map: more than one third of the faculty had studied, researched, or taught abroad in a formal program. In addition to the increase in international students coming to Athens and in Athens faculty going abroad, Ping hoped that more American students at Ohio University would choose to study abroad. In each year of his presidency, that number also increased as more options were added to the menu of opportunities abroad, from formal study, to internships, to work, to volunteering.

Ping's emphasis on international education was grounded on more than academic idealism. In the 1981 Convocation Address, after describing the university's latest developments in international education, he reiterated his determination to expand offerings. The Ohio University effort "reflects the hard fact that our world has changed and that the careers of current American students will unfold in a century that must find ways to resolve conflicts or it will destroy itself, a world that cannot exist simply as a series of national wills, because it is a world increasingly interdependent," he said.

In 1982 Ping's entire Convocation Address was devoted to international education. As the university's commitment to international community and education for interdependence had become many-sided, Ping advocated a self-assessment of the university's "complex set of agreements and formal ties with governments, universities and agencies." Citing four issues that needed to be addressed, Ping called for discussion that would advance the university's goals as a leader in international education. First was defining and clarifying objectives, a job he delegated to an ad hoc committee headed by Vice Provost for International Programs Felix Gagliano. The committee would survey and evaluate current international programs, find ways to encourage more interaction between international and domestic students, and study the variables in recruiting and admitting international students.

Second of the four overriding issues was devising "principles to govern our international activities." Rather than act as a free agent, Ping pledged to recommend to the trustees that the university adopt comprehensive guidelines that had been developed the previous year by the Association for Foreign Student Affairs. Curricular emphasis, the third area Ping listed for consideration, would go beyond the cursory choices of Tier II's category of Third World Cultures (later renamed Cross-Cultural Perspectives), especially in the professional schools. The fourth issue, service and outreach, addressed the university's charge to enlighten the region outside its classrooms and labs, to share its international knowledge with public schools and the community at large. This fourth initiative was implemented in 1982 with the founding of the Ohio Valley International Council, headed by Mary Anne Flournoy. Aided by a grant from the National Endowment for the Humanities, the general goal of the council was to increase international awareness in the region via programs in schools and businesses.

Ping concluded the address by grounding the university's international offerings on two American ideals, one he updated and one he affirmed in its original form. He rejected George Washington's admonition against "foreign entanglements" while upholding Washington's rationale of enlightened self-interest. "Today interdependence is a practical understanding of both our self-interest and our future," Ping said. The second maxim he cited was from a star student of the Enlightenment, Thomas Jefferson. Wording from the Declaration of Independence on the inalienable right to "life, liberty, and the pursuit of happiness" had value beyond its original purpose in the American colonies, Ping said. "Education for interdependence is the exercise of this conviction," Ping said. "It accepts difference, nurtures self-consciousness, and thus the recognition of difference. At the same time it teaches the common humanity and the shared interdependence of all people and all nations in the pursuit of happiness, life and freedom."

The university's president did not merely encourage other Athenians to become citizens of the world. In travels to Asia, Africa, and Europe throughout the 1980s and 1990s, Ping participated in several of the university's ventures abroad. Presenting Steiner's map as a symbol of Athens's stardom in education for interdependence, Ping paid personal visits to most of the sites of the university's far-flung educational empire. He strengthened existing programs and encouraged the establishment of new ones. He had long advocated integration of international students on U.S. campuses and had lobbied for federal support for international assistance programs as a member of the International Affairs Committee of the National Association of State Universities and Land Grant Colleges, a consortium of 149 U.S. institutions of higher education. In 1986 he was appointed chair of the committee.

Ping also was personally involved in arranging for internationally known speakers to travel to Athens. One of the best examples was former president Jimmy Carter, who spoke at the university in May 1989. Carter had been invited months earlier, chiefly for his prominence in championing world peace and democracy, but the timing of the trip to Athens brought another dimension of newsworthiness to his visit. Only four days earlier, Carter had led a team of international observers to monitor elections in Panama, a nation recently liberated from the dictatorship of Manuel Noriega. Overflow crowds filled both the Carter press conference and his public lecture. In demand by international leaders as well as by the world press, Carter nonetheless made the effort to keep Ohio University on his itinerary. Minding the manners his mother had taught him, the former president thanked university officials publicly for the kindness shown to his mother, Miss Lillian, who had received an honorary degree from Ohio University ten years earlier and who had been the guest of Charles and Claire Ping.

By 1991, students majoring in international studies were choosing not only courses in foreign languages, but also those with international emphasis in such subjects as history, geography, anthropology, economics, and ecology. An increase in new courses devoted to professional concerns, particularly in Business and Communication, helped students prepare for problem-solving projects abroad. Evidence that Ohio University was a star in international education was summarized in an article in the November 1991 *Chronicle of Higher Education*. After spending two days in Athens gathering information and impressions for a news feature, the reporter said of Ohio University, "The international feel of this Midwestern public institution is striking." The high percentage of international courses and visibility of international students were only two components of a total impression that was greater than the sum of its parts.

Educating for Democracy in Southern Africa

The first concentration offered in the university's interdisciplinary Center for International Studies was the African Studies Program, an Athens-based course of study that culminated in a certificate at the master's level. Begun in the 1965–66 academic year, the program attracted students from the United States and abroad, laying the foundation for an understanding of the cultures, philosophy, and history of Africa's nations. At its twenty-fifth anniversary in 1990–91, the African Studies Program hosted a lecture series that brought speakers from Ghana, Tunisia, Swaziland, and Liberia. Program chair Gifford Doxsee of the Department of History recalled that many of the program's graduates had moved into positions of influence in their respective home nations, whether in universities or in international development agencies. The importing and teaching of students was a start in Ohio University's participation in nation-building in Africa, albeit one graduate at a time. In addition to immigration, an emigration had developed as early as 1957, when the university sent faculty to Nigeria to train teachers, a partnership that broadened in the 1980s to training managers and staff in radio and television stations.

Throughout the 1980s, Ohio University took the lead in supplying expertise to train teachers in the nations contiguous to South Africa. While the former Dutch-then-British colony at the tip of the continent clung to apartheid and its selective democracy, its neighbors were building institutions requisite to democracy for all, universal public education being one of the most essential of those structures. Land-locked Botswana, about half the size of South Africa, had won its independence in 1966. In the subsequent fifteen years, it had proven its viability as the only democratically governed nation in southern Africa at that time and was determined to improve its educational system, especially at the primary level. In 1981 the U.S. Agency for International Development (USAID) proposed to aid Botswana's teacher training in partnership with an American university. Several U.S. universities competed for the five-year $7.3 million USAID contract that Ohio University won, in part because of prior experience in Africa and Asia by university faculty. Donald Knox of the College of Education, who had led similar ventures for the USAID in Nigeria in the 1960s and in South Vietnam in the 1970s, would lead the Botswana project as well.

Knox and four colleagues from the university taught in a new department of primary education at the university in Gaborone, Botswana's capital. The department held the distinction of being the first four-year training program for primary-level teachers at the university level anywhere in southern Africa. Three education professors had laid the groundwork in the preceding year. Milton Ploghoft, Reba Pinney, and Max Evans spent six weeks designing the initial phase of the project. Since Botswana's official language is English, professors from Ohio had less difficulty adjusting to their assignment in the decidedly non-Western setting. The bulk of their work was developing teacher preparation programs at the university level and curricular materials for elementary schools. For teachers already on the job, Ohio staffers provided on-site training in the primary schools to update skills and knowledge.

In October 1982, shortly before the president's three-month leave to teach at Harvard University as a visiting professor, Ping and his wife, Claire, were invited by the government of Botswana to formal ceremonies marking the establishment of the University of Botswana, where he also visited with the team from home. Reports even at that early juncture suggested that the university's five-year contract would be renewed. The new contract in 1986 was even larger—$8 million from the USAID and $2.7 million from the government of Botswana. It was the praise for Ohio University expertise by Botswani that probably discouraged other universities from making serious bids for the work in 1986, Education Dean Allen Myers said, noting the contract work was done entirely by telephone. To existing goals, the new project added in-service support for primary school principals via regional training centers and a master's degree in primary education at the University of Botswana. The number of staff and consultants who would move back and forth from Athens to Botswana also increased.

The success of the Botswana project spread, literally, to other nations. As Ping reported in the Convocation Address in 1984, "The external reviews, so high in their praise of our handling of the tasks in Botswana, were a primary factor in the recently announced Swaziland award." Only slightly larger than Connecticut, the nation between South Africa and Mozambique had set a goal: within the decade, Swaziland would achieve primary education for all. The USAID was there to help, awarding an $8 million contract to Ohio University for revamping the educational system of Swaziland. So that the programs would continue beyond the departure of Ohioans, the project included an exchange in which twenty Swazi teachers would study for advanced degrees at Ohio University.

The next year, Lesotho was added to the university's teacher-education client list. A nation within a nation, Lesotho had been carved out of South Africa by the British as the homeland of the Basotho, or Basuto, people indigenous to the mountainous region that covers about the same number of square miles as Appalachian Ohio. Again, the granting agency was the

USAID; the grant amount was $25 million and the grantees were a consortium of U.S. universities, including Ohio.

The three nations of Botswana, Swaziland, and Lesotho had more in common than contiguity to South Africa and assistance from Ohio University, a reality addressed in research projects presented at annual research symposia for graduate students coordinated by the university's College of Education faculty in southern Africa. The first of the conferences, in July 1987 in Lesotho's capital of Maseru, was opened by Ping, who promoted research-based decisions to the two hundred participants. He also advocated a collaborative approach to problem solving. The research symposium did become an annual event as planned, with the three sponsor nations rotating as host. An annual winter-break seminar offered by Ploghoft served both to germinate new research ideas and to fertilize ongoing research projects developed in the summer symposia.

Ohio University's role in assisting the nations in sub-Saharan Africa made it a leader in a part of the planet that was the focus of both world leaders and the news media that follow them. South Africa's neighbors were demonstrating success with nonracist and participatory social and political institutions. Comparisons were inevitable. As the credibility of South Africa's policy of segregation and nonparticipation for people of color began to sag, the nation at the tip of the continent circled its wagons. The university's role in what happened next in South Africa went further than merely assisting its neighboring nations in teacher training. In 1985 the Ohio University Press became the U.S. distributor for Ravan Press of Johannesburg, publisher of anti-apartheid South African authors Nadine Gordimer and J. M. Coetzee.

Perhaps the most cogent criticisms of South Africa of the entire era were not couched in negative terms at all, but in comparisons between South Africa and its democratic neighbor to the north. When President Quett K. J. Masire of Botswana addressed graduates and guests at Ohio University's commencement in June 1989, Ping's introduction emphasized the contrast between the two African nations. Masire's address included profuse appreciation to Ohio University for its role in bringing universal education to Botswana. He acknowledged that the fortunes of his nation, as well as other nations in the region, would depend on the right use of the knowledge accrued through the Ohio partnership. Masire spoke optimistically of the future in South Africa, saying that recent developments gave him hope that the region south of Botswana was on the road to democratization.

The following October, another speaker hit harder on South Africa's reluctance to modernize its government. Helen Suzman, Member of Parliament in South Africa for thirty-six years, brought her pro-reform but anti–economic-sanctions message to a near-capacity audience in Memorial Auditorium. Suzman had accepted a personal invitation from Ping, whom she had met earlier in the year in Africa, to be a Kennedy Lecturer. She explained that the U.S. economic sanctions had little effect on the white government because the resulting unemployment hurt only black South Africans, who furthermore had no safety net comparable to U.S. unemployment compensation or social security. Suzman proposed instead that U.S. businesses aid education in South Africa and assist in organizing trade unions. Like Masire, Suzman expressed optimism about the future of South Africa, especially under its new president, F. W. de Klerk. He had already released some political prisoners to test the mood of the electorate about freeing members of the African National Congress. Four months after Suzman's lecture, ANC party leader Nelson Mandela was released from prison, eventually to become president himself.

Another step toward democracy in southern Africa came with Namibia's independence from South Africa less than two years after Masire's and Suzman's prescient forecast. A region larger than Botswana to its east, Namibia did what most newly independent nations do to retain freedom—bolster the education system. An international commission on higher education was convened, with Charles Ping as the sole American member. Though the trustees gave Ping professional leave to participate, he had to miss the first meeting in February because of a second bout of degenerative arthritis in a knee. He made it to the second round of commission meetings in April, but the knee problems would eventually affect his own independence. At the end of fall quarter 1991, he underwent surgery at Cleveland Clinic to replace both knees. During Ping's winter quarter recuperation and rehabilitation, Provost James Bruning served as acting president.

By 1991 the university's contracts with Botswana and Swaziland had ended, but not the relationships. Because Ping had hoped for more two-way traffic on the routes between Athens and southern Africa, Donald Knox pursued USAID funds for an exchange program with Swaziland that would enable undergraduate students in education from the university to spend six weeks at Ngwane Teachers College. The venture was so successful that the university and the government of Swaziland pledged to continue it after the three-year USAID funding ended. Education for democracy was under way, but education for interdependence was just getting launched.

One spin-off of the university's accomplishments in southern Africa was establishment of a partnership at the University of Manchester on a master's degree in international education. Though England is as far from Botswana as Ohio is, the English had also shared educational expertise with emerging nations in southern Africa. The link in the trio was Ping's friend, Professor John Turner, who had been the first vice chancellor at the University of Botswana before becoming dean of the faculty at the University of Manchester. The connection across three continents was precisely the kind of interdependence Ping had hoped for.

Orienting Ohio to Asia

When Ping first sat at the antique table in Cutler Hall, Ohio University already had programs in Asia, most notably in Japan and Southeast Asia. Ping was determined to expand them. Mainland China, however, had been aloof from the world and even hostile to Western values until the late 1970s. In 1979, when the United States and the People's Republic of China (PRC) established diplomatic relations, Ohio University hosted a contingent of Chinese scholars who were scouting the United States for quality science programs. Arts and Sciences Dean William Dorrill used his contacts to insure that Ohio was on the itinerary along with Stanford and Massachusetts Institute of Technology. Ping packed the one-day visit with events to orient the Chinese to mid-America. The Chinese faculty on campus prepared a twelve-course meal at the president's home, followed by the first U.S. media conference held by the visitors. Echoing the sentiments of legions of American students who had chosen Ohio University, the president of Beijing University told the world, "We would much rather have our students here than in big cities. It is a much nicer environment."

The Asians liked the university's mid-sized nuclear accelerator so much that eight nuclear physicists from China returned to Athens three months later for a closer look. The visits were of course a prelude to sending students, and the PRC lost no time in sending its talent to America to catch up after the years of degradation wrought on its higher education system by the Cultural Revolution. In fall 1979, the first seven Chinese students from the People's Republic arrived in Athens—three undergraduates and four scholars who had chosen Ohio University for advanced work. Soon, dozens of students and scholars from the People's Republic were enrolling in faraway Athens. Six years after the university's first students had arrived from the PRC, Ping was invited by Governor Celeste to travel with Ohio's official trade mission to China in 1985. Ping was an educational delegate among the thirty corporate leaders who traveled to Shanghai, Wuhan, and Beijing, all of which had had some exchanges and connections with the university. By the end of Ping's term as president, students from the People's Republic constituted the largest contingent of international students at the university, even after the brutal suppression of the student demonstrations in Tiananmen Square.

A stop in Hong Kong at the end of the tour had included a meeting with Ohio University alumni in the British colony. Talks began that year to implement coursework for nontraditional students at Hong Kong Baptist University. What eventually matured was the Hong Kong External Student Program, which in 1991 awarded the first bachelor's degree to an Ohio University student who had never actually been in Athens, Ohio. Though the program began as a distance-learning venture geared toward working adults, it matured into an on-site program in which both Ohio University professors and Hong Kong Baptist University faculty taught a broad-based curriculum in Hong Kong, with all courses taught in the English language. The year the first baccalaureate was awarded, another 375 students were pursuing the bachelor of specialized studies, with about 60 percent of the students enrolled in business courses. Distance methods still delivered about 20 percent of the Hong Kong students' coursework, but the combination of Hong Kong and Athens professors teaching in the External Student Program enabled working adults to complete their degrees around their jobs.

News of another world first for the university came via a news release on March 17, 1980, made jointly in Washington, D.C., and in Malaysia. The first endowed faculty chair in Southeast Asian Studies at an American university was established at Ohio University in a partnership with the government of Malaysia, which granted $350,000 to fund the chair. That amount would be matched by gifts from American corporations doing business in Malaysia in a fund-raising drive by the university. In addition to funding the salary of the holder of the chair, the endowment would also provide income for library acquisitions to bolster international studies Named for the late prime minister, Tun Abdul Razak, the position was conceived as a way to bring Malaysian scholars from a variety of disciplines to the university's Center for Southeast Asian Studies, established in 1968, for a two- or three-year stay in Athens. To cement the bonds, the university invited Malaysia's minister of education, Datuk Musa Hitam, to be the commencement speaker in Athens three months later. Hitam had made the announcement of the Razak Chair in his nation on the day that Malaysia's Ambassador to the United States, Zain Azraai, had made the announcement in Washington, D.C., with Ping. The first Razak Chair holder, Syed Muhammad Naquib al-Attas, arrived in 1982 to teach Malay literature and Islamic philosophy. By the time of the university's Bicentennial, ten professors from five universities in Malaysia had shared expertise in economics, political science, business, literature, education, history, agriculture, and geography. With the chair comes the obligation of conducting the Tun Abdul Razak Conference, the themes of which vary with the chair-holder's expertise. Like any academic conference, the event brings together experts from academia, government, and the private sector to explicate a major topic.

The origin of the university's relationship with Malaysia is itself an illustration of global networking. It had begun halfway around the world in Nigeria, where the education program conducted by the university was thriving in the 1960s. A Malaysian ambassador to Nigeria learned of the program and thought the university's expertise might also serve his nation. With a grant from the Asia Foundation in 1968, the Mara Institute of Technology in Kuala Lumpur contracted with Ohio University for staff training, which opened the door for Ohio faculty to teach in a host of programs at Mara. One of those collaborative programs, business administration, was so successful that Ohio University soon offered a bachelor's degree at Mara, with junior- and senior-level courses taught by Ohio faculty in residence in Malaysia's capital. A master's degree in economic education, which focused on the development needs of Malaysia, evolved next. Another MBA program, a master's in business administration designed for graduates in science and engineering, was launched in 1991.

Felix Gagliano, who taught in the interdisciplinary Southeast Asian Studies Program for ten years, had spent two years in Kuala Lumpur coordinating the business degree program. When Gagliano returned to Athens in 1982, he became vice provost for international programs, a new position that elevated the status of international study at the university.

The Mara Institute programs and the Razak Chair had created bonds between Malaysia and Ohio University that were celebrated in a 1982 ceremony to confer an honorary doctor of laws degree on recently retired Prime Minister Tun Hussein Onn. The contingent from Ohio, led by Ping, included Trustee Kenner Bush, 1804 Fund Chair Wilfred Konneker, and Vice President for University Relations Wayne Kurlinski. They encountered more than the ordinary degree conferral, however, as the Americans experienced two hours of formalities governed by state protocol and attended by six hundred dignitaries. Among Ping's fondest memories of the occasion was the drive to Parliament House in Kuala Lumpur along a route lined with alternating flags of Malaysia and Ohio University. Another particular that signified the strength of the relationship was the inclusion of the Ohioans' wives in the opening procession, which was a gesture of respect by the Muslim Malaysians to their non-Muslim American guests.

The Mara connection was one of several the university had established in Southeast Asia, and the university's achievements in Malaysia seemed to rejuvenate existing programs. In 1981, the U.S. Department of Education granted $90,000 to the Center for Southeast Asian Studies. The same year, the Indonesian Studies Summer Institute was scheduled in Athens for the first of three annual meetings. The third coup in the university's expansion of international options in Asia was a gift from Chubu University in Nagoya, Japan, for 10 million yen ($92,000) to support an existing exchange program. Then in 1984 the university expanded its presence in the Philippines with a three-year grant from the United States Information Agency. In addition to strengthening the Southeast Asian Studies Program, the grant assisted De La Salle University in Manila in developing an American Studies program. Ohio professors in journalism, history, English, and sociology taught in Manila, and Filipino faculty from various disciplines came to Athens.

The expansion of the university's presence in Malaysia was nearly repeated in Japan, where an exchange with Chubu Institute of Technology (later Chubu University) had been established in 1973. A private engineering and architectural school, Chubu sent students to Athens for graduate school and Ohio sent faculty to Chubu to teach. By 1986, the university's linguistics department was so grounded in Japanese language and culture that it offered translation services to American firms doing business with Honda Motors in Japan. The expertise in Japanese led to another opportunity for education for interdependence when the Ohio Program of Intensive English in the linguistics department was chosen by Honda of America to conduct a fourteen-month English language training project at Honda plants in Marysville and Anna, Ohio.

In 1987, several U.S. universities were investigating the possibility of starting programs in Japan, as the U.S.-Japan Committee for Promoting Trade Expansion had advocated. Since Ohio was already known in central

Japan through its Chubu connection, the university was approached by leaders in the city of Komaki, a few miles north of Nagoya, to explore the possibility of a two-year branch campus at its university. The mayor of Komaki was among a group of mayors from several Japanese cities to visit the United States in July 1987, but the initial visit was merely introductory. Negotiations actually began later in the academic year when Ohio sent a delegation to Komaki for discussions. From 1988 to 1992, Komaki courted Ohio, working hard to craft an agreement that would satisfy the university's insistence that the program be self-supporting. With reluctance, the university withdrew its proposal once it became clear that the imbalance between the dollar and the yen would sabotage extraordinary efforts to operate within a balanced budget.

Though the work on a two-year branch came to naught, the discussions did produce some fruit. The city of Komaki subsidized an English language program taught by Ohio University professors that was well attended. Years after Ping retired, Japanese students at Komaki's university were still lining up for the Ohio University English language courses. The cordiality that had extended across four years of negotiations also resulted in an exchange of middle school students forged by the mayors of Athens and Komaki. Exchanging students and faculty was easy, however, compared to one swap the Japanese had requested—a shipment of gray squirrels. A delegation from Komaki had admired the bushy-tailed chatterers on the Athens campus of Ohio University and wanted to study them more closely, specifically in the city park on Mt. Komaki. After managing the myriad details of adaptation, transport, and export, the university's Vice President for Regional Higher Education, James Bryant, and his staff solved the problems, and twenty-three Ohio squirrels were shipped to Japan. Accompanying the Appalachian critters was a surprise gift to the Japanese—a videotape of a program about squirrels that Ohio University professors had translated into Japanese. The descendants of squirrels native to the Hocking Valley were soon scampering about Komaki Park, perhaps among the ancestors of the cherry trees that had been planted along the Hocking.

One of the stalwarts of Ohio's reputation in international education was the Center for Southeast Asian Studies. Founded during the presidency of Vernon Alden, it was one of the strongest of the international programs Ping inherited when he arrived in 1975. By 1987, however, four of the ten original faculty members had left or retired and not been replaced, leaving the program strong on library holdings but short on faculty, the Razak Chair notwithstanding. Funding from federal sources had declined for programs that reminded the government of its failures in Vietnam and neighboring nations. A private funding source, however, came to the rescue of Southeast Asian Studies programs nationwide in 1987 when the Henry Luce Foundation awarded $8 million to eight universities with centers devoted to Southeast Asian Studies. Ohio University got $268,500 of the total award, enough to fund four new positions and several fellowships for master's students. The university agreed to fund the positions in economics, philosophy, Indonesian language (part-time), and research bibliography after the Luce grant was spent.

In 1993, the university's partnerships in Malaysia reached the twenty-five-year mark. To observe the anniversary, Trustee Chair Jeanette Grasselli was invited to be the commencement speaker at the Mara Institute of Technology while Ohio alumnus Stephen Fuller spoke at the Malaysian House of Parliament. Capping the celebration was the awarding of an honorary degree from Ohio to Tuanka Ja'afar, who had been deputy king of Malaysia when officials first called on Ohio University to help their nation modernize. The year 1993 marked another anniversary, the twentieth year of Ohio's relationship with Chubu University in Nagoya, Japan. To mark the occasion, the university shipped a replica of Cutler Hall's cupola to the Chubu campus.

Improving Access to the World's Knowledge

Hwa-Wei Lee came to Ohio University to become director of Alden Library in 1978 with every intention of duplicating his accomplishments at a similar post in Thailand. As the founder of the graduate school library for the Asian Institute of Technology in Bangkok, Lee went from mere plans for a library to building one of the most technologically up-to-date facilities in Asia. It took him seven years. Conceived as the Asian equivalent of the Massachusetts Institute of Technology, the Asian Institute of Technology was a joint venture between the United States and Britain. Lee, a native of Taiwan, had been recruited for the job in Bangkok by the U.S. Agency for International Development.

Armed with his recently acquired know-how in retooling libraries, Lee aimed to put Alden Library in a league that matched the university's international academic status. In addition to installing information technology, Lee hoped to see Alden Library gain membership in the Association of Research Libraries, an elite group of a hundred or so libraries, most of them at universities. In took him little time to realize, however, that state funds in Ohio would never match the resources of the two world powers that had underwritten the library in Thailand. Undaunted, Lee set about raising money. He wrote annual proposals for grants from both the 1804 Fund and UPAC, and got windfall money from a sympathetic Provost Bruning that had been generated by growing enrollments.

Ping did his part to help the library by designating one anonymously donated 1804 Fund account for library use. The donor had stipulated that the president could decide how to spend the money, and Ping was committed to seeing the library join the ranks of research libraries. Lee said the funds "kept us at one point from abandoning the research status goal," the elusiveness of which persisted as the bar was raised each time the university got close to meeting the existing criteria. Lee rallied his staff to apply for outside grants, too, and by 1987 they had garnered a total of $600,000. One part of Lee's development efforts resulted in assistance from the local community. The Friends of the Library, founded in 1979, was a group of academics and nonacademics devoted to promoting and aiding Alden Library.

Lee spent some of the money he raised to computerize the card catalog, making Ohio University the state's second, after Ohio State, to switch to on-line cataloging. Despite the serious reservations of many library patrons, Lee forged ahead in 1983 with the on-line modernization, steeling himself for the slings and arrows of patrons' reluctance to give up something as familiar and tactile as cards in catalog drawers. Users did adjust to Alice, a system that functioned for thirteen years until the state paid for the next catalog iteration as part of a statewide network. The speed and ease of the on-line catalog also freed up Lee's staff to do what librarians do best—serve as mediators and facilitators between collections and their users. The consistently professional execution of duties by library staff was in fact one of the hallmarks of Lee's tenure as director (later dean) of libraries.

Internationalization of academic resources was one of the goals Lee and Ping readily agreed upon. Through his connections in Asia, Lee arranged a shipment in 1982 to Alden Library of 634 books from the national library of the Republic of China. That same year he got funding from the United Nations Educational, Scientific, and Cultural Organization (UNESCO) for two internships that enabled library school faculty from Southeast Asia to study new methods and technology at Alden Library. In 1983 and again in 1985, with Lee's guidance, Ping endorsed an exchange between Ohio University and Xian Jiantong University, one of the oldest and most respected universities in the People's Republic of China. The exchange of students, faculty, and library materials also opened the possibility for collaborative research on coal. The first Ohio professors to lecture at Xian Jiaotong under the agreement were chemistry professor James Y. Tong and Hwa-Wei Lee.

Lee had other dragons to slay. By the late 1980s, established libraries everywhere were facing monumental storage problems. Most libraries, and Alden was no exception, had been adding books, periodicals, and documents without subtracting anything while knowledge continued its explosion. Space projections of the library's current holdings, added to typical annual acquisitions, predicted maximum capacity by November 1988. Using extra space for temporary storage at the Innovation Center bought time for the library, as did accelerating the conversion of bound items to microfilm, microfiche, and CD-ROM disks. The stopgaps worked while the university scrambled to construct a storage building with high-density mobile shelving on Columbus Road (opened in 1998). Athens's remoteness, though, forced the university to act alone in finding a depository rather than collaborating with other academic libraries, as the board of regents had suggested.

Those were just the stateside challenges Lee faced. He often went abroad on academic missions, always on the lookout for exchanges to enrich the international offerings at Ohio, but he encountered Indiana Jones–style dangers in Asia in 1989. In June he was restricted to his hotel in Beijing as dissident students occupied Tiananmen Square. He left before the massacre began, but not before he had managed to sneak aid and comfort to the students. His second brush with danger that year came in Manila, when he was among Americans evacuated during an attempted coup to overthrow Corazon Aquino.

One of the causes for the space crisis at the library was simultaneously one of the library's strengths—its collections. Indeed, the Southeast Asia collection was one of the reasons Lee had been attracted to the job at Ohio. Already recognized by Asian scholars as one of the best research collections in the United States, the Southeast Asia resources became *the* best in 1988 when the Malaysian government designated Alden Library at Ohio University as the United States Depository for Malaysian Materials. Botswana followed suit and designated Alden Library as depository of its government documents in 1990. The next year Swaziland did the same.

Not all the collections at Alden came from abroad, though three of the

American collections were international in scope. Another gift from the Scripps family, the papers of E. W. Scripps, arrived at Alden Library in 1988 to be archived in perpetuity. The collection came with a $60,000 grant from the Scripps Howard Foundation to defray costs of archiving. It was the second journalistic collection the university had acquired, the first being the archive of Cornelius Ryan, which had been presented in 1981 by his widow, Kathryn. Ryan had been a war correspondent with John Wilhelm, first dean of Ohio University's College of Communication. Ryan incorporated his experiences into World War II novels, the best known being *The Longest Day, The Last Battle*, and *A Bridge Too Far*. A third gift of research materials to the library was the collection of musical instruments, scores, records, and papers from the estate of alumnus Sammy Kaye.

Lee also implemented two programs to circumvent what he called "Western biases" in the library. In 1986 he set up a program with the Chinese Academy of Sciences whereby Chinese librarians came to Athens and Alden staff visited China. Lee had a separate internship program that brought graduate students in library science from various Asian nations to Alden Library to learn new technologies. The library's Asian connections were bolstered in the early 1990s by two Hong Kong businessmen, father and son, who donated funds to the library. Dr. Shao You-Bao gave $500,000 to endow and establish the Overseas Chinese Documentation and Research Center that bears his name. The center's focus is Chinese people who live outside the Asian mainland. His son, Daniel Shao, Class of 1972, also donated money to Alden Library that was earmarked for internships to enable Asian librarians to learn Western library techniques. A timely gift by the younger Shao paid Ohio University's membership in the East-West Institute, a consortium of American universities that conducted academic exchanges with universities in Hong Kong.

The indefatigable Lee was named Librarian of the Year by the Ohio Library Association in 1987, an honor followed by a citation from the House of Representatives praising his fund-raising accomplishments. Those laurels notwithstanding, Lee continued to encourage his staff to raise funds. Associate Director of Libraries Gary Hunt landed a grant in 1988 from the National Endowment for the Humanities for $750,000, the library's second such award. Though the university would have to raise an additional $3 million, the challenge money was a measure of the library's quality. Research status was yet to come, but it did in 1996 before Lee retired. Ohio University's Alden Library then became one of only 122 research libraries in the nation and one of five in the state of Ohio.

Studying the World's Contemporary History

As a diplomatic historian, John Lewis Gaddis, Distinguished Professor of History, had accrued credentials that spanned the globe as well as the chasm between the United States and the Soviet Union. As well-known in historical circles as Wagner was in biological circles, Gaddis had an idea, germinated in his management of the Baker Peace Studies Program and nurtured in discussions in the Toward the Third Century Colloquium, for a new graduate-level program to be named the Contemporary History Institute. The interdisciplinary approach to world political problems would address the "widespread concern among scholars, government officials and major foundations over persistent failures to relate recent (post-1945) historical experience to current policy issues," he wrote in the proposal for the institute.

Gaddis had been a co-organizer of an American Academy of Arts and Sciences workshop that focused on linking historical fact to policy considerations. He also noted that two major foundations had established new fellowship competitions that emphasized the role of historical research in formulating policy. In short, the need existed for further study of the subject, but no academic institution had yet answered the call. Ohio University's Contemporary History Institute would therefore be unique in emphasizing the role history should play in policy development and would furthermore carve a distinctive niche in its era of study post–World War II history, politics, and economics. In addition, such a structure would fit the colloquium's call for interdepartmental cooperation and resource sharing. In this microcosm of global interdependence, faculty from the departments of history, political science, and economics would teach courses that satisfied requirements for a certificate in contemporary history. It was hoped that students from other disciplines—business, journalism, telecommunications, any program in which a "sense of the context of the recent past is useful"—might eventually seek the certificate.

A history professor at the university since 1969, Gaddis had made history for Ohio University in 1986. As coordinator of an international conference on the cold war, he broke new ground in arranging face-to-face discussions between American and Soviet historians and political scientists. The conference, sponsored by the Baker Peace Studies Program, focused on how the cold war might end. Nearly forty experts on the subject were invited to Athens in April 1986 for dialogue on differences between the superpowers and how to resolve them in a post–cold war world.

Opening the conference was President Emeritus Baker himself, who had devoted much of his twenty-four years since leaving Ohio University to the study of world peace. While President Ronald Reagan and his Soviet counterpart, Mikhail Gorbachev, conversed before the international press, an Athens form of *glasnost* was crystallizing between the two World War II allies. History itself interceded to mar the tenor of the discussions, however; the United States had launched a retaliatory strike against Soviet-backed Libya the week before the conference, riveting media attention to developments between America and Russia. Opinions of conference participants divided along political boundaries on whether the Libyan strike would jeopardize future summits between their nations' leaders. But there were disagreements that violated geopolitical lines, too, as Russian historians publicly disagreed with each other—another historical first—on interpretations of cold war events. However, on the issue of whether to hold future academic conferences on the changing relationships between their nations, there was unanimity. The academic rapprochement should continue. (History has shown that the political dialogue likewise continued.)

Scholars of the politics of the two global antagonists met again in 1987, this time in Moscow, to discuss the origins of post–World War II tensions between the superpowers. The facts about events in the Soviet Union before, during, and after World War II had been veiled in secrecy by the Stalin regime, obscuring the truth from citizens of the Soviet Union and the United States alike. Gaddis himself was surprised at the speed with which the openness between Reagan and Gorbachev had permeated discussions among the academics as well. The assembled scholars focused on the years 1945–1950 with an agreement to hold future conferences that would move the discussions forward in five-year increments. The Moscow conference also played a role in furthering *glasnost:* Soviet archives were opened to Western scholars.

Gaddis's prominence in the field was disseminated not only in conferences that assembled the experts, but also in an international accolade and in book-length treatises held in high regard by other scholars. In 1986 he earned a Guggenheim Fellowship Award, which would fund work on two new books: *The Oxford History of American Foreign Relations* and *The Long Peace: Inquiries into the History of the Cold War.* The latter book was summarized by Gaddis as the lead article in the November 1987 *Atlantic Monthly.* Titled "How the Cold War Might End," the article afforded the world an in-depth look at a future many had merely contemplated for forty years. The *Atlantic* article then became the source for a Public Broadcasting System documentary. Scholars knew Gaddis's works, but it was the *Atlantic Monthly* and PBS coverage that informed the general public's understanding of the forces at work in a changing world. The debut of the seminal work on the end of the cold war, however, was not in international media, but before an audience in Athens, Ohio, who heard the first draft of the *Atlantic* article at the Baker Peace Conference in 1986. (An earlier book, *Strategies of Containment: A Critical Appraisal of Postwar American National Security Policy*, published in 1982, had also received widespread notice from the daily press.)

The proposal to create the Contemporary History Institute therefore was not controversial. It went before two university boards in 1987—Trustees (for approval) and Fund (for start-up money). Approval was granted. Money came in the form of an 1804 Fund grant for $41,000 immediately and $27,500 across three years. Two months later the institute received $250,000 from the John D. and Catherine T. MacArthur Foundation. Gaddis had submitted a grant proposal for $200,000 and at first thought the extra $50,000 was a typographical error, he said. The five-year grant derived from the MacArthur Foundation's Program on Peace and International Cooperation, which had not erred in awarding the extra money. Sixty percent of the MacArthur money would fund $10,000 renewable fellowships for MacArthur Fellows, graduate students who could command such an attractive addition to a graduate stipend. The rest of the grant was earmarked for course development, library resources, and conferences.

The largest grant came at the end of the 1987–88 academic year in the form of $500,000 for an Eminent Scholar from the Ohio Board of Regents' Selective Excellence program. The university's second Eminent Scholar, in Contemporary History, validated the efficacy of the institute in its first year of existence.

The next meeting of the international scholars, to cover 1950–55, would double as the inaugural event for the Contemporary History Institute, in October 1988. Though the three-day meeting was a formal requirement for the thirteen graduate students studying for the institute's certificate, Gaddis opened the sessions to the public as observers and learners. Keynote speaker was George F. Kennan, former ambassador to Yugoslavia and the Soviet Union and, most significantly for the conference topic, author of the 1947 U.S. policy that ratified the cold war, the "Doctrine of Containment." An author with more than job-related policies to his writing credit, Kennan had chosen Gaddis to be his biographer.

Two years—and half a million dollars—later, the university had matched the state's grant and was ready to announce its second Eminent Scholar. In deference to the high-profile position of the candidate, the university had agreed to withhold announcement until January 1990. But a young *Post* reporter from Ohio's Academically Excellent journalism program broke the story in September. Albert Eckes, chairman of the U.S. International Trade Commission, had accepted the offer, but hedged when pressed for a quote by saying only that an offer had been made. After nine years on the commission, Eckes forwent more lucrative opportunities outside of academia because of the vital role the institute was playing in the education of future leaders in the global economy. It was actually a return to academia for Eckes, who had begun his postgraduate career at Ohio State University. He had also served for two years as editorial page editor of the *Columbus Dispatch*.

At the 1990 conference sponsored by the institute, the geographic scope of topics expanded to encompass the paradox of the domino theory in reverse, as the iron curtain crumbled between Communist and capitalist nations of Europe and freedom tipped eastward. Peaceful coexistence was the theme of the Changes in Europe Conference. Scholars marveled at the arrival of conversions that had appeared to be in the distant future—democratization in the Soviet Union and eastern Europe, the fall of the Berlin Wall, and the reunification of Germany. Many of the topics had been presented to the nation in the Gaddis article "Coping with Victory" in the May 1990 *Atlantic Monthly*, in addition to his writing in the *New York Times* and *Washington Post*. In early fall, the world's experts gathered in Athens to make predictions based on historical models while the general public listened. Scholars from the host university, in addition to Institute Director Gaddis, were institute newcomer Eckes and institute veterans Alonzo Hamby (biographer of Harry S. Truman) and Steven Miner (award-winning historian of Sovie diplomacy). Such integration of former diplomats, former government policymakers, and current academics shed light—and maybe some heat—that perhaps sped the global warming between cold war enemies.

The cold war was not the only topic of Contemporary History Institute programs. In December 1990, for example, the institute sponsored a conference attended by about forty Ohio legislators, titled "Ohio and the World: The Next Two Years." Co-chaired by Eminent Scholar Eckes and Distinguished Professor of Economics Richard Vedder, the conference assembled experts on international economic, educational, and environmental issues pertinent to Ohio.

Another development related to the end of the cold war was the surge of interest in English among people in eastern Europe, particularly those poised to conduct Western-style business. Ohio University's OPIE took the lead in a ten-university consortium to improve the teaching of American English behind the former iron curtain. Funded by a grant in 1991 from the U.S. Information Agency, OPIE teachers taught in Bulgaria and Hungary to satisfy some of the demand for English instruction in European nations that had been dominated by Soviet-style Communism until the cold war thaw.

Gaddis's stature in his field led to a visiting appointment at Oxford University in the 1992–93 academic year. Standing in for him at the Contemporary History Institute was Chester Pach, who succeeded him as CHI director in 1994. A specialist in U.S. foreign relations and recent U.S. history, Pach had capitalized further on the collapse of Communism by establishing exchanges with Leipzig University in a 1993 summer program sponsored by the United States Information Agency.

After twenty-eight years of building a research profile at Ohio University, Gaddis left Athens for a position at Yale University in 1997. His gratitude to the people who had encouraged his scholarship was known locally, but he announced it globally in the dedication of his 1991 book, *The United States and the End of the Cold War: Implications, Reconsiderations, Provocations*—

"For Charles and Claire Ping, who rebuilt a university."

CHAPTER SIX

REBUILDING A UNIVERSITY

Stabilizing Stewardship

The state of Ohio was very good to Ohio University when Charles Ping was sworn in as president. Institutions with fewer friends in Columbus might not have fared so well. Special operating supplements and purchases of residence halls by the state deserve credit for the early work of saving the university in the mid-1970s, but it was the philosophy, style, and integrity of the eighteenth president that helped lead a rebuilding effort for the future. The fact remains, however, that most of the years that Ping was president, all the universities in Ohio suffered from insufficient funding from the state. (Moreover, the record shows that insufficient funding of higher education had begun in Ohio in 1787, when the Continental Congress gave the university two townships and said in effect, "Fund thyself.") In lean years, the Ohio General Assembly usually put the state universities first in line for cuts when budget debits exceeded credits. In flush years, public universities still did not make up the ground they had lost in the lean years. Even when the state had the dollars to meet its obligations to its colleges, enrollment gains were not always rewarded with commensurate subsidy. The university responded to the shortfalls with aggressive fund-raising, grant writing, business incubation, and tuition increases, the last generating the same large headlines as disturbances on Court Street. The horrors of battling for money from the legislature, in fact, topped Halloween in Ping's ranking of "most difficult aspect of the job of president of Ohio University."

A litany of Ohio University's particular budget problems in 1975 has been recited elsewhere. While Ping was plugging the financial drains of low enrollments, empty residence halls, high-interest bonds, and gargantuan utility costs, he embarked on a concomitant strategy of (1) improving the quality of the university's academic offerings (as the preceding chapters have shown) and (2) trying to change the attitudes that were responsible for Ohio public universities' being perennially shortchanged. Following the first tuition increase of his presidency, Ping reminded parents and legislators that Ohio continued to rank forty-ninth among the fifty states in per capita expenditures for higher education. Tuition in fall 1975, Ping's first quarter at Ohio, had been $260 per quarter. Tuition increases brought the total to $290 per quarter for fall 1976, followed by surcharges of $10 each for winter and spring, necessitated by another $720,000 post hoc budget cut by the state in October 1976.

The story of tuition throughout Ping's administration was the same at all of Ohio's public institutions of higher education—it went up. It had to. By 1982–83, following several years of budget cuts, in-state tuition for a full load of classes for one quarter was $444. The year Ping retired, 1993–94, one quarter cost $897. (None of these figures has been adjusted for inflation.) The numbers that went down were the percentage of the overall state budget devoted to higher education, the percentage of university operating costs underwritten by the state, and the percentage of support Ohio gave to its universities compared to the rest of the nation, as measured by the per capita quotient. All three measures in Columbus, exacerbated by the lingering effects of inflation and de-industrialization, forced universities to raise money in any way they could.

A few numbers will illustrate the trends. During Ping's tenure as president, the state of Ohio ranked consistently in the upper forties among the fifty states in per capita expenditures for higher education. Only poverty-stricken southern states ranked below Ohio. National rankings, however, don't reveal the impact on students, who paid an ever-increasing share of the costs of a college education in Ohio out of their own pockets. Before 1980, for example, students paid about 35 percent of the costs. The House appropriations bill in 1981 drove that percentage up to 42. By the time Ping retired, students were paying more than 50 percent of the costs.

Though decreases in state support were not new, the reasons cited by the state took novel turns. In 1977, in a move more surreal than real, the legislature interpreted year-end balances at universities as evidence that they were over-funded. Never mind the unpaid bills that were due or inflationary pressure at work or the sensible stewardship of keeping a savings account. Ohio University was the exception to big year-end balances with an un-whopping balance of $80,000, an amount that might be viewed by a financial counselor as wholly inadequate as a reserve for a business with an operating budget approaching $100 million. Legislators slashed subsidy anyway.

"Erosion of public confidence in higher education" was the explanation Ping proffered for the state's ill treatment of its universities. Even though the university was funding programs from earned revenue (for the first time in six years), the cuts—coupled with veiled threats about unsatisfactory workload levels at universities—were reasons to fret about future funding for Ohio's public universities. For example, a parting of the clouds in the 1979–80 budget when the state awarded the university an increase was followed by a recession the next year. Massive and repeated cuts followed. Then a new instrument of financial pain was implemented—the *reduced* budget became the base for the next year. Though such planning structures as UPAC softened the blows at Ohio University, the climate in academia continued to be frigid in Ohio, not only for annual budgets, but also for capital improvements.

In the 1980–81 academic year, Ping argued eloquently about the role of higher education in helping the state adjust to the changes in its economic base as Ohio's industrialization corroded. University publications directed at students, parents, and alumni focused on the topic of the state's chronic under-funding of its universities, in hopes of getting the message to the public and the legislature through as many constituents as possible. The long-term solution to Ohio's problem, Ping said, was education. Re-industrialization was not an option. What Ohio (and its neighboring states) needed was "sustained investment in human capital, trained, educated men and women who can offer ingenuity, imagination and the disciplined use of human intelligence." Ping also argued these points before the House Finance–Education Appropriation Subcommittee, and it was not the last time he tried speaking directly to the people who enacted the budgets.

The budget that passed in 1981 looked like the nadir in the under-funding of universities in Ohio. (It wasn't.) After passing the July budget in November, the state Office of Budget and Management director announced in January that the budget for higher education, four months late ostensibly to insure accuracy, would have to be cut nearly 9 percent immediately and 16.3 percent for the next biennium. Ping's description of this budget reversal—"Whoops! Now you see it, now you don't!"—captured the absurdity in carnival-sideshow language. The university's subsequent 14 percent tuition increase in 1982–83 helped, but did not close the gap. From the perspective of the College Green, the ever-increasing enrollments at Ohio University looked like a restoration of confidence, not an erosion. Again, Ohio University was the exception to trends in Ohio higher education.

The erosion of confidence did not stop at the state line. On the federal front, the Reagan administration announced plans to cut student loans by a third, to whack work-study funding by almost half, and to eliminate Pell grants altogether. Speaking in Columbus would not suffice. Ping also went to Washington to meet with Ohio's senators and certain members of Congress to advocate that government help provide the means of access to college in order to reverse the vicissitudes in the economy, rather than let economic declines swamp the lifeboat of higher education.

The recession ended, but not the inadequate funding of higher education in Ohio. Tax increases had helped, but rollbacks were on the ballot in 1983. Again, Ping mounted an information campaign—not to tell people how to vote, but "to describe the consequences of the vote," in his words to the trustees. The tax rollback was defeated, as was the proposal to alter the vote required to pass new taxes from a simple majority to three-fifths, but the relief would be temporary. Also in 1983, the Celeste administration announced new and significant funding via the Selective Excellence competition and Edison partnerships, but the money was clearly aimed at making pockets of excellence better, rather than improving the entire higher education system across the board. Moreover, the Selective Excellence money aimed at an immediate economic goal, not a long-term intellectual one. Nonetheless, as the preceding chapters have chronicled, the headway Ping made in using scant resources to build strong programs did more than put the university on various cost-effective lists compiled by magazine sellers. Quality programs were the explanation for the success of capital campaigns and grant seeking detailed in chapters 2 and 4, respectively. Hard times would return, and Ping was building a foundation of excellence to withstand them.

When another recession did hit in 1990, the Ohio General Assembly returned to its sleights of hand. More seriously, the anti–higher education language reemerged in pronouncements that threatened actions beyond budget cuts. Vowing to set aside formula funding for the 1991–93 biennium, the legislature decided on a funding freeze. Universities would get the amount they had received in the previous year, never mind inflation or the mid-year 3 percent cut in subsidy a few months earlier. "This is the first time in almost three decades that politics has intruded so directly in the operating budgets of institutions," Ping told the trustees. July 1 came and went as Governor Voinovich pondered the appropriations bill that would cripple universities. The university budget already approved by the trustees anticipated the very real prospect of layoffs and hiring freezes should the will of the legislature prevail. In late July, Governor Voinovich signed the budget, but he used his line-item veto power to strike the formula set-aside. The relief was bittersweet, as Ping contemplated a future filled with "erosion of public confidence" despite the achievements at Ohio University.

The university braced itself for a return to major cuts. They came. For the first time since its inception, UPAC announced there would be no planning pool in the next year, 1992–93. But what followed was the worst blow yet. In a blame-the-victim model, the legislature suggested that state institutions of higher education were poorly managed. The board of regents asked each college to form "management task forces" that would find the fat and identify ways to contain costs. For a university that made the national short lists of "cost-effective," "best buy," and "best value," the mismanagement accusation was inaccurate and disheartening. As one of the elder statesmen in Ohio higher education, Ping was among the university presidents who spoke against this latest attack on universities by those who viewed higher education as a frill.

In the *déjà vu* scenario of the early 1990s, the federal government followed the states in reducing spending on higher education, specifically by reducing federal financial assistance programs for students. Sixteen university presidents were invited to address the Washington press corps on the matter. Charles Ping was one of them. His two key points were that federal money aided access to higher education, particularly in states that expected students to pay more of the cost (e.g., Ohio), and that federal assistance would be an investment that would pay off in a workforce better prepared to compete in a global economy. Countering the facts presented by university presidents were nationally disseminated ideas about rampant waste and abuses in universities. Books with titles like *Profscam* and *Tenured Radicals* were the popular versions of treatises like *The Closing of the American Mind* and *The Last Intellectuals*—all of them anti-university and all of them widely quoted. It was a bleak day for higher education.

The cyclical funding attacks on higher education during recessions were like recurring viruses that took hold when the body politic was run down. Though Ping-style planning had been the antidote to bouts of "now you don't see it" funding infection in Ohio, the virus was mutating into a more virulent form. In 1992 the efficiency fever spiked. Governor Voinovich named a task force that would review the reports of the "management task forces" written on college campuses a year earlier. "Managing for the Future" was the title of the 1992 document that resulted. It proposed radical changes in university administration, most notably a centralized management structure for all the state's colleges and universities in order to enforce efficiency. The legislative intrusion went further. A revamped super board of regents would have powers unheard of in the history of Ohio public higher education: assigning specific educational roles to individual institutions, culling graduate programs, and merging regional campuses with technical and community colleges. The centralized intrusion would not stop at programmatic power. Among its personnel mandates was an attack on tenure implicit in the proposed "time-limited contracts for faculty" and a call for 10 percent more teaching time by faculty.

Reaction to the report pivoted on its contradictions. The report itself praised the universities for good management, yet recommended draconian solutions predicated on the assumption that they were poorly managed. That was not the only paradox. As Ping pointed out, states that already had such centralization were spending *more*, not less, to administer higher education. He also took the lead in suggesting that more collaboration between and within universities was the cheaper and more direct path to both efficiency and excellence, and that cooperation would best be achieved by autonomous boards of trustees who knew their campuses' strengths and weaknesses. Superimposing a distant, all-powerful board would merely add costs without finding the most productive matches among academic partners.

Ping devoted his entire 1992 Convocation Address to the Managing for the Future threat. After citing background data on the state's reduced level of support for higher education, he summarized the persuasion efforts underway by the Inter-University Council, a group comprising the presidents of all the state's four year colleges and universities. Ping cautioned against a defensive posture en route to advocating that efforts be redoubled to inform the public about the benefits of higher education to the state. Then he focused on the specific dangers the report posed: (1) Centralization would open the door, wide, to political intrusion by removing the buffer of local boards. (2) The arbitrary designation of only two universities as "comprehensive research universities" would create a two-tier system. Ohio State University and the University of Cincinnati were nominated in the report to be the state's "comprehensive research universities." All others would therefore be second-class institutions doomed in the competition for research grants, quality faculty, and external gifts. (3) Bludgeoning all two-year programs into one system would erase the differences in function between regional campuses of universities, technical colleges, and community colleges. (4) The faculty workload proposals in the report revealed less about efficiency and more about distrust.

Ping decried the proposals' negative effects and recommended instead that universities explore ways to cooperate and collaborate. "Each university must demonstrate that it is a part of a larger whole of public purposes," Ping said, relying on his faith in a holistic philosophy to help defuse the crisis. "We have begun this pattern of creating systems for cooperation and sharing resources on our campus with shared equipment and resources and beyond this institution with the use of statewide resources of the super computer, library links, the aerospace institute and the Edison centers." But there was a broader task at hand in dealing with the external threats, and that was keeping the internal house in order for the present and in the future. The blueprint Ping sketched out was not new, and served more as a reminder: the university's strength was in the dedication of the members of the university community to a shared sense of purpose. With such a foundation, the university would adjust to any change.

Later that fall, public hearings statewide on the Managing for the Future recommendations rehashed the complaints against universities, but the voices of reason from the campuses were being heard. In a report that backed away from punishing universities and that moved toward the original goal of effecting efficiency, the board of regents drafted revised recommendations. Titled "Securing the Future of Higher Education in Ohio," the report focused not on taking over the governance of institutions or decreeing which ones could pursue research, but on saving money, most notably by eliminating duplication of expensive graduate programs. Programs deemed "not viable" would be eliminated by an institution's trustees, or by the state if trustees were slow to act. Left intact in the renamed efficiency document was a faculty workload increase and a persistent call to cut costs while increasing quality, though the language was not verbatim Voinovich's "work harder and smarter."

The very real threats to universities posed by the Managing for the Future report, and later the Securing the Future report, generated a positive benefit, too. Universities began cooperating immediately by speaking with one voice to challenge the more damaging proposals. As one of the presidents with a record of good management, Ping was chosen by the Inter-University Council (IUC) in 1993 to address the Senate Finance Subcommittee to lobby for universities. Alumni of Ohio University, more than 120,000 strong, also lobbied behind the scenes, armed with data and arguments culled from university publications.

The data that probably influenced the legislature the most during the budget wrangling were "economic impact statements" prepared by the IUC. Using readily verifiable, audited data, universities reported in dollars and cents the economic impact each had on its community and the state. The IUC reported that in the preceding year Ohio's investment of $1.19 billion in its fifteen institutions of higher education was returned *nine-fold* in a $10.72 billion impact on the state's economy. Using a model that accounts for spending by an institution, then calculates at least one re-spending before the money leaves the state, universities showed with numerical clarity that they were giving back far more than they took from the state economy. Ohio University ranked third largest among the fifteen in the economic impact ranking despite its medium size and its location in the state's poorest quadrant.

What was likely the key variable in budget decision making, though, was the economy itself, which improved somewhat the next year. The state did not cut university budgets, and even promised a bit of an increase that July, though it would take years to catch up from years of cuts. One development in budgetary decisions was met with cheers in Athens. Subsidy would be based on actual enrollment. As Ohio University's enrollment had increased every year, it stood to gain more than other universities. As Ping explained to Faculty Senate, "The pie of state support has shrunk, but we will get a larger piece of that smaller pie."

The 1993 budget bill also included two riders that had less to do with money and more to do with distrust: (1) Universities must demand that faculty spend 10 percent more time in the classroom, the amount the legislature alleged was equal to the decline over the past decade. (2) Universities must develop and implement annual performance reviews of faculty. Both stipulations, which were to take effect in fall 1994, would be executed under the guiding hand of Elaine Hairston, chancellor of the Ohio Board of Regents. Hairston recruited James Bruning, recently retired provost of Ohio University, to head a committee charged with writing guidelines on the two personnel policies.

Meanwhile, convinced that the 10 percent drop did not apply in Athens, Ohio University administrators conducted their own study of faculty workload. After reviewing the data, Associate Chancellor of Regents Howard Gauthier conceded, "Ohio University was the only four-year campus without a drop in classroom time." Being the exception to the facts, however, did not allow the university to become an exception to the new rules. Advising duties were also included in the committee's document, but Ohio University already had that responsibility covered as well. The Bruning committee completed the workload job in six months. The guidelines, described first and foremost as flexible, allowed universities to incorporate differences in faculty talents, fluctuations in a university's programmatic needs, and differentials in degree levels in formulating their policies. One example of the last, accounting for teaching load variances between a department's undergraduate and graduate components, became central to the university's compliance proposal, which permitted the trustees to sign off on a faculty workload policy that fit the regents' bill.

The second mandate, faculty performance review, culminated in the Bruning committee's call for incentives to encourage more undergraduate teaching. Devised as a means to balance among teaching, service, and research in tenure, promotion, and salary decisions, the second goal likewise had little negative impact at the university, which already had an annual review process in place. The work of the committee completed, the regents ended the year by announcing the next front in its accountability crusade. The board promised to revamp the funding formula so that various "performance goals," such as graduation and retention rates, would be factors, along with enrollment gains, in determining state subsidy in the future.

Ping did not singlehandedly change the minds of those in power in Columbus, though his reasoned arguments had a significant impact, as several people in the political arena would later testify. One seasoned journalist who covered state budget jockeying said all the reporters respected Ping. Trustee Jeanette Grasselli Brown summarized the opinion. Ping was one of the most influential people to advocate university issues before the legislature and regents, she said. After she became a regent herself, she said, "They still talk in Columbus about his wise leadership."

In for the Duration

That Ping managed Ohio University ably was never in doubt. Among the most impressive testimonials to his job effectiveness was the attempt by other university boards of trustees to hire him away from Ohio University. The first of three inquiries (that were made public) came after only three years at the helm in Athens. Michigan State University wanted Ping to apply for its presidency, reported a Lansing newspaper. He was already respected in Michigan's higher education circles for his success as Central Michigan's provost. For a month the press speculated, and Ping listened to Michiganders. When he withdrew his name as a possible candidate, he cited the unfinished tasks at Ohio University as one reason for staying. He also praised the trustees, writing that their "commitment to the University rather than to personal agendas, the character and quality of board work—so much in evidence on this campus and so lacking elsewhere—were primary factors in the decision to withdraw my name." Trustee commitment to Ohio University was one of the factors that had attracted Ping to the job of president in the first place. Unique among public university charters in the state regarding the constitution of its board, Ohio University's policy stipulates that five of the nine trustees must be alumni of the university.

Ping's five years of rebuilding at Ohio University also caught the attention of the trustees at Ohio State University. An Associated Press report listed Ping as a likely candidate, but the wire service had to report the very next day that Ping had asked that his name be withdrawn from consideration. It was not a difficult decision, as Ohio State dealt with the same legislature that had just perpetrated a tardy budget followed by an early cut.

Oregon State University came calling in 1984. The president and Claire spent the weekend in Corvallis being courted, but Ping withdrew from consideration on the Tuesday after the couple's return to Athens. Even though he had served at Ohio nine years and had turned an ailing university into a healthy one, he still thought there was more work to do at Ohio. Besides, he liked the place and its people. Ping even revealed that former president John Baker had warned him, "If you stay in Athens more than five years, you're not likely to leave." Five years turned into nineteen, fourteen years longer than the national average for years in office for college presidents. The only suitors, in fact, that might have succeeded at luring Ping away were private universities that weren't beholden to politicians for operating money. One such private university came very close to landing Ping, albeit out of the public eye.

The 1992–93 battles had been particularly wearying, but it was not the political wounds that led Ping to consider stepping down. In April 1993 he told the trustees that the next academic year, 1993–94, would be his last as president. A constellation of health problems—shoulder surgery, knee replacements, herniated disks—were conspiring to rob him of time, energy, and freedom from pain. "Two or three years from now my ability to assist in a smooth transition may be uncertain," he said. Planning for transition would be seamless this way, at a time when uninterrupted leadership was more crucial than ever. His guidance in the search for a successor would go beyond years of general experience in hiring administrators. As an often-courted candidate, Ping knew through the grapevine who was in the market to be a university president and which universities had interviewed people from the presidential candidate pools.

Ping also announced his intention to take a year's leave in 1994–95 so that the new president would have the campus to him- or herself. Then he would return to Athens to teach because he did not want to retire completely, and the Pings had no intention of leaving the community they loved. Besides, being relieved of the time-consuming duties of president would enable him to focus on both the Cutler Scholars Program, which he had helped found, and the Institute for the Teaching of the Humanities, which would soon bear his name. Ping would leave the office in order. The new president would have an interim provost (David Stewart, as Bruning had retired), no budget campaign (as it would be the second year of the state biennium), and no union contract to negotiate (as the next three-year contract would be signed in Ping's last year).

Newspapers across the state were filled with homage when the story broke in April 1993 that Ping would step down as president. The *Cleveland Plain Dealer*, always the first to trumpet trouble on Court Street, listed the nationally recognized academic programs at Ohio University, crediting Ping with leadership it described as "nothing short of remarkable" in an editorial headlined "Leading a College Comeback." The *Columbus Dispatch* called Ping's presidency "legendary among the nation's universities." The Associated Press wrote that Ping's actions at the university "transformed it back into a respected institution that is lauded in the United States as well as abroad."

The news stories also quoted trustees, the people who had worked with Ping in what was often called the "turnaround." Jody Galbreath Phillips, the former trustee who had chaired the search committee that recommended Ping for the job of president, said he had put Ohio University back on the map. "To me, he is and has been the perfect president," Phillips said. Trustee Charlotte Coleman Eufinger used the adjective "extraordinary" to describe Ping. "He is able to see the best in everyone and draw those qualities out of them. The university works so well under him."

Former presidents also spoke up when Ping announced he would step down as president. "Although I have been away from the University for 25 years, I feel possessive about OU. I have been pleased with the way Charlie has moved it ahead," Vernon Alden said in a *Columbus Dispatch* article. "Ping was the ideal president who put the school first," John Calhoun Baker said in the same article.

Other verbal tributes were a year off, but the trustees acted immediately to honor the man who had "brought the university immense stability," in the words of Trustee Jeanette Grasselli Brown. Following a model set by other universities, the trustees voted to give Ping a 15 percent salary increase, to take effect during his last year as president. His title would double: President Emeritus and Trustee Professor of Philosophy and Education. Actions that would honor him for perpetuity were the naming of the new student recreation facility and the naming of the new humanities program for Charles J. Ping.

The Charles J. Ping Student Recreation Center

Students themselves articulated the need for a new student recreation center. Across the nation colleges and universities were constructing multi-use facilities to meet student demand for space for intramural athletics as well as just "working out," which had become popular among young people of traditional college age. The university's 18,000 Athens students had outgrown Grover Center and its outdated equipment. To make sure there was demand for new physical fitness equipment, however, Vice President for Administration Gary North experimented. Two rooms in Grover were rigged temporarily with weights, treadmills, stair-steppers—all the machinery students preferred to use to stay in shape. The response was overwhelming. On weekdays 600 to 800 students showed up to take their turns, while more than 1,000 lined up on Saturdays and Sundays. North concluded that the students who were asking President Ping for a new recreation center were indeed representative of large numbers. Student leaders who advocated the construction of a new center also asked that the facility be named to honor their president.

The groundbreaking for the Charles J. Ping Student Recreation Center in January 1994 was covered by news stories that detailed the features of the building. Built at the edge of the university golf course near the

Hocking River, the imposing structure on the campus's southern border would cost $24 million. One measure of student desire for the center was the endorsement by student leaders of a dedicated increase in the quarterly activity fee, especially since the center was not eligible for state funding. The Ping Center would house fifteen athletic courts, a suspended jogging track, a climbing wall, a weight room, a fitness-equipment room, game rooms, campus recreation offices, and a central lounge—larger than the ballroom in Baker Center—for campus events ranging from banquets to dances. A portrait of Ping by John Michael Carter at the second-floor level above the open lobby shows those who enter what the eighteenth president of Ohio University looked like when the building was named for him.

The Charles J. Ping Institute for the Teaching of the Humanities

Though fund-raising efforts for an institute for the teaching of the humanities had implied to donors that the new program would be named for Charles Ping, a formal announcement of the tribute was withheld until the fund-raising was completed. An initial grant of $300,000 from the National Endowment for the Humanities formed the basis of an endowment for the institute. The required match of $900,000 in private gifts was surpassed quickly, said Jack Ellis, vice president for development. In less than two years the endowment total was $1.4 million, oversubscribed, Ellis said, because the mention of Ping's name had an effect on donors, the most generous of whom were those serving on the boards of trustees and foundation. Ping was officially informed only *after* the institute was fully funded, in late 1992.

No other academic program could have been a more fitting tribute to Ping. The institute's dual focuses on the academic disciplines in which he was steeped and the practice of imparting knowledge gave him the opportunity to spend his post-presidential career immersed in the teaching of the humanities, both in principle and in practice. When told about the endowment, he remarked, "Teaching is important throughout the university, but it is particularly important in the humanities, which deal with the judgement of values." He would also have a hand in the job descriptions for the three institute professorships funded by the endowment. Two current faculty members named to professorships in the institute in 1994 were Alan Booth, History; and Lois Vines, Modern Languages, whose specialty was French. The third of the teaching positions, appropriately named the Charles J. Ping Professor for the Humanities, was designated for a new, senior-level faculty member. Following a national search in 1997, Thomas Carpenter, holder of the doctor of philosophy degree in classics from Oxford University, was appointed the Ping Professor. In 1999 Carpenter succeeded Ping as director of the institute. In addition to the three faculty positions, the institute endowment funded library support, money for projects—such as colloquia on teaching and curriculum revision—and the means to encourage the improvement of secondary education through summer workshops for high school humanities teachers.

Recognizing Ping's Leadership

A senior in journalism was one of the first commentators to record for posterity that the eighteenth president at Ohio "had righted a foundering ship." Peter King, a *Post* writer who eventually landed at *Sports Illustrated*, arrived in Athens the year Ping did. Commissioned by the university's alumni publication, *Today*, in fall 1979, King wrote an assessment of Ping's first four years at Ohio in which he interviewed students, faculty, and staff about their impressions of the president's job performance. Though there was a bit of residual grumbling about the fizzled faculty union initiative, the consensus was that Ping was doing an admirable job. Perhaps the most cogent quote in King's story came from Mary Corrigan, a secretary who had observed several presidents at the university. "He's not a politician. He's a good manager. He's getting things done through others."

The laudatory front-page item in the *Wall Street Journal* about UPAC appeared at the end of the next academic year, in May 1981. Though it is detailed in the chapter "Collegially Speaking," it is appropriate to note here that reporter John A. Prestbo credited President Ping for the idea and implementation of UPAC as the sort of collegial process that assured widespread participation by others in decision making.

Probably the person in the best position to observe presidents of Ohio University was Marie White, who retired in June 1992 after serving forty years as assistant to five presidents—Baker, Alden, Sowle, Crewson, and Ping. All five praised her when she retired, using such descriptions as extremely efficient, totally reliable, very discreet, and always gracious. When she was asked to talk about her last boss, she emphasized the role of the 11:30 Group in creating a team with "a common responsibility for the whole university." White described Ping as calm, considerate, and humorous. From transcribing his handwritten scholarly writing, White learned that the president was still passionate about philosophy, the subject he had studied and taught for more than forty years.

Though praise and tributes appeared in various local, state, regional, and national forums over the years, the most reflective and comprehensive were made publicly in 1993–94, Ping's last year as president, and after he returned to the classroom. Opinions from both within and outside the university summarized his most important qualities as a leader and the most lasting accomplishments at the university during his tenure as president.

Described by those familiar with him as extremely modest, Ping tried in his last year as president to deflect the homage to come by emphasizing that he was only one of many who had contributed to the university's improvements. In a *Post* article early in the school year by Laura Jacobs, Ping said he did not want the credit for the university's turnaround. "It was a far better university than it led itself to believe—and far better than the people of Ohio believed," he said. "My role was to bring into focus and to quicken—that is, to make more lively—what was already here. I don't want the people who were here to lose sight of the fact that everything [renowned about the university] was already here." He admitted that some of that opinion likely stemmed from his background in Calvinist theology. "You work as if everything depended upon you, but you live secure in the knowledge that nothing ultimately depends on you," Ping said.

Those who worked with him, however, were not as reticent about giving Ping the credit for the state of the university in the years 1975 to 1994.

> Charlie brought us an institutional sense of self. Through consultation and some hard-nosed management, he helped this institution determine a set of priorities and then follow them. Now, as an institution, we have a strong sense of what we are and how good we are. As a result, I think we teach better.
> —Alan Booth, Hamilton/Baker and Hostetler Professor of History, former Faculty Senate Chair, and member of the 1974 presidential search committee

> Slowly, steadily, carefully, Charlie brought stability to the institution. The values we cherished when we entered teaching are the values we cherish today—collegiality, openness, taking seriously the input of colleagues, caring about students, wanting this place to be

the finest institution it can be in terms of teaching and scholarship.
—Donald Borchert, Department of Philosophy, vice chair of the Ohio Education Association in 1975 when it advocated a faculty union

I will remember Charlie because he helped us recover a sense of value and decency that made everybody believe it was worthwhile to be here, that what we were doing counted for something, and that it was terribly important to do something with these young minds. I honestly think Charlie Ping will be remembered as one of the great university presidents in this country. You think of John Hannah at Michigan State. You think of Robert Maynard Hutchins at Chicago, Charles Eliot at Harvard. Charlie is in that league in my opinion.
—Nicholas Dinos, Professor of Chemical Engineering, member of the original General Education Program Committee

President Ping knew what was going on all of the time. He didn't look over my shoulder or those of faculty. He just expected accomplishment.
—Lloyd Chesnut, Vice President for Research

Throughout his 19 years as president, Charlie Ping's character, honor and vision became the standards at Ohio University. All would agree that his decisions were always made with the best interests of the university at heart, even if one did not always agree with the decisions. He created a unique, wholesome bond among faculty, staff, students and alumni—a bond that made the university very special as a friendly, compassionate place to teach, work and learn.
—Jack Ellis, Vice President for Development Emeritus

UPAC was one of the best things he established. It was expensive in terms of the amount of time required of its members, but it was a deliberate way of getting things accomplished. Much more important was the stature he personally brought in his own dedication and personality and depth.
—Ted Bernard, Assistant Dean of University College, former Faculty Senate Chair

Part of Ping's legacy is that he did not have to take credit for everything. He didn't want to be on the front page. People had said UPAC would never work, but it did. It's a remarkable piece of his personality that he can sit at a table and blend into the background, contributing to the discussion but never dominating.
  —Samuel Crowl, Professor of English, former Dean of University College

There are some interesting ironies in the success of the institution. One is that during our academic successes, our athletic program has not done well. I think it's significant that our institution has prospered and become popular, and one cannot say that it's because of the success of the football team. A second irony is the successful fund-raising campaign, despite the won-lost record in the major sports.
  —Roger Rollins, Professor of Physics, two-term former Faculty Senate Chair

Before Charlie Ping arrived, there had been strong voices among faculty for re-instituting basic requirements. A lot of us felt that students needed some breadth that they didn't have. Then Charlie came in and gave focus to a General Education program. Even more important, he gave the support you have to have to get things going. There is no question that it has clearly helped strengthen and broaden the education of our students.
  —Eric Wagner, Professor of Sociology, former chair of General Education Council

I don't think so much about his contributions as I do the man himself. Words are not adequate to express fully what Charles J. Ping has meant to Ohio University and me personally. Dr. Ping is a most decent man, one who is committed to and honors God, country, family, Ohio University and all those he encounters.
  —Alan Geiger, Assistant to the President and Secretary to the Ohio University Board of Trustees

Jeanette Grasselli Brown, trustee and later regent, shared one of her fondest memories of Ping. "I remember Charlie's delight in talking about President Baker. He had such a warm, special relationship with him. I can never forget Charlie's laugh—you know that deep throaty laugh he has—when he would talk about President Baker. There was the story of Baker helping him get out of a car when Charlie had his knee surgery. Baker, in his mid-90s, said, 'Charlie, be careful how you're walking.'"

> Quality and excellence are the two words that, in my mind, most clearly describe Charlie Ping. Charlie seemed to make every decision against these two standards. His example set the tone for the members of his administrative team so that our actions also focused on promoting, enhancing and affecting the quality and excellence of Ohio University. His words, his actions and his influence on others—students, faculty, staff, alumni and friends of Ohio University—always reflected these two guiding concepts.
> —James Bruning, former Chair, Department of Psychology, former Associate Provost, former Provost

While those quoted include several former members, some of them chairs, of Faculty Senate, the members of that body in 1993–94 chose a collective and more lighthearted tribute—a loud hip-hip-hooray. While the mood was still jovial, the senators extended to Ping "a lifetime invitation to senate meetings," a 180-degree turnaround from 1976 when Ping had to ask, in writing, to address that body on the issues of the freshman grading policy and composition requirements.

Rebuilding a Town—Claire Oates Ping

The compound subject of every sentence Ping uttered after 1951 dealing with major life decisions was "Claire and I." Though the public and press usually saw only the man of the couple at microphones, on camera, on stage at public events, and quoted in print, those close to him knew that he was one member of a partnership despite Claire Oates Ping's preference to remain off camera. Ping's letters to the trustees, which were always off the record, are full of references to his wife, to their travels, to their family milestones, to their decision making. "Claire and I" may not have been what most of the campus saw, but it was the reality behind the scenes.

The college student Ping married on the day he graduated from Rhodes College did not see herself twenty-five years later entertaining state officials, nationally known scholars, or world leaders. Claire had simply wanted to be Mrs. Charles J. Ping, to live happily ever after with the classmate who was a football star and who occasionally preached at the Presbyterian church in her hometown. The "happily ever after" happened, but not the "simply," as she gave up about 125–150 days per year for nineteen years in Athens to her husband's job-related entertaining. (And that doesn't include the years as a provost's wife or interim president's wife that preceded the move to Athens.) When Ping left the President's Office, he and Claire estimated they had entertained about 50,000 guests in the official president's residence on Park Place. Some of the social functions bridged campus and community, such as thank-you receptions for volunteers in town-gown organizations like Athens Friends of International Students and Friends of Trisolini Gallery.

"I loved the entertaining," Mrs. Ping said. "It was something Charlie and I did together. He had his job; I had my volunteer work, but the events at the house were ours." Not unlike other couples who talk into the night after the visitors have gone, Charlie and Claire would talk about the evening's events, the guests, the university, and their stewardship of the historical institution and town for which they cared so much.

Being hostess while trying to preserve some privacy for a family of four was difficult. Living in a house with neighbors that included a fraternity, Alden Library, one other private residence, the Honors Tutorial College House, and two major classroom buildings (Scripps and Gordy) was about as different from her home in western Tennessee as a setting can get. Little Kerrville, where Claire grew up, was surrounded by cotton fields. Her father managed one of the largest plantations in the area before his death during her freshman year at Rhodes.

She admitted that balancing her public and private lives wasn't always easy. Yet she took on another job—improving the community—before Ping children Andy and Ann Shelton left Athens for college. (Born in Durham, North Carolina, Andy Ping holds degrees from Brown University, Ohio University, and Duke University Medical School. Born in Alma, Michigan, Ann Shelton Ping Venable holds a degree from Wittenburg University.)

"The town was in bad shape along with the university," she said, but Claire saw the value of the historic structures of both the university and Athens, and she worked harder than any other transplant to see her adopted hometown flourish. What's more significant is that she didn't have to. With various constituencies praising the job her husband was doing (and with various universities trying to hire him away), she could have stayed on the third floor when there wasn't an official function at 29 Park Place.

Her first project in preserving the heritage of Athens came in 1976, when Claire and campus planner Alan Geiger initiated the process of placing the buildings on and facing the College Green on the National Register of Historic Places. She had already met local historian Marjorie Stone, who was busy trying to establish a county museum, and Claire quickly became steeped in the historical details of the area. One historical project she immersed herself in, along with Ann Lee Konneker and Ann Grover, was restoring and decorating, to historical accuracy, the Grosvenor-Leete Home on University Terrace and its companion carriage house for use as alumni facilities.

Other women in Athens also saw potential in restoring the architectural gems in town. Claire led eight of them to form a group, which eventually grew to fifty members, called Community Scope, dedicated to exploring ways to preserve Athens's heritage. In addition to Claire Ping and Ann Grover, the original members included Margene Bush, Verda Jones, Nada Kerr, Marion Lavelle, Mary Ellen Rohr (Dudley), Rose Rutherford, and Jean Sprague. "One factor that made Community Scope so effective was its informality," Claire said. "There were no by-laws to follow, no quorums to count, no committees to give reports. Reaching consensus within a small group—whatever the number in attendance at any given luncheon meeting—was a lot easier," she said. Another factor in Community Scope's effectiveness was its leader's background in economics, which had been her major. Claire had been enrolled in three colleges and two universities as she pursued a degree in tandem with Charlie's career.

One early project of the group was to commission a study of downtown Athens that would catalogue restoration needs, costs, and priorities. Many of Athens's landmarks were suffering from the same deferred maintenance the university's buildings exhibited. Worse, two major fires had ravaged sections of North Court Street. To implement the findings, however, some formal structures were required. The women's group formed a separate corporation in conjunction with the Chamber of Commerce called Community Design, which focused on restoration of Athens's unique business district. Community Design spearheaded the makeover of about 20 percent of the downtown buildings by 1984. As different projects were completed and new ones moved up the list, new ways of accomplishing tasks were created. Several years after the original Scope members highlighted goals with broad brushstrokes, the Architectural Preservation

Committee was formed in order to keep Athens's nineteenth-century character on the civic agenda.

There was a lot to save in Athens and at the university. Claire wasn't done in 1984, but the Athens Chamber of Commerce was so appreciative of her accomplishments to that point that she was named Person of the Year. Claire had saved a lot of bricks and mortar, it was true, but her signature achievement was to create a means of improving the quality of life in Athens. Claire and her compatriots in community restoration had formed the Athens Foundation, a nonprofit entity designed to garner and husband an endowment, the earnings of which would be awarded to community projects in annual grants. Funds for the foundation came from the pledges of individuals, as is typical of such development efforts, but Scope members also took the project to the entire community via elaborate shows and sales of antiques in the Convocation Center. The Person of the Year citation also praised Claire's fund-raising for a community cultural arts center, called the Dairy Barn because it had always been just that at the Mental Health Center on The Ridges. Also in the list of jobs well done in the Chamber citation was a "Charlie and I" project—the Pings' co-chairing of the United Appeal campaign for Athens County in 1981.

Claire's efforts never ended. She had overseen the renovation and decoration of the house the university owned on Elmwood as a residence for the visiting Razak Chair holder. She was one of the prime movers in the extraordinary effort to salvage and relocate the Silas Bingham cabin during the Northwest Territory Bicentennial in 1987. She orchestrated the landscaping of a rose garden to remember Rose Rutherford and a daffodil garden to memorialize Alberta Grones, both of whom had contributed to making Athens known far and wide as a charming and distinctive place to live.

Before Ping's final commencement as president, the trustees had voted to name the cottage behind the Konneker Alumni Center in Claire's honor. When her husband gave the Commencement Address in June 1994, Claire knew that the trustees had voted to award her an honorary degree as well. But knowing the recognition was coming did not change the emotions she felt on the stage that day as the crowd of nearly 15,000 people gave her husband a standing ovation at the end of his speech. She had left her home to marry Charlie and follow him in a supporting role wherever his career took them. "He has a combination of philosophy and theology that serves him so well," she said later. "He starts each day with prayer. He is committed, determined, dedicated."

In the opinions of those who knew her, Claire too was committed, dedicated, and determined. She listened to the honorary degree citation that gave her credit for "modeling the evolving role of First Lady." She heard the words "No alumna has demonstrated more loyalty and selflessness to her adopted alma mater." She was aware that the cavernous Convocation Center was filled with people who had worked tirelessly for the university in the past and with new graduates who would serve the university in the future. But all she could focus on was Charlie as he smiled, recited the words, presented the degree, then kissed her in front of all those people.

An Everyday Citizen

After Ping announced his intention to leave the Office of the President, he told the trustees early in 1994 that the decision he and Claire had made "was the right one for the university's future and for us personally." He described the job as completely absorbing, demanding, yet satisfying. "Both of us look forward to greater control of our calendars, and I am eager to have time for serious study and reflection," he said. "The prospect of returning to the Ohio University campus in the fall of 1995 to teach, to contribute to the Ping Institute for the Teaching of the Humanities, and to help start the Cutler Scholars Program excites us greatly. We look forward to being part of the beginning of Ohio University's third century."

In 1994, after nineteen years at the helm of Ohio University, Charles Ping moved into an office in the southeast corner of the second floor of Trisolini Gallery, across the street from the College Green. Now that the university had spacious quarters for an art museum at The Ridges, Trisolini was retooled again. It had served as home to three presidents of the university—Elmer Bryan, Herman James, and John Baker—before its two decades as an art museum. The location on West Union, distanced from Baker Center only by the site of Howard Hall, was ideal for the professor who preferred lunch in the Elizabeth Baker Room.

The Pings spent the 1994–95 academic year out of Athens. Half the year was spent in faculty leave at their cottage in Eastport, Michigan; half in Namibia, Lesotho, and Botswana, where Ping was Fulbright Senior Research Scholar for Southern Africa. His official mission was to explore the role of the university in less-developed nations, but he put his updated knowledge to additional uses. Upon his return to Athens, he chaired the committee that reviews and nominates candidates for Fulbright Scholar appointments in Africa as part of his term on the board of directors of the Council for International Exchange of Scholars.

When the president emeritus returned from Africa, he settled into three new jobs for the 1995–96 academic year: Trustee Professor of Philosophy and Education, Director of the Ping Institute for the Teaching of the Humanities, and Co-Director of the Manasseh Cutler Scholars Program. Ping's favorite topics in philosophy, after nearly half a century of teaching in the discipline, were nineteenth-century philosophy and the history of philosophy. In education, he taught higher education administration, with emphases in the history of American higher education, educational planning, and the role of the university in contemporary society. At the Honors Convocation in October 1995, his successor Robert Glidden presented Ping an honorary Doctor of Humane Letters degree from Ohio University. The citation that came with the degree conferral reiterated the comments made by dozens of Ping's colleagues in 1994:

> Internationally recognized teacher and administrator, you have brought distinction and honor to yourself and to Ohio University.
>
> As Ohio University's eighteenth president (1975–1994), you have set an example for many with a constant striving for excellence in such matters as holistic planning, general education, development and scholarship.
>
> Under your exemplary leadership, Ohio University enjoyed stability and prosperity.
>
> Your generous contributions of time and energy to the life of Ohio University over the past two decades instilled among the faculty, staff and students a sense of community that will be your legacy to the university.

After 1995, Ping continued to contribute his time and energy to a host of endeavors. By the turn of the century he was chair of the board of directors of the Council on International Educational Exchange, which kept him focused on his longtime interest in the internationalization of universities. He was a member of the Board of Trustees of Louisville Presbyterian Seminary and Muskingum College. In 2001 he began a three-year term on the Ohio Humanities Council, which gave him an opportunity as one of the state's experts on the subject to share his expertise statewide. He did take some time off to read and reflect. Every spring and summer the Pings spent as much time as possible at the cottage in northern Michigan where they are simply Charlie and Claire to their longtime friends and neighbors.

In 2001 Ping attended the fiftieth reunion of his graduating class at Rhodes College. "I thought about all those reunions I had attended as president of Ohio University. At my own 50th, I faced the reality that nobody wants to hear the college president speak. They want to talk to each other," said the president of the Rhodes Class of 1951. Mr. and Mrs. Ping also celebrated their fiftieth wedding anniversary in 2001.

Ping had used his leadership talents to position Ohio University for permanent excellence in a situation where change was the sole predictable variable. His recipe was as easy to describe as it was hard to effect: make the educational function primary, build a holistic sense of community, practice superior stewardship of resources, and use sound data in proactive planning. In theory, any college president could read the recipe and try to follow it, but few have been as effective as Charles Ping. What then, made him different? Various published testimonials clarify that consistency of message was one of his most important qualities. There was never a "now you see it, now you don't" tenor to his philosophy of what was best for the university. He simply wanted everybody involved to recognize that they shared responsibility for their community. And he said it with conviction again and again, year after year. Underneath the consistency of message, as colleagues knew, was a consistency of feeling as well. Charles Ping loved Ohio University. He said it best in a speech before the Toward the Third Century campaign council September 23, 1989. "This place has held both Claire and me with a passion born of the very special qualities of this university and nurtured by the loyalty that it generates. I sensed this special-ness early," he said, explaining his role as one of many whose efforts achieved a whole greater than the sum of its parts.

Perhaps the best expression of his penchant for giving others credit appears in his 1992 Convocation Address:

> What is truly distinctive about Ohio University is the degree of dedication and loyalty offered by a great many individuals. This distinctiveness is the acceptance by these individuals of responsibility for the mission of the University, the giving of years of life and energy to the University as an institution. At its heart a university is people, the touch of life on life: students with students, students with faculty and staff, faculty and staff with each

other. This is true of all educational institutions, but it is a particularly powerful force in the life of a university like this one. A great many talented, capable and dedicated people have accepted the claim of Ohio University on their lives and efforts.

As various university committees planned bicentennial activities, President Emeritus Ping continued to touch people. He engaged in discussions with students in his classes, talked with alumni about the value of the Cutler Scholars Program, and contributed to intellectual dialogue with faculty colleagues. In fall 2002 he taught History and Philosophy of Higher Education with such zeal that Tracy Reedy, 2001 Outstanding News-Editorial Senior in the E. W. Scripps School of Journalism, described it as the capstone of her graduate degree in higher education. "I learned more from his course than most of my other courses combined," Reedy said, recalling the heft of reading assignments as well as Dr. Ping's insistence that students critically analyze what they had read.

Also that fall, the philosophy teacher took renewed interest in the Marching 110, for one of its percussionists was freshman Sam Venable, first grandchild of Charlie and Claire. When fall quarter 2002 ended, Ping was given the Ohio University Foundation's highest honor, the John C. Baker Award. Unveiled at the 1995 birthday party celebrating John Baker's hundredth birthday in tandem with the fiftieth anniversary of the foundation, the Baker Award recognizes individuals who have provided exemplary philanthropy and service to the foundation.

When Ping walked the campus byways early in the university's third century, many students thought that the tall man carrying a briefcase was just another teacher, one of many in the constant stream of people on campus. As he had concluded in the 1992 Convocation Address, "We who are momentarily privileged to be part of that constant stream rejoice in what has been given to us by those who have gone before and in the promise of what lies ahead in the life and mission of Ohio University." He was happy that he had earned the role of everyday citizen in the community that claimed him.

APPENDIX A

103 Goals of the Educational Plan of 1977

Liberal and Fine Arts Education, by Samuel Crowl, English

Goal 1. To identify and support, as the keystone and foundation of the university's central educational mission, those educational experiences which provide our students with the knowledge and skills which are the essence of a solid liberal education.
Goal 2. The faculty should recommend ways in which the university's general education curriculum can be reformed to provide students with a more rational, integrated, and meaningful exposure to the liberal disciplines and the fine arts.
Goal 3. Greater integration within and between the curricula of liberal and creative studies and the professional schools should be accomplished. The deans should be charged with establishing the devices and mechanisms, perhaps by inter-college committees and task forces, by which the faculty can identify the specific objectives and the procedures which would accomplish the aims of curricular integration.
Goal 4. The existence of the professional programs in art, dance, film, music, and theater are of great importance not only to their own students but to the cultural life of the campus as well. All colleges should examine the methods by which their students can develop a greater literacy of the eye and ear through exposure to the visual and performing arts.
Goal 5. The excellence of the faculty must be maintained and encouraged through increased support and recognition of distinguished teaching, research, scholarship, and creativity.
Goal 6. A strong system of academic advising by faculty members should be established.
Goal 7. A variety of courses and programs in liberal studies for adults should be established.
Goal 8. As a means of recognizing the value of integrating experience in life with knowledge gained from creative or intellectual inquiry, all

departments, schools, and colleges are asked to create the mechanisms which will offer the opportunity for students to put their education at the service of experience.

Graduate and Professional Education, by Svenn Linkskold, Psychology

Graduate Programs

Goal 1. To set criteria and standards for regular evaluation of graduate programs so as to define needs and objectives within programs and to guide the distribution of resources across the university.
Goal 2. To support the achievement and maintenance of quality in programs where there is evidence of student interest, scholarly and creative accomplishment, and societal need.
Goal 3. To develop financing for graduate education.
Goal 4. To achieve flexibility in programs, built around a stable core, and to combine resources into new programs.
Goal 5. To support and encourage research, scholarship, and creative activity.
Goal 6. To make graduate programs attractive to quality students.

Professional Programs

Goal 1. To set criteria for regular evaluation of professional programs so as to define needs and objectives within programs and to guide the distribution of resources within the university.
Goal 2. To support professional training at a high level.
Goal 3. To provide basic liberal and fine arts and science programs to support professional programs.
Goal 4. To make professional programs flexible, around a stable core, so that resources can be best utilized in serving needs of society and interests of students.
Goal 5. To foster community contacts for service and training.
Goal 6. To foster extended learning opportunities in professional education.
Goal 7. To set standards for achievement by students.
Goal 8. To provide up-to-date practical counseling to students in professional programs.

Science and Technology, by Nicholas Dinos, Chemical Engineering

Goal 1. The general education plan for the university will include, as integral parts, such studies as lead to understanding of science and technology. Support will be for faculty to create curricular materials as well as other required efforts.

Goal 2. Research activities of faculty and students (especially undergraduates) will be encouraged to meet the commitment of the university to contribute to the development of knowledge, and to the vitality of the educational environment.

Goal 3. Science, technology, and medicine will be enabled to explore areas in research and education of mutual interest.

Goal 4. Science and technology programs will seek and maintain all appropriate accreditations. The university will provide whatever facilities and resources are required to meet this commitment.

Goal 5. The university will establish activities designed to encourage research in applied and service areas. Cooperative relationships with other institutions (academic and others) will be strengthened and augmented. The scientific and technological concerns of Southeast Ohio are central to this goal.

Goal 6. New programs in science and technology may be required to serve societal needs and student interest. The university will encourage and support such programs when the need can be demonstrated and where quality already exists in related university efforts.

Goal 7. The university will support extra-academic relationships that provide learning experiences in career areas as a supplement to formal curricular programs. These could include internships, cooperative education, workshops, etc.

Goal 8. Science and technology programs will take the initiative for the updating, career changing, continuing education, etc., of practicing professionals in the region.

Goal 9. Relationships with international groups will be strengthened and incorporated into the educational and research planning of the university.

Goal 10. A learning center function will be established that will incorporate museums, hands-on devices, films, lectures, demonstrations, etc. The center will extend across the entire university's concerns.

Health and Human Services, by Donald Fucci, Hearing and Speech

Goal 1. To establish a sound structure that assures appropriate identification, coordination, and development of those programs directly involved in the education and training of health professionals.

Goal 2. To place heavy emphasis on an interdisciplinary approach to the education of students involved in health and human services.

Goal 3. Eventually to house all units identified as health and human services contingents within a comprehensive health education complex.

Goal 4. To seek and maintain appropriate state, national, and professional accreditation for all units identified as being health and human services.

Goal 5. To maintain an effective balance between quality education and numbers of students involved in any given health program.

Goal 6. To maintain an overall health training system of a size necessary to help in the provision of personnel sufficient to meet the health care needs of those not presently receiving proper services in Southeast Ohio, the entire state of Ohio, and the nation.

Goal 7. To be allied with and involved in appropriate university research activities that will lead to the best and most advanced education in all health-related fields and contribute to the general understanding and application of knowledge in health and human services.

Goal 8. To develop additional sources of funding for all aspects of the health and human services contingents.

Goal 9. To develop through present branch campus affiliations and other logical channels relations with external programs within Southeast Ohio that can contribute to and benefit from quality education of health-related professionals.

Goal 10. To serve as a significant center for the provision of experiences in continuing education for the practicing health professional.

Goal 11. To provide public service that is of the highest quality through all clinical outlets that are a part of health and human services training at Ohio University.

Goal 12. To show and demonstrate through all endeavors the utmost respect for the educational process, its traditions, its principles, its potential, and its proper application toward the training of those who will devote their lives to the physical and mental well-being of others.

Lifelong Leaning and Regional Higher Education, by George Klare, Psychology

Goal 1. Establish a university office concerned with lifelong learning.
Goal 2. Assign responsibility to the lifelong learning office for collecting and evaluating information about this rapidly growing area.
Goal 3. Review existing university offerings in the light of the needs of lifelong learners.
Goal 4. Develop and use a set of systematic procedures for surveying the need for new courses and programs that may be proposed.
Goal 5. Attempt to determine, for each new course or program being proposed, the medium or media that are likely to fit best the instructional needs involved.
Goal 6. Consider new and flexible methods of offering and financing instruction that relies less upon departmentally based FTE (full-time equivalencies).
Goal 7. Help to provide broad university involvement and cooperation in planning, funding, preparing, and offering correspondence coursework.
Goal 8. Help to provide broad university involvement and cooperation in planning, preparing, and offering instruction via radio and television.
Goal 9. Develop further the system for providing cooperation between the regional campuses, the Athens campus, and other institutions of higher education in the region.
Goal 10. Develop courses in regional higher education and lifelong learning to meet two needs: skills for taking undergraduate and graduate college courses and prerequisite knowledge required for enrollment in undergraduate and graduate college courses.
Goal 11. Explore existing and new systems of crediting for prior learning outside the college setting.
Goal 12. Offer opportunities for career education of the sort that cannot easily be provided on the Athens campus.
Goal 13. Offer opportunities for both career change and related multiple career training.
Goal 14. Offer instructional opportunities to professionals and paraprofessionals who wish to upgrade or update their training.
Goal 15. Offer additional instruction to adults who wish to cope more effectively with a changing society.
Goal 16. Explore the possibility of setting up an external degree program.

Residence Life Programs and Services, by James Hartman, Education

Goal 1. To provide living accommodations to various groups of students and to promote housing arrangements designed to complement the academic programs of the university and to respond to students as consumers.
Goal 2. To provide for the basic food needs of resident students and other outside guests residing in the halls.
Goal 3. To provide adequate care, maintenance, and improvements in the residence hall facilities, thereby providing a satisfactory physical environment.
Goal 4. To encourage the development of an environment within the residence halls that reflects a vital commitment to learning and provides a "community" life for students.
Goal 5. To provide opportunity through the residence halls for individual learning and development of attitudes, capabilities, etc. Such opportunities are developed through information, personal advising and counseling, educational programs, social activities, etc.
Goal 6. To develop residence life programs based on identification and assessment of the needs and interests of students and to evaluate the effectiveness of programs and services in the residence life and residence service area.
Goal 7. To promote greater input, communication, and expanded responsibility to representative students, faculty, and staff in the planning and program development for residence halls.
Goal 8. To achieve fiscal and planning accountability and solvency of auxiliary operations, thereby serving students well and efficiently, and fulfilling the commitment to the state legislature, bond holders, and the university that the residence halls be self-supporting.
Goal 9. To accommodate outside groups desiring temporary residence with the university for educational, developmental, and recruitment programs.

Academic Support, by William Allen, Associate Dean, University College

Goal 1. To support the library at a level which assures that it meets both the qualitative and quantitative standards necessary to provide quality academic programs.
Goal. 2. To provide funding support to those units of the university the special mission of which is to obviate educational and cultural deficiencies.
Goal 3. To assist faculty in the utilization of instructional media and tech-

nology through the establishment of the center for instructional development.

Goal 4. To encourage the use of instructional media and technology in meeting the academic needs of students.

Goal 5. To encourage the development of a centralized academic advising center.

Goal 6. To encourage effective faculty advising.

Goal 7. To upgrade existing facilities and equipment and to design new facilities to accommodate multi-media presentations.

Goal 8. To develop an awareness of the special advising needs of women, minorities, older students, international students, and other non-traditional participants in higher education.

Goal 9. To encourage the development of a learning center, suitably equipped with course materials, educational media, and supportive apparatus.

Goal 10. To encourage the adoption and use of teaching formats that speak to the diverse ability levels present in the student body.

Goal 11. To create attractive, comfortable, secure, and functional learning environments.

Goal 12. To encourage the use of computer applications in areas that directly support the ongoing instructional mission of the university.

Goal 13. To provide effective and efficient library service.

Goal 14. To expand the level of faculty and student awareness with regard to library holdings, services and methods of access, and utilization.

Goal 15. To provide continuing encouragement to those programs that lend distinction to Ohio University, to provide opportunities for students to practice their skills, and to provide a public service.

General Administration, by Dale Mattmiller, Health, Physical Education, and Recreation

Goal 1. To exert decisive, professional leadership, appropriately utilizing consultation and interaction with all university constituencies while improving and implementing the effective utilization of communication processes and channels.

Goal 2. To coordinate the total activities of the university in order to: (1) facilitate the mission of the university relative to instruction, research, and public service; (2) insure ongoing innovative but realistic planning that avoids *ad hoc* decision making; (3) convert planning into action that insures a balance between the interests of the several parts and the university as a whole through resource allocations reflecting university priorities.

Goal 3. To insure accountability of the public trust while: (1) maintaining the essential independence and integrity of the institution and academia; (2) effectively advocating university interests; (3) necessarily anticipating, influencing, interpreting, and implementing legislative and judicial interpretation of the public interest in higher education.

Goal 4. To maximize the efficiency/effectiveness of university operations through ongoing review of all programs, including the administrative organization and structure of the institution and all its components, concordant with established criteria of accountability.

Goal 5. To maintain sound fiscal management, including: (1) ongoing income projections, (2) debt service supervision, (3) responsible allocation and expenditure controls through appropriate budget development processes, (4) building of an adequate university reserve and (5) accounting of all revenues.

Goal 6. To exercise efficient, enlightened, professional personnel management that emphasizes staff/human development and satisfaction and is consistent with the university mission, goals, and priorities.

Goal 7. To provide energetic, progressive, cost-effective management of plant and all other physical resources.

Goal 8. To assure the availability of essential services to support the administration and activities of the institution as a total entity as well as each of its component parts.

Goal 9. To seek increased institutional support by relating the university to the general public; local, state, and federal government agencies; alumni and friends of the university; and those private individuals, agencies, corporations, and institutions willing to provide assistance through their financial support.

Student Services, by John O'Neal, Registrar

Goal 1. Provide a comprehensive and integrated system of student services programs and activities that are responsive to the educational needs and interests of students, faculty, and staff and are supportive of the academic mission of the university community.

Goal 2. Adopt organizational structures that emphasize and encourage careful planning and efficient, effective use of resources within student services programs and activities.

Goal 3. Actively promote communication between student services programs and activities and other offices and persons within, as well as outside, the university community.

Goal 4. Utilization of more advanced data processing techniques and equipment in an effort to develop an orderly, responsive, and systematic information system.

Goal 5. Support a high quality admission process through extensive programs of visitation and articulation with high schools, community, technical, junior, and four-year colleges. Enhanced by hosting visiting groups of prospective students and their parents, and establishing close working relationships with alumni, high school teachers and guidance personnel, and friends of the university.

Goal 6. Provide the broadest scope of need- and achievement-based financial assistance possible for all student ranks through an efficient and effective financial aids program.

Goal 7. To maintain and promote comprehensive health programs that provide students and staff medical, dental, health education, counseling and psychological, and environmental health and safety services.

Goal 8. Provide a placement and internship program that assists all students seeking career information.

Goal 9. Development of student life programs that, through viable extra-class activities and educational programs, can help students learn skills necessary to design and manage their own environments and to help students recognize and create environments that encourage unique, creative ideas and experiences conducive to individual growth.

Goal 10. Provide and encourage professional development and high standards consistent with the educational goals of the university among the student services staff in their responses to students, faculty, and other staff.

APPENDIX B

EDUCATIONAL PLAN II

Toward the Third Century: Issues and Choices for Ohio University

A REPORT TO THE UNIVERSITY
BY THE COLLOQUIUM ON THE THIRD CENTURY

Resolution of the Board of Trustees

WHEREAS, the Board of Trustees incorporated the *Mission Statement*, the convocation address on The Search for Community, and the *Statement on Goals and Directions for Ohio University* into *The Educational Plan 1977–87* and on October 1, 1977, adopted *The Educational Plan* as a guide for planning and program development of the university, and

WHEREAS, the Colloquium on the Third Century, after over two and a half years of debate and discussion, reported to the university community in October, 1987, on issues and choices for the third century of Ohio University, and

WHEREAS, this report was widely discussed and revised following suggestions developed in discussions and written comments, and

WHEREAS, the Board of Trustees had an opportunity to study and to discuss the original report and the revised document,

NOW, THEREFORE, BE IT RESOLVED that the Board of Trustees reaffirms the goals and commitments described in *The Educational Plan 1977–87*, and adopts the revised report *Toward the Third Century* as the *Ohio University Educational Plan II*.

BE IT FURTHER RESOLVED that the Board of Trustees directs that these statements of goals and principles be used in the preparation and review of planning documents and recommendations on resource allocations.

Adopted January 30, 1988

MISSION STATEMENT FOR OHIO UNIVERSITY

Ohio University is a public university providing a broad range of educational programs and services. As an academic community, Ohio University holds the intellectual and personal growth of the individual to be a central purpose. Its programs are designed to broaden perspectives, enrich awareness, deepen understanding, establish disciplined habits of thought, prepare for meaningful careers and, thus, to help develop individuals who are informed, responsible, productive citizens.

Undergraduate Education

Ohio University offers undergraduate instruction on both the Athens campus and the regional campuses. Undergraduate programs, designed to contribute to intellectual and personal development and career goals of students, emphasize liberal studies.

Undergraduate major programs, preprofessional, and professional programs prepare students for employment in a variety of careers and for continued study. Two-year technical and associate degree programs, reflecting employment opportunities as well as the general career interests of students, are taught primarily at the regional campuses.

At the Athens campus instruction is combined with residence life and other extracurricular programs in an effort to create a collegiate experience integrating learning and living.

Graduate and Professional Education

Ohio University offers graduate and professional education. The primary forms of activity are advanced and specialized courses of study, supervised practical experience, and research.

The essential concentration of faculty, material, and space resources dictates that the activity associated with graduate and professional education will be centered on the Athens campus. This activity is not limited to that campus; research and instruction are carried out at various locations.

Scholarship, Research, and Creative Activity

Ohio University is a center for scholarship, research, and creative activity involving the creation, testing, and dissemination of knowledge, understanding, expression, and technique.

As a public university, Ohio University has a particular responsibility to address societal issues and needs through such scholarship, research, and creative activity. The scholarly and artistic activity of the faculty enhances the teaching function at all levels of student experience.

Extended Community

Ohio University serves an extended community. The public service mission of the university, expressed in such activities as public broadcasting and continuing education programs, reflects the responsibility of the university to serve the ongoing educational needs of the region. The regional campuses perform a critical role in serving this extended community.

The university has a state-wide responsibility for an extended university program using independent study through correspondence.

It is the purpose of these extended university programs to serve a diverse range of educational needs, from professional groups requiring continuing courses of study related to the practice of their professions, to individuals desiring occasional or special interest study.

By service to the extended community, Ohio University contributes to cultural and economic development, health care, and to other human services.

Adopted January 15, 1977

Colloquium on the Third Century

Charles J. Ping, President
Joseph H. Berman, Director, J. Warren McClure School of Communications Systems Management
James L. Bruning, Provost
G. Kenner Bush, Trustee Emeritus
Richard R. Campbell, Trustee
William A. Day, Dean, College of Business Administration
John L. Gaddis, Distinguished Professor of History
Wilfred R. Konneker, Ohio University Fund Board Trustee
Richard I. Miller, Professor of Applied Behavioral Sciences and Educational Leadership
Marjorie E. Nelson, Assistant Professor of Family Medicine
Roger Radcliff, Associate Professor of Electrical and Computer Engineering
Jacobo R. Rapaport, Distinguished Professor of Physics
Duane B. Schneider, Director of the Ohio University Press
Gary M. Schumacher, Professor of Psychology
J. David Stewart, Associate Provost
Thomas E. Wagner, Professor of Chemistry, and Director, Edison Animal Biotechnology Center
Dora J. Wilson, Dean, College of Fine Arts

PROLOGUE
EXTERNAL ENVIRONMENT
1. Economic Factors
2. Social Environment
3. Educational Factors

UNDERGRADUATE EDUCATION
1. General Education
2. Disciplines and Professional Programs
3. The Internationalization of Undergraduate Education
4. The Libraries and a New Literacy
5. The College Student and Campus Life
6. Minority Access
7. The Nontraditional Student
8. Funding for Quality
9. Education and Values

GRADUATE EDUCATION
1. The Relation to Undergraduate Education
2. Professional Training
3. Medical Education
4. Interdisciplinary Programs
5. International Connections
6. Faculty and Staff Renewal
7. Resources for Graduate Study and Research

RESEARCH, SCHOLARSHIP, AND CREATIVE ACTIVITY
1. Areas of Inquiry
2. The Support for Scholarly Inquiry
3. Research and Society
4. Research and University Values

INSTITUTIONAL SUPPORT AND SERVICES
1. General Administration
2. Academic Support
3. Residential Life Programs and Services
4. Student Services
5. University Relations and Development

EPILOGUE

EDUCATIONAL PLAN II: TOWARD THE THIRD CENTURY

PROLOGUE

Issues and choices which can shape the third century of the life of Ohio University are the subject of this report. It is not an effort to predict the future. The starting point is an examination of factors already much in evidence. A critical observation is that we are in an age of wrenching change and that this has important consequences for the work of the university. What results is an agenda for action. Implementation must be the product of the periodic review of the goals of the various organizational planning units and continuous dialogue on priorities of the university-wide planning process. Rather than a blueprint for specific decisions, the report represents an analysis of structural change together with an exploration of the consequences for university planning.

Ohio University faces its third century with many strengths: an outstanding faculty, a diverse student population, an impressive array of programs, a residential campus in an idyllic setting in Athens and developed commuter campuses throughout the region, a history associated with the development of the state and the nation, and a pride in a sense of mission and place.

Decisions made in recent years have contributed to the university's strengths as it enters its third century. These decisions have resulted in controlled enrollment growth with an accent on increased standards for admission and for performance. During the past decade the university has implemented a general education program, increased the breadth and quality of its undergraduate majors, established major new curricula for health careers, and strengthened graduate and research efforts. University programs have attained national and international visibility and are a critical factor in the success of the institution in recruiting and retaining both students and faculty.

The university pursues a broad teaching and research mission based on planning that emphasizes interaction and interdependence among programs, schools, and colleges. Despite its size and complexity, the university remains flexible and responsive. Location and campus life contribute to a distinct sense of community. Shared purposes are shaped by institutional history, setting, and heritage as Ohio's first university and one of the earliest land-grant institutions.

It is reasonable to expect that the university will face different conditions in its third century from those that have allowed it to prosper in the closing decades of its second century. A changing external environment will call for internal changes. Needs of students, faculty, and staff, as well as the expectations of society, will require changes in curriculum, research, and professional training. These conditions present challenges as well as opportunities for the university. The consensus of the colloquium is that the strengths of Ohio University will enable the university in its third century to enhance its service to students and society and to participate in the creation of a better world.

One word consistently dominates every section of this report: *quality*. The insistence on this measure is not new. It continues the theme central to *The Educational Plan 1977–87*. The initiatives of that document are prologue to the challenges that the institution faces at the end of its second century and the beginning of its third. It is neither possible nor desirable to recreate the institution every ten years. The passage of a decade rather allows us the opportunity to be both retrospective and introspective. The past and the future provide a dialectic that presents us with opportunities for change, but change based on what has gone before as well as response to the challenges of the new.

This report reaffirms the binding of the life of Ohio University described in *The Educational Plan 1977–87* as a community committed to an *idea of a university*, a residential university joining liberal education and graduate and professional education in a campus setting, a university committed to teaching and to research; to *quality and the willingness to make the judgments* so necessary to defining and sustaining quality; to the search for *intellectual community*, the interaction and the integration of knowledge; to *international community* and to education for interdependence; to *lifelong learning* and to the creation of a broad community of learners; to *educational justice* and the effort to become a just and socially responsive educational community.

EXTERNAL ENVIRONMENT

The university will face significant modifications in the external environment in its third century. Signs of these changes already are apparent: alterations in federal aid for students and programs; new and expanded federal and state investment in research and development; increased emphasis on technology; heightened competition from other campuses and from alternative education programs provided by corporations and professional associations; greater attention to assessment and measurable outcomes; demands to demonstrate the cost effectiveness of programs; expectations of linkages between the university's programs and economic development, particularly economic development which affects the competitiveness of the United States in the world. The national emphasis on quality and performance, unprecedented in strength and scope in the history of education in this country, continues and will likely increase. Many factors important to planning for the third century of Ohio University are already much in evidence.

Expectations addressed to education provide the primary external environment for university planning. These expectations, presented in a variety of ways, are seldom stated with precision or clarity. They come as changing patterns of student course or major selection, as priorities for funding from governmental, corporate, and foundation sources, as public statement and discussion in political campaigns or media analysis, as legislative incentives and mandates. The economic, social, and educational expectations for university life will be met. The expectations will be served either by existing institutions or, as the history of American colleges and universities suggests, by the creation and support of new institutions to meet changing expectations.

1. Economic Factors

From its beginnings as the first university north and west of the Ohio River, and one of the first institutions founded by a grant of public land, Ohio University has throughout its history been responsive to public expectations. The state's current attempt to establish a partnership with educational institutions to address pressing economic problems is not a radical departure either from the history of Ohio University or of higher education in the United States. The earliest institutions in the nation were founded to provide educated persons for the professions and an educated leadership essential for the survival of democratic institutions. The Morrill Act, by federal grants of land, supported in the second half of the nineteenth century the establishment of institutions which brought the resources of education to bear on the need to increase the nation's agricultural and industrial productivity. The land-grant institutions were uniquely designed to serve the needs of a developing nation. The structure combined university instruction and research with the transfer of new knowledge and technology by extension agents. Now institutions and government must search for a contemporary counterpart. What form this will take is not clear, but it is obvious that the national and state agendas are enlisting educational institutions in economic revitalization and the effort to adapt to structural changes in the world economy.

The principal base of support for Ohio University is the state of Ohio. Given its dependency on subsidy for instructional and general needs, public education in Ohio cannot be strong if the state is economically weak. In the search for new economic initiatives, the state will likely continue to support partnerships drawing together university instruction and research with private and public support. It is imperative now, and will remain so into the twenty-first century, that the university contribute to finding new possibilities for the generation of economic activity and jobs. Economic dislocations will be accompanied by other challenges facing the state, such as an infrastructure in need of repair and a shrinking tax base brought about by the shift from manufacturing sector jobs to service economy employment. All have implications for funding education.

It is assumed that educational institutions will play a pivotal role in helping the state solve its complex economic problems. Higher education is regarded as a unique resource in developing new economic potential through instruction and research. Efficient use of technology will be one key to keeping Ohio's industries competitive and profitable. In addition to technology, the generation of basic knowledge and the creation of new understanding will be crucial for anticipating and dealing with an age of discontinuity. The beginnings of these new relationships involving education, state, and private sectors are already in place with state funding for Edison centers, business incubators, eminent scholar programs and Research Challenge funds.

2. *Social Environment*

Economic stresses have their social counterparts. Structural changes and dislocations in the United States affect the work force. The implications for education are clear. Workers will need different skills to preserve their jobs and the competitiveness of the industries in which they work. Research has shown that one million Ohioans, representing twenty percent of Ohio's workers, will need retraining to be employable. While much of the responsibility for skills development will fall on Ohio's two-year colleges and regional campuses of universities, advanced study and research centered on the main campuses will play a central role in preparing the state to deal with these pressing economic and social issues.

Education is no longer primarily the activity of the young. The constituencies of universities are changing: the overall population is growing older; many have two years of entry-level education and want more. Patterns of attending college also are shifting, especially at urban universities and the branch campuses of universities where the average age is steadily rising. Other changes and urgent issues are the increasing presence of minorities in the school age population and the decreasing participation of these students in university education.

The challenges from the changing social environment to education are diverse. Potential social problems are many: the erosion of values; the emergence of a permanent underclass with the division of society into haves and have-nots; the shrinking of the middle class; the growing number of single parent families; the continued threat to society posed by public health problems and substance abuse. Such social changes may have far-reaching political ramifications and will affect the educational services demanded from Ohio University.

3. Educational Factors

While university students always have been interested in careers, the contemporary student generation now seems to have stronger, more precise career plans and specializes its studies accordingly. Again economic expectations seem dominant. The university cannot ignore these interests. The challenge is to channel them into a broader participation in university education.

The general public sees higher education as more important today than in past decades. One outcome of this perception is the increased participation rate of high school graduates. Having consistently lagged behind the national averages in percentages of graduating seniors attending college, Ohio is currently enjoying an improved participation rate. These increases have altered decade-old projections of reduced college enrollments based on a shrinking pool of young people. Working against the continuation of such improvements are the shifting of a larger percentage of the costs of higher education to the students themselves, potentially limiting access; increased opportunities for entry-level employment which may alter the attractiveness of attending college for recent high school graduates; or such unpredictable events as an economic recession or the reinstatement of a military draft.

Coupled with the public's acceptance of the importance of a college education is an insistence on quality and accountability. Excellence is a recurrent theme. It translates into varied expectations for quality: the preparation of entering college students; teaching, especially at the undergraduate level; graduates described in terms of mastery of content as well as employability; the results of basic and applied research. Accountability defined as measures of performance is increasingly part of the expectations.

Conditions that contribute to excellence in education are much discussed. The pressure is to conform to prescribed definitions and to assess performance according to preset conditions. This is as much an internal institutional problem as it is a matter of external expectations. University education could easily fall prey to the danger of a narrow definition of excellence and resulting invidious comparisons of particular public universities with institutions such as liberal arts colleges, highly selective private universities, and the limited number of comprehensive national research centers that are offered as models of excellence but which have different missions and circumstances. One of the major challenges during Ohio University's third century will be to strive for excellence by realizing the university's distinct potential as a particular institution with its own history and characteristics.

Education is high on the nation's agenda. The current interest in performance at all levels of education has produced a public awareness that quality in primary and secondary education is in part dependent upon university teacher preparation programs. What is new is a quickened sense of partnership of public schools and the university and the recognition on the part of the faculty that university programs are tied directly to the success of the primary and secondary schools. The partnership is a shared task across the several levels of education and within the university among various colleges active in the preparation of teachers. The public demand for improvement in education is addressed to all who share in the responsibility for education.

The environment is charged with calls for the reform of public school education and teacher preparation. With a long history of preparing teachers and administrators for public schools, Ohio University bears a responsibility for active leadership in these efforts at reform. The university has a particular role in working with the schools in the immediate areas of the five Ohio University campuses and with school districts throughout southeastern Ohio. The calls for formal school-university linkages and programs, the efforts to develop discipline based seminars bringing together university and public school teachers, the establishment of resource centers and curriculum projects, the pressing need to find ways to reach that large number of students in the southern part of the state who see neither the possibility nor desirability of continuing on to post secondary education illustrate expectations which must be met.

Increasingly society looks to universities to provide a wide range of services. From public broadcasting to ambulatory and rural clinics; from the university library serving as a regional center for local public libraries to the tasks of assisting in development of information seeking literacy for students, teachers, business personnel; from demographic studies and training programs for local government officials to issues of conflict resolution in labor management relations to small business development, Ohio University has a steadily expanding service mission to the region. This service mission is basic to the land-grant tradition to which Ohio University belongs.

The primary service the university renders is providing educational opportunities for all students who can profit from university education. The role of the public university in America has been and continues to be the nurture of an aristocracy of talent, rather than of wealth or privilege. Access is open to all who give strong evidence of such talent without economic or gender or racial barriers. The public university should be a place of opportunity where students can prove themselves, an environment marked by racial, economic, and ethnic diversity. In a democratic society a passion for excellence must be reconciled to the determination to provide educational opportunity.

A strong insistence on the internationalization of university curricula is yet another expectation in the educational environment. Ohio University, with world-wide interests and relationships, mirrors a new world order of interaction and interdependence. This is reflected in both the mix of the student population and the content of educational programs. The United States is the country of choice for many international students for education. This provides a continuing opportunity for Ohio University to internationalize the campus and the person-to-person educational experiences. The attractiveness of the American model of higher education will likely make education a major item of international exchange well into the future. To be effective, this exchange must increasingly involve a flow of American students and faculty abroad. Basic to the educational tasks of

Ohio University in its third century will be the response to an increasingly interdependent world, the urgent imperative to prepare students to live and work in the world of the twenty-first century.

UNDERGRADUATE EDUCATION

Change and the insistence that universities respond are dominant contemporary themes. The environment points university planning in two different directions: the reform of undergraduate education and the development of research, graduate, and professional education. Both are important to planning the future of Ohio University. But since so much of the life of the university centers and will continue to center in the undergraduate experience, the quality of this experience must be the starting point for any exploration of the future.

The primary task of Ohio University is undergraduate instruction. This is true generally of American higher education. Discussions of the present state of higher education share a broad judgment that undergraduate colleges have serious shortcomings in both general education and specialized studies. Critics note with alarm the absence of a base for continued learning and the inability of undergraduate institutions to educate to the full obligations of civic and personal life.

Openness to critical examination is the first condition of reform. But equally important is the intense exploration of implications and the resources necessary to institute needed changes. Competing interests are identified in calls for breadth and depth, diversity and coherence. The effort to reform undergraduate education, given these competing interests, strains resources and decision-making processes.

As Ohio University approaches its third century, a variety of factors will direct decisions affecting undergraduate programs. Funding sources and student interests will influence these decisions, but so too will a determination to state and sustain a shared sense of the purpose and nature of a university education. Some of the imperatives for education come with additional resources; most do not and will require internal reallocations. The institutional challenge is to understand the enduring mission of the university and, to the degree it is consistent with that mission, to respond to the changing expectations of public mandates and student interests.

Those who define the university mission over an extended time are principally the trustees and the faculty. They must assume responsibility for an insistence that the university only serves its students and its era well when it is an independent critic as well as a servant, that the university only responds to the times when it is a community of senior and apprentice scholars seeking timeliness through enduring wisdom.

It is a foregone conclusion that Ohio University cannot resist change or cling stubbornly to current offerings or patterns of life. Nor can it surrender the direction of the university to the constantly changing interests of the public or students. The uncritical acceptance of external expectations or students' choices can compromise the ideal of the university as an independent critic and scholarly community. The structure and content of undergraduate education can only be defined as the result of a constant dialogue between contemporary expectations and the mission of the university. What is new as Ohio University prepares for its third century is not this tension but the power and influence that student choices and external expectations exert upon university life. The issues involve weighing institutional circumstances and potential, the consequences of not responding, and the costs of responding too completely.

1. General Education

General education describes a structure, typically some arrangement of course requirements common to various undergraduate curricula. But the actual content is not any particular set of courses; rather it is the objectives described by the requirements. Purpose, clearly defined and understood by students and faculty, is essential to a general education program. Such education is designed to contribute to that breadth of knowledge and that active engagement with ideas so essential to liberal learning. The extent of student involvement in learning sets the conditions of excellence in undergraduate education. These conditions include the investment of time and effort in learning; they are present when students discuss what they read and hear and see on campus; they are expressed in the pursuit of the consequences of ideas. The search for the conditions which contribute to such learning constitutes the central challenge to the reform of undergraduate education.

A major theme in the current discussion of the quality of undergraduate education in America is the need for an integrated common core in the curriculum. Prior to the current debate regarding the importance of general education, the faculty of Ohio University recognized this need and adopted a general education requirement for all students that called for three tiers or types of learning experience. All are now in place. The reform, however, is far from a finished product. It must be subjected to rigorous evaluation and, when necessary, reasoned change.

A number of continuing challenges are apparent. One is the definition and communication of goals. Another is evaluation and the use of the results of existing assessments. A third is the reallocation of the faculty time and institutional resources necessary to carry out the program. There is also a critical need for ongoing course development. But again, the most important issue is involvement. The problem is how to create, or in some cases sustain, enthusiasm for general education on the part of faculty preoccupied with research and teaching in their disciplines, or students primarily concerned with their special interests and careers.

The goals of general education require ongoing reinterpretation and communication. The present structure reflects a strong conviction that developed skill in the use of language and mathematics should be required of all university students. Beyond this, there is some agreement that undergraduate programs should be designed to insure both breadth and coherence, but there is little agreement on how to achieve this.

The original consensus which gave rise to the distinctive elements of the Ohio University general education curriculum remains strong—intellectual disciplines of analysis and synthesis should be a common expectation for all undergraduate students. But even this basic agreement is challenged by widely divergent understandings of the objectives, by the specialization necessary to the growth of knowledge, by the influence of the self-interests of academic departments or accrediting bodies on the design of undergraduate curricula, and by the almost universal student preoccupation with vocational relevance.

The rate of knowledge growth and its corollaries—accelerating obsolescence, the increasing specialization of knowledge, the steady erosion of any shared literary or common cultural heritage—give added urgency to the call for the reform of undergraduate education. Insofar as liberal education can contribute to the ability to learn, to evaluate new knowledge, to adapt to change; insofar as liberal education develops critical intelligence and imagination; insofar as it nurtures language and awareness, such education responds to the needs of the times. Specialized and general knowledge are both essential elements of the needed reform. The strength of university programs has been in specialized understanding. The area most in need of development is the general education component of the curriculum.

To meet this challenge Ohio University will have to make extensive new investments of time and resources in its general education program. Ongoing curriculum workshops, faculty seminars, careful orientation of students and faculty to the goals of general education, a reassessment of faculty-student interaction, and the exploration of the relation of residential life to educational goals are all essential aspects of this effort. The expansion and strengthening of the general education program will require diversion of faculty time and energy from departmental programs. A closer integration of campus life and academic goals will dictate a reorientation of student programming. All this and more is needed. The end sought is an active, vital, involved intellectual community with, in some measure, a common base of understanding and interests.

An important part of the educational impact of a university on students is the formal and informal structures of advising. At a most stimulating level the faculty member takes on the role of tutor. More commonly, the role is as a departmental or general advisor. But the task is too narrowly defined when it is seen only in terms of a professor of a particular discipline. It is as a mentor to the intellectual life that the relation is most critical to the undergraduate experience. Not all faculty or staff can do this well, but those who devote time and energy to the task and are effective should be recognized and rewarded. Intellectual values, the involvement in learning so basic to excellence, are nurtured by the availability of faculty and by the nature of the out of class contact between faculty and staff.

2. Disciplines and Professional Programs

A university, in contrast to a liberal arts college, organizes its life around colleges and professional schools. For an institution of its size and setting, Ohio University offers an unusual breadth of majors and professional degrees. This contributes greatly to the richness and variety of its intellectual life and its ability to respond to a changing environment. It also strengthens the university's competitive position in student recruitment and in the ceaseless search for external funding. But breadth and diversity must be maintained at a level of high quality. Breadth has a price. Ever increasing faculty specialization is expensive, and the costs of essential library materials have exploded. The need for equipment in laboratories and studios, and for new and renovated facilities, strains operational and capital budgets. Legitimate needs must be met program by program to insure high quality.

Can quality be sustained throughout the broad range of majors and degrees at Ohio University? As new majors or programs are proposed reflecting the development of knowledge or new opportunities, can the university respond? To sustain what already exists or to develop new programs requires a steady growth in resources. Whatever options are explored, high quality must be the constant standard. The recent calls for the reform of undergraduate education are unequivocal on this point: the nation requires excellence in disciplines and professional studies.

If choices must be made, then student interest, external reviews, and state and federal funding priorities can help frame the criteria. But the decisions will be campus-based given the statutory provisions for university autonomy in Ohio. This freedom to decide brings a difficult responsibility when resources are strained.

The guideline seems self-evident and deceptively simple: Ohio University will have to limit itself to achieve greatness. At the same time breadth and diversity of programs at the undergraduate level are recognized as desirable characteristics of Ohio University, it must be accepted that, if the university tries to do too many things, it will do nothing well. The critical choices are dictated by the commitment to quality and the will to make judgments based on that commitment. Breadth and diversity of program are acceptable only to the degree they are consistent with the quality of program.

Another issue for disciplines and professional programs is how to accommodate nontraditional, multidisciplinary, and interdisciplinary interests within a structure designed to serve established disciplines. Some combinations attracting interest reflect a joining of academic and job considerations; for example, a student combines the study of literature or philosophy with accounting. This is an important but relatively easy restructuring of curricula. Sometimes the degree represents a combination of several disciplines, drawn together not on the basis of the relatedness of disciplines but the needs of career preparation.

Topical, interdisciplinary, area studies are likely to grow in importance in the years ahead. These will require a rethinking of discipline-focused faculty training and evaluations based solely on departmental criteria; it will also require the removal of organizational barriers, for example, the allocation of positions and operating budgets exclusively to departments. To be able to adapt to new combinations will require the development of different patterns and multiple assignment of positions and budgets. Flexibility and adaptability are important in a rapidly changing intellectual landscape. The encouragement of multidisciplinary programs can create, with modest investments of additional resources, possibilities for new programs.

3. The Internationalization of Undergraduate Education

Both the general education core and requirements in professional curricula need to be internationalized. The literacy required to function well in the modern world begins with a solid grounding in a particular cultural tradition. But at best this can only be partially understood when seen in isolation. The richness and variety of cultures, the mutual dependency of the world dictate increased emphasis on cross-cultural content and global awareness.

Language study is a primary component in internationalizing undergraduate education. Unconditional admission to the university now has language study as an expectation, but for too many students the development of cross-cultural literacy stops at this point. Advanced levels of language competency should be a more common expectation for most students, and certainly for students in business and communication and in many other professional programs. More emphasis on the languages of Asia and of developing countries is essential to preparing students for the emerging new world order.

The internationalization of undergraduate education can be greatly enhanced by opportunities to live and study abroad for extended periods of time. On campus, person-to-person contact in a close university community offers valuable opportunities for expanding the awareness of Ohio University students. The presence in Athens of a large number of students from many different cultures is a major asset of the university.

4. The Libraries and A New Literacy

The rapid expansion of knowledge and information in the twentieth century has made the library and information systems even more central to university education. Education for an information age can never be a completed process. It is an ongoing, lifelong activity. As a consequence, the effort to provide students with a base for continued learning becomes the primary task of undergraduate education. The process begins with the use of the library. The steady growth of a well-balanced collection of books and periodicals designed to serve the needs of a comprehensive undergraduate program is a necessary condition for quality in education. But the collection itself is of value only as it is used. Library usage is a critical measure of excellence in undergraduate education.

In the era of computers a base for continued learning also requires developing what has been labelled as "information-seeking literacy." No one can carry away from the campus experience an adequate knowledge or information base. What university education can and should provide is a developed capacity to search for what is needed, an ability to find, interpret, and evaluate information. The Ohio University libraries have a key and expanding role in providing access to books and periodicals as well as access to and training in the processes of information seeking so essential to contemporary life.

5. The College Student and Campus Life

The character of Ohio University as a residential campus is more than a historical accident of location; the quality of campus life more than a practical necessity. Residential life, embracing both on campus and nearby community housing has important educational potential. Ideally, such a setting offers unique opportunities for intellectual and personal development as a product of close human contact. It offers the possibility of education in the tasks of leadership as a result of the myriad of campus activities. A residential university can help create a sense of responsibility and involvement in the larger society and enthusiasm for the creation of a better world.

Identifying and nurturing the distinct qualities of campus life is a matter of necessity for Ohio University. What to emphasize is the issue. The place to start is with the primary value of a residential university—the close association among students themselves as well as students with faculty and staff. Additional strategies need to be developed to insure close integration of residential life and educational goals, and to continue to encourage student involvement in co-curricular activities, such as broadcasting, student publications, performing arts, athletics, and campus organizations. The end sought is a rich intellectual, cultural and recreational environment for the campus.

Diversity contributes directly to the quality of community life at Ohio University. The maintenance of a diverse undergraduate student population ultimately depends upon choices made in the admissions processes. An insistence upon high standards of pre-college preparation, standards that predict degree persistence, is accepted practice; however, admission based on high school rank or test scores, untempered by other factors, can present a threat to diversity. Overall, maintenance of diversity will require active recruitment of well-prepared students from a variety of geographic, social, and economic backgrounds and active outreach to sustain the institutional ties which have brought significant numbers of international students to Athens.

A balance as well as a range of academic interests give a distinct character and quality to campus life at Ohio University. This balance requires constant monitoring. A basic judgment already made is to maintain that balance by limiting the growth of individual professional colleges to fifteen to twenty percent of the total undergraduate enrollment and to sustain the strong, central position of the disciplines of arts and sciences for all university degree programs.

Attention to the physical attractiveness of the campus and its facilities—the constant renovation and improvement of campus buildings, both residential halls and academic space, and the development of recreational space—all contribute to the quality of campus life.

Extensive student involvement in co-curricular activities, and, most importantly, the close contact of students with faculty and staff combine to set Ohio University apart. The perceived and actual character of the residential life and its interpersonal contact is critical to the university's future.

There is a strong practical reason for special attention to campus life. Ohio University is by history and design a residential institution. A diminished number of college-age students, increased competition for this shrinking pool of young people, and the relatively high costs of education at a residential campus point to the practical imperative that Ohio University pay particular attention to the quality of student life on campus. Only as the total educational experience is something of exceptional value can the high cost of a residential undergraduate education be justified. The issue will become more acute in the years ahead as the cost differential grows between commuter and residential education. All of these conditions reinforce the goal that students, faculty, and staff of Ohio University be actively involved in shaping campus life.

Closeness, diversity, balance of programs, physical setting, involvement in activities all combine to give a distinct character to campus life at Ohio University. Size is an uncertain but important factor determining campus life. Carefully controlled growth over the past decade has allowed the university to expand without changing the character of its life. The determination to grow in size only insofar as such growth was compatible with improving quality described in *The Educational Plan 1977–1987* now raises a new set of issues. Growth in numbers must not be allowed to alter the residential character of Ohio University or diminish the values of campus life.

6. Minority Access

As an institution committed to educational justice, Ohio University faces a challenging set of issues in minority access to the campus. Population studies uniformly project a growing minority population for America in the twenty-first century, and educational statistics document the increasing underrepresentation of this population in university programs. The trends of the closing decade of the present century point not just to underrepresentation but also to the declining presence of minorities on campuses.

The issue is how to reverse those trends in order to create a more just and socially responsible educational institution. Recruitment of minority students must continue to be emphasized. Constant evaluation of current efforts and a resolute search for new and more effective strategies are basic to the response.

Another set of choices revolves around the removal of economic barriers to education for minority students. Ohio University has increased financial aid for the support of minority students with funding from the general operating budget. Such support is limited, however, and increased corporate, foundation, and individual giving for minority scholarship programs must be sought vigorously and creatively.

A third set of issues is the effort to address individual support and degree persistence. Standards for admission should provide reasonable expectation of success, but compensatory education in language, mathematics, basic science and other areas must be made available. Opportunity and assistance, however, are not enough. The need for effective role models for the minority student population to increase the likelihood of their completing degrees will require an increased presence and integration of minority faculty and staff in the life of Ohio University.

7. *The Nontraditional Student*

The changing nature of the population served by undergraduate education points to the need to give more attention to older students, individuals who already have employment and need to upgrade their skills, and to many students who cannot come to the Athens campus as full-time residents. The delivery of educational services will have to be significantly modified if Ohio University is to serve this population.

Rather than occupying a time period prior to joining the work force, education in the years ahead may well become a lifelong activity. If this proves true, education for more people over longer periods of time will make education a major growth area in the twenty-first century. Some will seek the opportunity for additional education because they want to re-enter the work force; others because they want new opportunities; still others will require additional education to maintain employment in a rapidly changing and increasingly technological society; some, whatever their age, will seek education for personal satisfaction and growth.

Since most older students are limited either by work or family responsibilities, the choices facing Ohio University will involve a continuing search for the best methods to deliver educational services to this population. Appropriate teaching, advising strategies, and the effective use of educational technology are among the issues. Educational television and the possibilities it creates—for example video cassettes, the two-way interactive microwave system computer assisted instruction—will become increasingly important.

While the location of Ohio University in sparsely populated areas is a disadvantage in serving the nontraditional students in the state of Ohio, the university has developed several special initiatives and capacities to serve this student population. One is decades long, and involves experience in the creation and use of correspondence courses. A second and more recent initiative is the design and implementation of degree programs and options for the nontraditional student. A third involves the pioneering use of television and educational technology. A critical element in the overall strategy is Athens campus interaction with regional campuses. These campuses are central to the university's ability to serve the nontraditional student population throughout southeastern Ohio.

8. Funding for Quality

Long-term trends in funding higher education are not easy to predict, but several characteristics of university budgets in the state of Ohio suggest that difficulties may lie ahead. For a number of years Ohio has been a high tuition state with the result that its public universities have become heavily dependent on tuition as a principal source of income. State funding has been uneven with recurring cycles of relative prosperity and then austerity. New initiatives to support quality or to lower the share of the cost borne by students have been difficult to sustain across budget cycles.

A second problem comes directly from the funding models themselves.

While the formula budgeting approach employed by the state is rational and analytical in its use of enrollment and average costs by instructional areas to define support levels, the formulas themselves do not provide additional support for high quality. The limited support of initiatives for excellence requires special line item appropriations. The Ohio University *Educational Plan 1977–1987* described an intent to focus institutional life on growth measured in terms of increases in quality. It resulted in a decision carefully to control enrollment in Athens while maintaining open enrollment for the regional campuses. After a sharp drop in the early 1970s, enrollment at Ohio University has increased by twenty-five percent over the past ten years. The proposed fifteen thousand ceiling for the Athens campus was reached by the mid-1980s. The size of the freshman class has been rigidly controlled, but improved retention and other factors have continued to push enrollment upward.

Enrollment growth and the additional funding it generates have been an important base of new resources for improving institutional life in the past. An enrollment-driven formula for budgets, combined with steady enrollment increases, translates into new dollars for qualitative growth and new initiatives. But even if Ohio University can define conditions that would make expansion in size consistent with its life as a residential university committed to quality, the demographic facts suggest that the potential for enrollment growth and therefore the potential for additional dollars from enrollment increases is limited.

Additional resources do not assure increased quality, but few would quarrel with the judgment that adequate resources are an important condition. If major enrollment growth is neither possible nor desirable for the Athens campus, then alternate sources of funds to enhance quality must be identified.

Two possibilities for funding seem consistent with the basic goal of the institution for its third century. Efficient and effective use of existing resources is the most obvious. This includes the reallocation of funds in the interest of improved quality. Such a process, while sensitive and difficult, is a most important source for funding growth in quality. But efficiency and reallocation are unlikely to produce adequate new support. Private support offers the potential for margins of difference in the search for excellence. Such support is already an important factor for Ohio University and will become crucial for the years ahead. Quality in the third century will require successful efforts to dramatically increase the endowment and the annual gift income.

9. Education and Values

If quality is the basic value, actual performance becomes a critical measure. High standards, rigorously applied, combine with the assessment of individual and institutional performance as necessary conditions for excellence in undergraduate education.

The affirmation of high standards of performance leads logically to the insistence that the university measure its impact on students by ever more rigorous processes of assessment. When such evaluation indicates a need, the standards require that the university take corrective measures and dedicate what is required for good quality. If the resources are not available, the standards dictate that the university face the always difficult judgment about continuing particular programs.

The search for excellence in university education goes beyond academic standards. It requires a willingness to make judgments on acceptable conduct. This is a particularly important issue on a campus distinguished by the close contact of students with students and with faculty and staff. Codes of conduct for students, faculty, and staff need to be demanding and should be applied with a determination to preserve the values of a university community.

Undergraduate education is both an end in itself and a means to various ends. It should contribute to a delight in knowledge, an expansion of the capacity to value and enjoy the fullness of human life. Undergraduate education is also preparation for employment, for careers and for the exercise of a responsible and productive participation in society.

The values that Ohio University seeks to communicate through its undergraduate academic programs and campus life are the values of a whole person, a sense of purpose larger than individual interests, and a feeling of obligation derived from that special opportunity which talent and education provide.

GRADUATE EDUCATION

As the twentieth century draws to a close, it is increasingly clear that the future well-being of humankind is dependent upon a steady growth in the pool of well-educated and highly skilled people. The distinct university contribution to the development of this pool is its capacity to direct students beyond the general knowledge of subjects gained during their undergraduate years to the advanced understanding, skill development, and research activity of graduate education.

Graduate education comes in a number of different modes. For the sciences and engineering, it centers in laboratory and problem-oriented research. For some of the social sciences, graduate education assumes a training function in addition to basic research. For the humanities, graduate education focuses on the preparation of teacher-scholars who have a command of the content and are skilled in the methodology appropriate to the disciplines. For the arts, graduate education may follow the patterns of the humanities, or it may center in performance and practice. The professional schools and applied disciplines work to develop both the skills and the understanding required to perform tasks as business professionals or educators, professional artists, broadcasters, journalists, health-care professionals, and engineers. Graduate education in the creative arts nurtures the abilities of students to understand, interpret, and create in both the visual and performing arts.

Access to leadership roles in the professions—medicine, engineering, business, university teaching—is often through graduate education. A growing presence of minorities and women in the professions is dependent upon their increased participation in graduate programs. The issues of educational justice, acute at the undergraduate level, are magnified at the graduate level because of under-representation. Strategies to address the situation include the earmarking of funds, the early identification of possible candidates for graduate study, providing role models, and the dedicated effort of all members of the academic community to recruit and support both female and minority students. As the university searches for quality in graduate education, it will do well to remember that women, although they represent more than half the undergraduate population, have not gone on to graduate education to the extent that their numbers and talents would indicate.

Strong graduate education goes hand in hand with research and service programs of the university. Without the constant supply of graduate students, research and service activity would wither. As research assistants and collaborators, as apprentice scholars and teachers, as interns in the professions, the graduate population continually renews the university community.

The issues of education to values—intellectual standards, personal conduct, social responsibility—raised in the context of undergraduate education are equally relevant to graduate education and education to the professions. As noted earlier, such education leads generally to the exercise of leadership and, accordingly, carries added obligations for responsible, moral behavior. Ethical concerns for the practice of business, journalism, public service, medicine, teaching, and research are raised from a variety of perspectives. To neglect these issues in graduate education is to ignore the role and the power created by advanced understanding, skill development, and research. Whether it is possible, and, if so, how to teach virtue has been long debated. Given the turmoil of our times, what cannot be debated is the importance of raising ethical issues and expecting reflection and thoughtful value judgments.

1. *The Relation to Undergraduate Education*

The emphasis on the importance of strong graduate programs for the university in its third century creates the danger of dividing the institution into two universities, one undergraduate, the other graduate; or into two faculties, one a teaching faculty and the other a graduate and research faculty. Strong graduate education programs cannot be emphasized at the expense of undergraduate programs. To have strong graduate programs the university also must have strong undergraduate programs. Greater integration of graduate and undergraduate education is possible. Indeed a common theme in the literature exploring the future university is the argument that institutions of higher learning must involve students in research and creative processes beginning in their undergraduate years and continuing throughout their university experience.

Excellent teaching relies on research. When these values are supported by faculty and students working together, the result is a community of scholars. To achieve strength in both graduate and undergraduate education, Ohio University will have to forge linkages between the graduate and undergraduate programs and involve undergraduate students, wherever possible, in inquiry, search and creative activity. Such intermeshing of the graduate and undergraduate programs will not only strengthen undergraduate education but also help to overcome the erroneous assumption that good teaching and research are incompatible.

2. *Professional Training*

Graduate education traditionally has focused on scholarship and scientific inquiry. Today graduate education is much broader in scope and varies in emphasis from advanced inquiry to detailed study of specialized techniques to the learning of skills necessary for professional success. There is every reason to believe that society's expectations for highly trained specialists in the professions will place even greater emphasis on intellectual and skill development in business, education, communication, health services, medicine, engineering, and the arts.

As it approaches its third century, Ohio University will have to include in the curriculum, to an even greater extent, programs of training and education for those practicing the professions. It is a matter of high priority that the university develop methods of delivery of specialized programs to individuals already engaged in the professions. In-service programs that make extensive use of technology and communications systems will become important if the university is to meet the needs of the times. One issue is the maintenance of quality in the face of many demands on time. The special interests of disciplines and professional accrediting agencies present a potential distortion in university programs. Another issue is maintaining the balance between training in specific skills and educating for scholarly inquiry. Similarly, a basic issue for professional education is the proper balance between professional specialization and the need for a generalist's perspective.

3. Medical Education

The mission of Ohio University's College of Osteopathic Medicine, as set forth by the General Assembly of Ohio, is to provide instruction in the practice of osteopathic medicine in such a way that its programs will "emphasize the training of osteopathic doctors who will engage in the family practice of medicine." The college is also to "encourage its graduates to practice medicine in those areas of the state where the greatest need exists for osteopathic physicians."

The need for physicians in under-served areas of the state will likely continue into the twenty-first century, providing an ongoing affirmation of the college's assigned mission. If it is to fulfill its distinct charge, the college must educate students to become well-rounded osteopathic physicians who will in significant numbers enter family practice in under-served areas following postdoctoral training. The college also has a responsibility for the discovery and dissemination of new knowledge, especially in the areas of traditional concern to osteopathic physicians. Through the Athens campus and its seven regional training centers dispersed throughout the state, the college is an important resource for osteopathic medical education and research in the state.

Planning and development over the past decade have emphasized the linking of the College of Osteopathic Medicine with the College of Arts and Sciences and the university as a whole for the enrichment of instruction and research in both clinical education and basic sciences. This is consistent with the enabling legislation. Only a few universities have attempted an integrated physician education program. The experiment has proved successful but requires continued attention in the years ahead.

4. Interdisciplinary Programs

There are intellectual and practical reasons for an emphasis on interdisciplinary programs of graduate study and research at Ohio University. Much of the intellectual ferment of contemporary campus life has not been narrowly identified with disciplines. It has crossed disciplines and provides for more encompassing considerations of topics, issues, phenomena. It has led to the creation of structures within university organization—institutes and centers designed to support interdisciplinary teaching and research. The processes have redefined discipline relationships. The practical reason derives from limitations of resources and the importance of realizing the greatest return by sharing, by coordination, and by collaboration.

It is clear that flexibility will enhance the university's ability to respond to future needs in graduate education. Ohio University has gained national prominence in several programs that have interdisciplinary components, reflecting a recognition that it can best remain competitive by pooling its resources across colleges and departments. The integration of the basic sciences faculty of the College of Arts and Sciences and the College of Osteopathic Medicine illustrates an effort to maximize gain from new resources and avoid needless duplication. Allied to this concept is the development of the graduate program in molecular and cellular biology which involves the cooperation of our academic departments. Similar programs exist in other areas, such as international studies and communications. Interdepartmental cooperation serves to consolidate resources and to strengthen graduate education beyond the capability of a single department or a single college. As Ohio University moves toward its third century, the choice to build interdisciplinary and cross disciplinary graduate programs will be part of a fundamental decision to remain competitive in an environment where the costs of graduate education and research are very high.

5. International Connections

At a time when the United States has come to be the country of choice for graduate study in many areas, Ohio University has profited from its many connections around the world and from the excellent reputation its programs have gained abroad. It is anticipated that the demand for graduate and professional education from international students will remain strong. Most of the increase in the numbers of international students coming to the United States in recent years has been at the level of graduate and professional study. One of the keys to Ohio University's participation in this developing trend is university outreach abroad through projects, faculty overseas assignments, faculty exchange, cooperative programs, and research collaboration.

At issue is how best to respond to this surge. The questions include how to respond with integrity and state support. Graduate and professional programs are highly specialized and frequently culturally determined. This is not true in all areas of study, and, in any case, is not important to a number of international students who consciously come to study in an American setting. Most of the work in the sciences and in engineering present no problems since they offer an easy transfer of knowledge and research across national boundaries. For other areas this is less true. The recognition of this fact raises questions of how effectively the university can serve large numbers of international students, and questions of relevance and transferability of United States–based graduate and professional study. At issue is the capacity of Ohio University to provide instruction, supervision of research, practical experiences, case studies, data, and other research materials relevant to the needs of developing countries. In some areas of study, Ohio University faculty members have the experience, partly as a product of the university's international connections and, typically, in such areas, the university also has a good base of data and materials for research. In areas where this is not true, to serve students and countries well, Ohio University will have to work to establish formal ties with other institutions both in the United States and abroad. To be functional, the connections may well require the development of patterns of alternation of study in Athens and on site for practical experiences and observations, the gathering of data and relevant materials for graduate projects.

In addition to being specialized, graduate and professional programs are also expensive. They require major state subsidy to insure good quality and integrity of programs. Questions continue to be raised by state officials about the return on the investment by the state of Ohio in foreign students. Perceptive state officials recognize the critical importance to the state of strong international connections for trade, job creation, and continued economic progress. This perception of the value of strong international connections extends to university education. No one questions the importance or value of foreign students to the urgent tasks of internationalizing the curriculum and experiences of American students. But, given the costs, there are questions about state support, direct or indirect, for the graduate and professional education of international students. To sustain support, Ohio University, together with other institutions in the state, will have to defend forcefully the importance of these students in these programs to the international connections of the state, to present the case convincingly that it is desirable, not just for the students and countries served, but for Ohio University and for the state of Ohio.

6. *Faculty and Staff Renewal*

Continual growth and development is a necessary condition of participation in university life. Through professional leaves, research by assignment, and external programs such as the Fulbright fellowships and exchange programs, faculty have been able to keep abreast of their fields and to develop new areas of expertise as their careers as university professors mature. The accelerating growth of knowledge, the development of new technologies for research, the increased availability and uses of technology, the rapidity of change and new developments, will require an institutional effort to insure that faculty and staff are sufficiently knowledgeable to make the necessary adjustments in teaching and research. In a similar way, individuals will have to pursue carefully planned programs of professional development to keep abreast of changes in their fields.

Given the rate of both knowledge growth and obsolescence, helping faculty and staff grow during the thirty years or so of their careers is a major issue for university life. It will require funds to support new initiatives. These initiatives should include opportunities to bring mature faculty into contact with new developments and new technology; support for junior faculty to branch out beyond the specializations of graduate education to establish themselves in their research; and, most importantly, encouragement for mid-career faculty and staff to follow shifting interests even if this leads them outside their current departmental boundaries. It means facilitating the movement of faculty members into new areas of teaching and research.

Curriculum development and cooperative research projects can stimulate interests. A recent example of multiple benefits is the seminars held to develop Tier III courses. While the seminars were funded for undergraduate course development, the most important result was sustained interaction among faculty from different departments and colleges. That interaction provided stimulation for new interests.

7. Resources for Graduate Study and Research

Faculty knowledgeable and active in their fields provide the essential base resource for graduate education. But there are other important factors. Two critical measures of quality are the availability of library holdings and access to equipment. Both must be sophisticated and current. In the modern world this dictates a reliance on a third resource—computer capacity. How to make comprehensive, up-to-date library materials available and how to provide access to the latest technology and equipment will continue to be major issues for graduate education.

Well-documented needs exceed resources on even the best endowed campuses. While it seems to be a variable standard, clearly the requirement of basic quality of resources must be met for a university to have a credible potential for graduate education.

Since needs continuously exceed the resources of a unit or a single institution, choices must be made. Prospects for the future suggest a growing dependency on consortia arrangements, the sharing of library resources, interdepartmental and interinstitutional use of major laboratory facilities and equipment.

Collection-building for a research library is frustrated by costs of printed material and by the exponential growth in the number of journals and books published. Behind this frustration is the operating assumption of local availability and comprehensive coverage for all collections. Except for a very few major depositories of printed and microform materials, this Alexandrian Library approach to collection-building will not be a model for the next century. Adequacy is required, but it will be adequacy within newly defined limits. Interinstitutional arrangements are already in place for bibliographical information sharing and for interlibrary loan of material. Indexing and searching collections increasingly are machine based. Planned division of responsibility for research collection-building seems likely. As much as anything else, costs of space are forcing choices. Expensive patterns of shelf storage of all materials, including seldom used materials, will have to be altered to accommodate continued growth. The next generation of facilities and technology for this revolution is already being planned. In the third century of its life the Ohio University Libraries will be part of a mutually dependent network of libraries. Particular specialized collections in individual libraries will reflect the interests of the faculty and the strengths of the programs of a campus and, at the same time, be a resource for all institutions in the network.

This assessment of change does not diminish the university commitment to building the best possible collection for the Ohio University Libraries. Books and periodicals, readily available for local use, provide an essential resource for instruction and research. But a potential for access expands dramatically by the addition of data and information systems and by the linking of Ohio University to the library resources of many campuses.

A similar set of issues is evident in the requirements for sophisticated and up-to-date facilities, equipment, and computer capacity. Support for quality continues to be an elusive ideal. In many cases the required facilities, equipment, or capacity far exceed the resources of a single unit. Interdepartmental cooperation and sharing is required to provide graduate students access to expensive equipment. This is particularly true when the equipment can serve multiple needs. Intrainstitutional cooperation and interinstitutional sharing is one of the choices to help the university keep pace with the expansive growth of the equipment needed for graduate education and research.

RESEARCH, SCHOLARSHIP, AND CREATIVE ACTIVITY

Developed intelligence and imagination are critical for the struggle to survive and prosper in an era of rapid change. Research results provide discoveries, essential new knowledge; university education joins students and faculty in research contributing to the development of intelligence and imagination. The presumption that research and teaching interact, together with the clustering of graduate education and professional schools around undergraduate departments and majors, defines the idea of the modern university. It is interesting to note that this configuration of collegiate life is little more than a century old and that it continues to develop and change. The era now unfolding has been described as "the information age," an age distinguished by a flood tide of new knowledge, incredible new instrumentation, and an almost unlimited capacity to store, retrieve, manipulate, and transfer data. To participate in this contemporary revolution, universities must educate new generations of researchers and create new knowledge.

The term "research" in ordinary usage is too narrow to capture the diversity of scholarly creativity used to characterize the ongoing inquiry and creativity of various kinds, all of which are vital to the life of the university. Although the term "research" is used throughout this discussion, the reference is intended to be inclusive and to apply to the activity of faculty in those disciplines where a narrow definition, implying scientific research, does not adequately describe their contributions.

1. Areas of Inquiry

Generally, campus-based research directly mirrors the particular interests and gifts of the individual researcher or groups of researchers. It is a free, unstructured initiative only indirectly affected by institutional decisions. If there is an institutional force it is that existing strengths in research tend to attract people with like interests to campus and that reputation and funding, once established, tend to be perpetuated. The organization of research has been principally within established academic disciplines and departments. These conditions, unstructured initiatives, and present patterns of organizing research will and should continue, but need to be modified in the years ahead.

Advanced scholarship, research, and creative activity are dependent upon insight and talent. Such factors cannot be planned. But the conditions which support and encourage them, and the dedication of university resources to particular emphases for research, are important issues in planning for the third century of Ohio University. The essential strategy is to build on existing strength. However, the university cannot successfully compete for the resources required if it locks itself into overly specific goals for research, or if the university's human and material resources are so tied to previous success that the university cannot respond to emerging areas of inquiry and opportunity.

Flexibility and adaptability are critical factors in weighing investment in staff, equipment, or facilities. A rapidly changing environment and limited resources dictate that the dedication of university resources reflect judgments based on criteria such as estimates of personnel and equipment costs required to contribute actively to particular resource areas; in the case of areas requiring high capital investments, evidence of a sensible strategy to secure funding; potential for research grants and contracts; prospects for private and corporate as well as public funding; contributions of a particular emphasis to cognate areas; the value of the research emphasis to faculty and student development and to the reputation of Ohio University; and, if a particular research emphasis is offered as a theme for the University's life, the potential importance of research results in addressing urgent public issues, questions, or problems.

These criteria describe major institutional decisions on specific resource allocations. The mission of the modern university requires support for unfettered inquiry and creativity. The forms of support, however, are less specific than research emphasis and centers and are described by a dispersed investment in studios, laboratories, equipment, faculty time, and faculty activity. Research activity in this sense cannot be planned, but the conditions which support and encourage such research and the dedication of significant institutional support to particular emphases, as noted above, can and should be the result of careful assessment.

For many of the same reasons that multidisciplinary approaches are important to graduate education, they are also important to the organization of research. Such approaches open new possibilities and maximize return from equipment and facilities. Interaction among faculty and the formation of interdisciplinary teams can provide flexibility and responsiveness. The complexity of major research areas suggests that the research organization cannot be defined by structures of university organization.

2. The Support for Scholarly Inquiry

Ohio University has a long tradition of supporting research, scholarship, creative activity, and other professional endeavors in a variety of subjects and disciplines. This has been accomplished notwithstanding the fact that the state of Ohio does not have a history of direct funding of research and scholarship. In the 1980s, state policy shifted with the endowment program for eminent scholars and direct funding of research for the Edison Advanced Technology Centers. Among the new initiatives, the Research Challenge is the most direct form of research support. The university determines how to use these funds to increase outside grants and contracts. As vital as this program is to encouraging research, it clearly is designed to provide a lever to achieve greater external funding for research, and cannot be regarded as a primary source of institutional support for ongoing research.

The cost of research in the laboratory sciences and in engineering and technology requires that funds from outside the institution and from sources other than the state subsidy be vigorously pursued. Ohio University's research leadership has been in fields where there are faculty members of unusual abilities on campus and where their work has attracted funding from both private and governmental sources. Grants and contracts have more than doubled in the last decade. But this can only be regarded as a modest beginning. What is reflected in this trend is movement and direction for the third century.

The combination of funds generated from the state, outside funding from grants, contracts, and private sources, plus the use of graduate students as research and teaching assistants, must cover the costs of graduate research and education. Funds generated from fees and state subsidies do not fully meet costs of graduate education, let alone the additional expense of supporting research. The cost offset most commonly employed by universities is the use of graduate students for teaching and supervision of laboratories. Within limits, this is a desirable and effective educational practice, but the key is the recognition of these limits. Planning starts at Ohio University with a basic commitment to improving the quality of the undergraduate experience. The forced conclusion is that cost alone of graduate education and research cannot be used as justification for the practice of using graduate students in class. This judgment underscores the need to develop strategies to increase funding for research.

External support for research is heavily concentrated in science and technology. Only limited grant funds are available for scholarly and creative work in the arts or humanities. It is unlikely that this distribution of support will change in the years ahead. The counterpoint is that the costs of supporting inquiry and creativity in these areas are relatively low, instrumentation requirements modest, and the work largely the product of an individual scholar or artist. Accordingly, relatively small investments in research in these areas can produce important results. Major funding for the arts and humanities is most likely to come from private sources generated by Ohio University. Funding for scientific and technological research by contract, will come primarily as a result of proposals developed by the researchers themselves and then only after the success of individuals and groups of researchers, by the concentrated efforts of Ohio University to institutionalize strengths of researchers into major research centers.

3. Research and Society

The quest of the state of Ohio to find alternatives to the manufacture of durable goods as a basis for its economy has focused attention on the universities as partners in research activities with the investment of both private and state dollars. Ohio University has already begun to move to respond to these new expectations with such initiatives as the Innovation Center, the Avionics Center, the Edison Animal Biotechnology Center, and plans for a research park. If it is to be successful, the university will need to reach out to business and industry, and to utilize faculty expertise in technology transfer and planned efforts to address the interests of both the private and public sectors. The need for specific job preparation has already been referred to as a role to be borne principally by the two-year and regional campuses; basic and applied research as a base for economic development will be a responsibility of the graduate and research concentration on the main campus.

While such interactions with the business community will require strategic planning, the initiatives largely will be in response to opportunity rather than detailed planning. The institution can devise ways to give assistance and direction to such initiatives, but success will depend on entrepreneurial activity. A key expectation which addresses the future of the university, which if successful will influence and shape the role of the university, is the translation of research and expertise in terms of their potential for economic development.

4. Research and University Values

The university values basic research and scholarship primarily because it is a community committed to inquiry and discovery. To support the open pursuit of knowledge, universities have zealously defended objectivity, academic freedom, and the open sharing of the results of research. This openness, freedom, and objectivity may well be tested by society's expectations, especially if resources supporting research are allocated to obtain particular results. The challenge will be to find the proper balance. The university cannot compromise its commitment to basic research and to the free pursuit and exchange of knowledge. At the same time, it must responsibly aid the state and nation in the search for solutions to the urgent public issues.

The university exists to promote human development through instruction and research. Accordingly, the institution has not only an obligation to encourage the development of knowledge but also the responsibility to aid in its effective dissemination. Centers for advanced research combined with technology transfer and product development describe new roles for the university. The efforts to incubate and to assist small businesses are contemporary adaptations of the mission of a land-grant university. Telecommunication and computer networks reflect new possibilities for the dissemination of expertise and research results. A more traditional form, but central to the mission to disseminate the results of scholarship, is the Ohio University Press. The search for contemporary strategies of dissemination is a major issue in the effort to plan the third century of the university.

Graduate programs and research are dependent ultimately on the quality of the faculty and students in those programs. Consequently, recruiting of outstanding staff and students becomes the first order of business. The original responsibility rests with academic units. Each position to be filled or student to be admitted represents an opportunity to strengthen the program. While salary and stipend levels are obviously important, as are the level of research support, laboratory and studio equipment and library holdings, the essential condition is people with an enthusiasm for what is being accomplished at Ohio University and a conviction, supported and documented by institutional decision making, that Ohio University values scholarship, research, and creative activity.

INSTITUTIONAL SUPPORT AND SERVICES

The preceding descriptions of the challenges and opportunities facing the university in its third century have focused on academic issues—the undergraduate experience, graduate education, and research. Any institution is in large measure a sum of its parts, and the strengthening of university instruction and research is possible only as they are supported by a broad range of services. The university describes its values not just by academic programs but also, for example, by care in the design and maintenance of physical plant, by responsible servicing of debts and administering of budgets, and by the provisions of its personnel policies.

1. General Administration

Administration, like the technique of an artist, is most effective when least noticed. *The Educational Plan 1977–1987* spoke of the necessity for well-developed processes for decision making that consider the institution as a whole. The planning process put in place following that plan has served the institution well, but the process must be constantly under scrutiny to avoid rigidities. Just as adaptability is important to the development of strong programs of instruction and research, so also this quality is required of effective administration. If the analysis of the previous sections of this document is correct, flexibility and responsiveness will be even more important as the university prepares for its third century.

2. Academic Support

Several of the more prominent academic support units, such as the library, admissions, and computer center, have already been discussed in the previous sections of this document. These units, which participate directly in the educational process, are clearly vital to the university's health in its third century. But no less vital are the smaller units providing academic support in a variety of ways. The goals statements of *The Educational Plan 1977–1987* point to the importance of creating attractive and comfortable learning environments, encouraging the integration of technologically aided instruction into the curriculum, improving services to students, and strengthening a faculty-based advising system. Success in meeting these goals does not diminish the importance of continuing to enhance this support in the university's third century. The improvement of facilities, the encouragement of sensitivity to special student needs, and the providing of opportunities for students to develop and practice necessary skills are continuing imperatives for the university in its third century.

3. Residential Life Programs and Services

Long before The National Institute of Education's report, *Involvement in Learning*, highlighted the importance of the residential experience in undergraduate education, Ohio University had emphasized the significance of the role of the residence and dining halls. Residential facilities play a significant role in the educational process and help students mature by developing independence, social sensitivity, and adaptive skills. The residential life programs at Ohio University during the past ten years have made significant contributions to strengthening the educational environment, and this role will continue to be critical to the undergraduate experience as the university enters its third century.

Among the strategies that are important are the further involvement of faculty with residential life programs, the integration of the residence hall experience with classroom activities, and the continuation of programs of renovation, refurbishing, and upgrading of the physical facilities themselves. Whereas ten years ago the looming concern was the financial solvency and viability of the residence hall system, these problems have now been solved, allowing the institution to turn its attention, as it is already doing, to the qualitative improvement of the residence experience at the university.

4. Student Services

A danger inherent in the kind of enrollment pressures the university is currently enjoying is the temptation to fall into complacency about student services. Especially at residential campuses, student services will continue to be an important ingredient in the institution's ability to speak to the whole life of the student. The trends of recent years indicate the growing importance of increased programs of financial aid, counseling and health education, as well as internship and placement services. As the previous sections of this document indicate, the demand of students for services that integrate their educational achievements into campus life and careers beyond college experience is a challenge that will fall heavily on the Student Services areas of the institution.

5. University Relations and Development

The concern to tell the university story effectively and to advance the interests of the institution led, following the adoption of *The Educational Plan 1977–1987*, to the expansion of two key support activities: university relations and university development.

The Office of Development provided the leadership for the successful 1804 Campaign. The dramatic increases in endowment income and annual giving which this campaign produced are much in evidence in the life of Ohio University. The continued efforts to build a broad base of private support for the university will be even more important in the years ahead. As noted earlier, private support can provide the margin of difference in support for the third century of the life of Ohio University.

The opinions and interests of constituencies, starting with the alumni and extending to the general public, are important to Ohio University. The university has a unique tie to its alumni. Alone among the Ohio institutions, Ohio University is required by state statute to have a majority of its trustees be graduates of the institution. The alumni on the Ohio University Fund Board and the National Alumni Board both monitor and serve the institution well. Among the issues for the future are the changing character of alumni activities, the development of constituent alumni groups for colleges and schools, and the search for strategies which relate alumni to the university in its distinct life as an educational institution.

The perception of the university by its many constituencies is the focus of the responsibilities of university relations. The development of quality can be greatly assisted by the effective communication of the Ohio University story.

EPILOGUE

We report with a sense of excitement. The discussions of the Colloquium over the past two and a half years have brought into sharp focus the promise and the challenge of the years ahead for Ohio University.

The Colloquium on the Third Century was established in February, 1985 in response to a review of the university planning process the year before. There is a need, the critique concluded, for sustained discussion of issues and choices without the deadlines of annual planning reports and budget recommendations.

The intended outcomes of the discussion begun by the Colloquium are decisions made as a result of the weighing of issues and choices. The report is a sequel to *The Educational Plan 1977–87* and, as was true of that document, is designed to inform the goals and objectives of the various planning units of the university. It also is intended as a guide for the ordering of institutional priorities and resource allocations as recommended by the university planning process, and the annual planning reports, and recommendations to the Board of Trustees.

The continuing effort to shape the future of Ohio University assumes the broadest possible discussion of issues and choices. The discussion must develop at least a functional consensus for decision making on that future. It is the hope of the Colloquium that the discussion will go beyond the need for decisions and produce a convictional consensus among the various segments of the university community. The links between discussion and decision are the planning units, which are responsible for the entire range of activities of the university; the University Planning Advisory Council, which provides a critical focus on university priorities in the planning process; and the Board of Trustees, which holds the university as a public trust.

Each has a set of related tasks. The Board of Trustees establishes direction for the institution as a whole by the adoption from time to time of broad statements of principles and goals for Ohio University and by the annual review of resource allocations recommended in planning reports. These recommendations are strategies for implementation based on the principles and goals. The twenty-three planning units which encompass all the activities of the university define the ways in which each separate group or cluster, such as departments or schools within a college or divisions within student affairs, serves the ends of the university. The formulation or restatement of goals for each planning unit, some on an annual cycle and all within a five-year cycle, are critical translations of university goals into ongoing activity. Given the importance of this translation, the statements require constant internal discussion by units and periodic review from a university perspective. The University Planning Advisory Council annually prepares a three- to five-year action agenda and specific recommendations to the President on budget priorities. The final recommendations are presented annually to the Trustees as part of the budget and planning cycle for the university as a whole.

What are the essentials of the principles and goals set forth in this report?

The recognition that Ohio University is a *singular place with a history, setting, and distinct characteristics which largely determine its future* is a constant in the face of change. The life of Ohio University centers in a residential campus in southern Ohio. The university consciously seeks to serve the community and the region but has a larger role in the world. Those who teach and those who work on its Athens campus, those who come to study, at least for a period of time, make this place their home. The university provides a diverse, cosmopolitan community with a setting conducive to close contact and interaction in its intellectual, cultural, and recreational life. That setting defines both its history and its future. An essential characteristic is the development over two centuries of educational programs which reflect a joining of professional preparation to a primary role in liberal learning, of research to the basic task of teaching.

The agenda for action described in the report calls for *continuing analysis and reform of undergraduate education and, at the same time, the strengthening of graduate education and research*. Both are essential to the future of the university.

The rate and the consequences of change force *flexibility* on university programs and planning. Innovation, adaptability, cooperative use of resources, and multiple departmental and interdepartmental programs need to be emphasized.

The public agenda looms large and argues for a *responsiveness* on the part of the university. These external expectations help to define the current tasks of the university. The order of topics in the report underscores a perspective encompassing a historic and contemporary mission. The focus is on the imperative to respond to these expectations.

Quality, the dominant theme of this report, provides direction for the future. It calls for a striving for excellence:

- high standards of performance for students and faculty; rigorous and yet sensitive requirements for admission; demanding standards for courses, for campus life and student-faculty and staff conduct, for scholarly activity and research.
- high expectations for the effectiveness of teaching and learning, for professional skills, for the development of capacities for research, interpretation, and discovery.
- the use of examinations and assessments to evaluate and to assist in the improvement of the performance of individuals and of programs.
- quality as a value, performance the critical measure, and assessment and feedback as imperatives.
- diversity of student and faculty with the campus serving as a mirror of the complexity and the challenges of our modern global society.
- a range and balance of programs that respond both to the need

for common learning and varied opportunities for productive work; a range and balance that join research and teaching, undergraduate and graduate education.
- an ideal for university life which insists that whatever the university does must be measured against the standard of its contribution to human development; that education is dedicated to the values of a whole person and the creation of a sense of purpose larger than individual interests, a feeling of obligation derived from that special opportunity which talent and education provide.

Those who would shape the third century of Ohio University hold a trust from the past for the future. This legacy demands much of those who would establish the priorities and plan the programs of the university. Born of a revolutionary understanding of government and the role of education in society, the university owes its life to the conviction that knowledge is ". . . necessary to good government and the happiness of mankind."

INDEX

Academic Excellence program, 29–30
Affirmative Action, 22–23
African American(s): faculty recruitment of, 24; first OU graduation by, 22
African National Congress, 143
African Studies Program, 139–40
Ahlquist, Jon, 128
Alden, Vernon R., 5–6, 53, 100, 148, 169, 171
Alden Library project, 149–52
Allen, William, 19
Alma College, 3
alumni, OU, 57; Alumni College and, 58–59; center for, 56–57; state lobbying by, 165
American Arbitration Association, 14
American Association of University Professors (AAUP), 12, 38
American College Test, 88, 89
American Federation of State, County, and Municipal Employees (AFSCME), 50–52
American Western University, 55
Ameritech, 69
Anderson, Cortland, 124
antiwar movement, 8
apartheid, 142–43
Appalachian Regional Commission, 111
Aquino, Corazon, 151
Architectural Preservation Committee, 177–78
Arkes, Hal, 80
Asian Institute of Technology (Bangkok), 149
assessment: California Psychological Inventory as, 31; COMP/ACT as, 31; task force for plan, 30–31; value added theory and, 30
Associated Press, 168
Association for Ambulatory Health Care (AAHC), 107
Association of Research Libraries, 149–50
Association of University Technology Managers, 134
Athens, Ohio: The Village Years (Daniel), 54
Athens County Community Urban Redevelopment Corporation, 71
Athens Friends of International Students (AFIS), 137
Athens International Film and Video Festival, 72
Athens Messenger, 28, 124
Atlantic Monthly, 154–56
Attas, Syed Muhammad Naquib al-, 146
Axline, Robert, 61, 65–66, 100
Azraai, Zain, 146

Baker, Elizabeth Evans, 64–65
Baker, John C., 53, 59, 100, 167, 169, 171; endowment by, 64–65; Third Century Campaign and, 65
Bald, Richard, 12, 14
Barr, Ronald, 118, 126
Baum, Edward, 18
Bergman, Lawrence, 127–28
Bernard, Ted, 173
Bingham, Silas, 55
Bingham house, 55–56, 178
Blackburn, David, 99
Blackburn, Martha Jane Hunley, 22
Bohm NBBJ, 47, 71
Boorstin, Daniel J., 55

Booth, Alan, 5, 58, 170, 172
Borchert, Donald, 82–83, 173
Botswana: and OU, 140–41, 142
Bowers, Frank L., 57–58
Bowling Green University, 113
Boyd, William, 3–5
Boyer, Ernest L., 53
Brown, Jeanette Grasselli, 129, 149, 166, 169, 174–75; faculty recruitment by, 25; gift by, 68
Bruning, James, 16, 29, 41, 80, 83, 90, 119, 143, 150, 175; faculty recruitment and, 24–25; faculty reviews and, 165–66
Bryan, Elmer, 179
Bryant, James, 114, 148
Bucklew, Neil, 15–16, 28, 80, 109, 111
Bush, Gordon, 124
Bush, Kenner, 119, 146
Bush, Margene, 177

Campbell, Dick, 115–16
Campus Compact, 97
Cappelletti, Ron, 83
Carnegie Foundation for the Advancement of Teaching, 130
Carpenter, Thomas, 171
Carter, Jimmy, 48, 139
Carter, John Michael, 170
Carter, Lillian, 139
CASE (Council for the Advancement and Support of Education), 74
Case Western Reserve University, 131
Celeste, Richard, 30, 71, 99, 145; bicentennial celebration and, 55; Edison Partnership Program and, 130; Selective Excellence Program and, 121, 123
Central Michigan University, 3–5, 76, 167; unionization of, 4, 11–12
"Challenge and Response: Opportunities for Excellence" (Ping), 37–38
Challenge grants, 125–26, 129
Change, 84
Chapman, Barbara, 26
The Charles J. Ping Institute for the Teaching of the Humanities, 170–71

Chesnut, Lloyd, 129, 173
Chronicle of Higher Education, 139
Chubu University, 149; exchange program with, 147; gift from, 53–54
Cleveland Plain Dealer, 78, 168
Cleveland State University, 9
Coetzee, J. M., 142
Cohn, Margaret, 26, 123
Cohn, Norman, 83
Cohn, Walter, 117
colleges, 8–9; management task forces for, 162–63; unity between, 164–65
Columbus Citizen Journal, 115
Columbus Dispatch, 156, 168–69
Commager, Henry Steele, 53
Commencement(s), 91–93
Committee for Independent Faculty (CIF), 13
Community Scope, 177
COMP/ACT (College Outcomes Measurement Project of American College Testing), 31
Contemporary History Institute, 153–56, 157
Cook, Raymond C., 69
Corrigan, Mary, 171
Coulter, William, 90, 118, 125
Council on International Educational Exchange, 180
Creer, Thomas, 127
Crewson, Harry, 8, 12, 53, 104, 171
Crowl, Samuel, 77, 58–59, 82, 83, 174
Culver Academy, 2
Cutler, Manasseh, 52, 53; and Northwest Ordinance, 54–55; scholarship named for, 100
Cutler Scholars Program, 100–102, 168, 182
Cuyahoga Community College, 9

Danforth Summer Institute on Liberal Arts Education, 3, 76
Daniel, Robert, 54
DARS (Degree Auditing Reporting System), 75–76
de Klerk, F. W., 143
De La Salle University (Manila), 147

INDEX 237

Diagnostic Hybrids, Inc. (DHI), 121, 132
Dinos, Nicholas, 19, 77, 81, 173
Dorrill, William, 76, 118, 119, 144
Duke University, 2–3
Dunigan, George, 104

East-West Institute, 152
Eckes, Albert, 125, 156
Edison Biotechnology Institute (formerly Edison Animal Biotechnology Center), 130–34
educational plan of 1977, OU, 17–20, 26–30, 32, 109. *See also Toward the Third Century*; University Planning Advisory Committee
Edwin L. and Ruth E. Kennedy Museum of Art, 72–73
1804 Campaign, 59–64, 150
Eiler, Terry, 123
11:30 Group, 10, 16–17
Ellis, Jack, 59, 62–63, 100, 170, 173
Embryogen, 131
Eminent Scholar awards, 124–25
energy crisis, 48–50
Engle, W. E. "Gene," 69
enrollment, OU, 7–9, 11, 88, 90. *See also* selective admissions
Eufinger, Charlotte Coleman, 168–69
Evans, Max, 140
E. W. Scripps School of Journalism, 123, 124, 182

faculty, OU, 13, 24, 38–41, 80
Faculty Senate, 12; General Education debate by, 78–80; Ping addresses to, 85–86, 175
Fairbanks, Douglas, 69
Family Health (radio program), 107
Faverman, Gerald, 105–6
Federal Aviation Administration, 128–29
Fenn College, 9
Finlay, Roger, 118, 128
Fiske, Edward B., 90–91
Flournoy, Donald, 18
Flournoy, Mary Anne, 138
Food and Drug Administration, 132

Friends of Alden Library, 53, 150
Fries, Tom, 104
Fucci, Donald, 19
Fuller, Stephen, 65–66, 149
Fund for the Improvement of Secondary Education (FIPSE), 82

Gaddis, John, 81, 153–56, 157
Gagliano, Felix, 137, 146
Galbreath, John W., 57, 62
Gault, Janice, 118
Gauthier, Howard, 166
Geiger, Alan, 2, 44, 72, 119, 174; historical registry and, 56, 177; OU building plan and, 46–47
gene transfer, 116–18, 132
General Education component, 33, 75–78, 83–84, 124. *See also* Tiers, General Education
Glenn, John, 106
Glidden, Robert, 180
Goldman, Sam, 18, 109
Goll, Lawrence, 124
Goll, Milton, 124
Gorbachev, Mikhail, 154
Gordimer, Nadine, 142
government, state, 115, 162–66; education spending by, 159; ILGARD funding by, 112; Selective Excellence Program by, 121–26; subsidies by, 11, 27–28, 158, 159–61
government funding, federal, 82, 161–62
Grlic, Rajko, 125
Grones, Alberta, 178
Grover, Ann, 57, 177
Guide (New York Times), 90–91
Gusteson, Raymond, 14

Hairston, Elaine, 165
Hamby, Alonzo, 156
Handler, Philip, 2–3, 117
Hannah, John, 173
Harbarger, Arthur L., 68
Harrington, Charles, 29
Harter, Carol, 16, 25–26, 43, 51, 98
Harter, Michael, 111

Hartman, James, 19
Harvard University, 4–5, 100, 173
Harvey, Richard, 83
Haynes, Fred, 51
Health and Human Services, College of, 109–11
Hecht, Martin L., 16, 60
Henry Luce Foundation, 149
Herpes Probe Test, 132
Hitam, Datuk Musa, 145–46
Hodinka, Richard, 118
Hogan, Terry, 97
Holden, Ellsworth, 118
Honda of America, 147
Hong Kong Baptist University, 145
Honors Convocation, 91
Hoppe, Peter, 118, 133
How to Get an Ivy League Education at a State University, 91, 100
Hughes, Leona, 66
Hunt, Gary, 152

Innovation Center and Research Park (ICRP), 118–21
Institute for Local Government Administration and Rural Development (ILGARD), 112–13
internationalization, 136–39; educational plan importance of, 33; Ping's emphasis on, 40, 137. *See also* African Studies Program; Southeast Asian Studies; *and individual nations*
Inter-University Council, 163, 165

Ja'afar, Tuanku, 149
Jacobs, Laura, 172
Jacobsen, Edna Parker, 68
James, Herman, 179
Japanese cherry trees, 54–55
Jeffers, Dean, 62
Jefferson, Thomas, 54
John C. Baker Award, 182
John C. Baker Fund, 73
John D. and Catherine T. MacArthur Foundation, 155

John Grenzebach and Associates, 66, 68–69
Jollick, Joseph, 116–18, 121, 132
Jones, Bill, 90
Jones, Verda, 177
Jordan, Mary Kaye, 137

Kaye, Sammy, 152
Kellogg Foundation and UPAC, 26
Kennan, George F., 155
Kennard, William, 43, 45–46
Kennedy, Edwin L., 5, 62, 65, 67, 73–74; art museum donation by, 73; Third Century Campaign and, 65, 67
Kennedy, Ruth E., 67, 73–74
Kennedy Presidential Library, Boston, 54
Kent State University, 8, 50
Kerr, Nada, 177
Kibble Foundation, 69
King, Peter, 171
Klare, George, 19
Klinder, John, 68
Knox, Donald, 140
Konneker, Ann Lee, 57, 177
Konneker, Wilfred, 121, 131, 146; alumni center and, 56–57; Cutler Scholar Program and, 100–101; 1804 Campaign and, 60–62; innovation center and, 119; Third Century Campaign and, 65
Kopchick, John, 124, 133
Kotses, Harry, 127
Kurlinski, Wayne, 16, 29, 53, 146

labor relations, 49–52
Lasher, George Starr, 124
Lavelle, Marion, 177
Lee, Hwa-Wei, 149–52
Leipzig University (Germany), 157
Lesotho: and OU, 141–42
libraries: educational plan for, 19, 33. *See also* Alden Library project
Lifelong Learning, 114–15
Liggett, Carr, 53
Lilley, Robert, 127
Lilly Foundation, 76

Lin, Henry, 73
Lin, Maya, 73
Linkskold, Sven, 18
Louisville Presbyterian Theological Seminary, 1

Malaysia. *See* Southeast Asian Studies
"Managing for the Future" report, 163–64
Manasseh Cutler Scholarship, 66
Mandela, Nelson, 143
Mara Institute of Technology, 146
Marty, Martin, 55
Masire, Quett K. J., 142
Massachusetts Institute of Technology, 149
Mattmiller, Dale, 19
McClure, J. Warren, 60–61, 68
McCutcheon, Bill, 68
McDaniel, Drew, 123
McFarland, Richard, 127, 128–29
McGeogh, Lyle, 26
media publicity, 28–29, 90–91, 117–18
Miami University, 50, 87, 113
Michigan State University, 52, 105, 167, 173
microwave landing system (MLS), 127
Miner, Steven, 156
minorities: educational plan for, 34; faculty appointments and, 24; MITCO and, 23; student outreach and, 23; University Council and, 22
Minority Introduction to College (MITCO), 23
Mitchell, Edward, 114
Moden, Gary, 89
Money Magazine, 90
Moss, Cruse W., 64
Myers, Allen, 141
Myers, Frank W., 106–7

Nab, Adrie, 16
Namibia: and OU, 143
National Academy of Sciences, 128
National Aeronautics and Space Administration (NASA), 127
National Association of State Universities and Land Grant Colleges, 139
National Business Incubator Association (NBIA), 120
National Endowment for the Humanities (NEH), 82, 138, 152, 170
National Heart, Lung, and Blood Institute grant, 127
National Institutes of Health (NIH), 121, 127–28, 133
National Register of Historic Places, 70
National Research Council, 25
National Science Foundation, 27, 83, 128
Newell, Robert, 55
New York Times, 73, 156
Ngwane Teachers College, Swaziland, 143
Nigeria: and OU, 140
Nixon, Corwin, 104
Noriega, Manuel, 139
North, Gary, 16, 52, 169
Northwest Territory Ordinance: bicentennial of, 55, 178; passage of, 54–55

O'Bleness, Charles G., 69
O'Bleness, Henry, 69, 70
Ocasek, Oliver, 105–6
Ohio Board of Regents, 9, 41, 118, 163–65; Program Excellence Awards and, 83–84; Selective Excellence Program and, 29, 122, 155
Ohio Department of Development, 128
Ohio Education Association (OEA), 12
Ohio Farm Bureau Federation, 131
Ohio Humanities Council, 180
Ohio Osteopathic Association (OOA), 104
Ohio Program of Intensive English (OPIE), 137, 157
Ohio State University, 131, 167
Ohio University (OU). *See* educational plan, OU; research, OU
Ohio University Foundation, 65
Ohio University Inn, 57
O'Neal, John, 19
The 100 Best Colleges for African-American Students, 90
101 of the Best Values in America's Colleges and Universities, 90

O'Neill, Thomas, III, 54
Onn, Tun Hussein, 146
Oregon State University, 167
Osteopathic Medicine, College of, 103–8
Overby, Charles, 83
Oxford University, 69, 100, 157

Pach, Chester, 157
Peebles, Gene, 16, 26
People's Republic of China (PRC), 145, 150, 151; extended student program with, 145; students from, 144–45; visit by educators from, 21, 136, 144
Perotti, James, 18, 26
Peterson's Competitive Colleges, 90
Phillips, J. Wallace, 106
Phillips, Jody Galbreath, 5, 106, 168
Ping, Andy, 3, 176
Ping, Charles Jackson: accolades to, 168–69, 171–75; administrative model by, 15; Alma College and, 3; awards bestowed upon, 106, 182; Central Michigan University and, 3–4; Challenge grants and, 125; class reunion of, 181; dedications to, 169–71; educational focus of, 180; educational studies of, 1–3, 5; 1804 Campaign role of, 63–64; enrollment turnaround and, 88; gene transfer and, 117; General Education foundation and, 76, 84; Harvard University and, 4; health problems and, 143, 168; honorary degree for, 180; job offers to, 167; management report criticisms by, 163–64; marriage of, 2; Ohio University vision of, 9–10; ordainment of, 2; postpresidential career of, 179–80; retirement of, 167–69; scholarship of, 1; student board representation and, 99–100; travels of, 138–39, 145, 179; Tusculum College and, 3. *See also* The Charles J. Ping Institute for the Teaching of the Humanities
Ping, Claire Oates, 1–2, 175; awards bestowed upon, 178; community groups founded by, 177–78; educational background of, 177; fundraising projects by, 178; hosting duties of, 176; preservation projects of, 56, 57, 176–78
Pinney, Reba, 140
Ploghoft, Milton, 140
Porter, Thomas, 118
Post (student newspaper), 22, 28, 78, 83, 99, 156, 171–72
Precollege, 75, 81
Presidents Council, 98
Prestbo, John A., 28, 171
Proceedings of the National Academy of Sciences, 116–17
Procter and Gamble, 133
Profiles of American Colleges, 90
Progenitor, 133
Program Excellence Award, 83–84
Putnam, Rufus, 54, 55

Quattrocki, Edward, 58–59

Rapaport, Jacobo, 128
Ravan Press (Johannesburg), 142
Razak, Tun Abdul, 145
Reagan, Ronald, 154
Reedy, Tracy, 182
research, OU, 127–30
residence halls, 42–45, 46–48, 90, 96–98
Reynolds, John E., III, 65–66
Rhodes, James A., 106
Rhodes College, 1, 92
Richard, Patricia, 26, 83; learning communities and, 97–98
Richard Fleischman Architects of Columbus, 46
Richards, Hilda, 26, 111
The Ridges, 70–72
Riedel, Alan, 65–66
Riedel, Ruby, 66
Riffe, Vernal, 47, 105–6
Robe, Richard, 44–45, 64, 119
Rohr, Mary Ellen (Dudley), 177
Rollins, Roger, 174
Ross-Lee, Barbara, 26, 106

Rovner, Jerome, 58
Rudy, Joel, 16, 28; codes of conduct and, 95–96; residence halls and, 96–98
Rural Universities Program (RUP), 113
Russ, Dolores, 64
Russ, Fritz, 64, 119
Rutherford, Dwight, 57
Rutherford, Rose, 57, 177, 178
Ryan, Cornelius, 152
Ryan, Kathryn, 152

Sanford, Elise, 53
Savage, Robert L., 118
Schaefer, Laurel Lea, 68
Schey, Ralph, 65, 119
Schmidt, Mike, 68
Scholastic Aptitude Test, 88
Scholl, David, 118, 121
Schumacher, Gary, 31
Scott, Byron, 77
Scott, Chuck, 123
Scott, Damon, 99
Scott Fetzer Company, 65
Scripps, Edward Wyllis, 64, 152
Scripps Howard Foundation, 64, 124, 152
Secrest, Robert T., 103–4
selective admissions, 88–89
Selective Excellence Program, 29, 121–23, 129, 161; Challenge grants in, 125–26, 129; Eminent Scholar awards by, 124–25; Program Excellence winners and, 123–24; Selective Excellence Grant, 84, 122–26, 155–56. *See also* Challenge grants
Sensus, 133
Sesquicentennial Campaign, 59
Shevlin, Thomas, 118
Silver, Gerald, 18
Sinclair Community College, 9
Smith, William Y., 22–25
South Africa: apartheid policy in, 142–43; Namibia independence from, 143
Southeast Asian Studies, 145–47, 149; Malaysian partnership and, 145–47
Soviet Union: cold war conference with, 153–54; 1990 conference with, 156

Sowle, Claude R., 8, 53, 171
Space Utilization and Management Study (SUMS), 45–48
Sports Illustrated, 171
Sprague, Jean, 177
Stanford University, 44
State Teachers Retirement System, 39
Steiner, Catherine, 135
Stevens, Scott, 78
Stewart, David, 16
Stinson, John, 119
Stocker, Beth, 44, 61, 65
Stocker, C. Paul, 44, 60–62
Stone, Marjorie, 177
Student Senate, 98–99
students, OU, 23–25, 93–99, 115, 159; international, 136–37, 147; nontraditional, 11, 34
Sub Cycle static frequency converter, 61
Summer Institute for Liberal Arts Education, 5
Supercomputer Network, 129
Suzman, Helen, 143
Swaziland: and OU, 141, 142, 143

Templeton, John Newton, 22, 55
Tevis, Walter, 58
Third Century Campaign. *See* Toward the Third Century Fund Campaign
Third Century Colloquium, 32–33
Third Century report. *See Toward the Third Century*
Thomas Alva Edison Partnership Program, 130, 132, 161. *See also* Edison Biotechnology Institute
Tiers, General Education, 75–85; creation of, 76–77; debate over, 78–80, 82; implementation of, 80–82; Tier I goals and components, 77, 80–81; Tier II goals and components, 77, 79, 81, 84–85; Tier III, conception of, 78, 79, 80, 82; Tier III, courses in, 82–83
Today, 171
Tong, James Y., 151
Toward the Third Century (Third Century report), 32–38, 127, 153

Toward the Third Century Fund Campaign (Third Century Campaign), 65–69, 181
transfer, knowledge, 115–18, 130–33; Edison Partnership Program and, 130–31; gene transfer and, 116–18; research parks and, 118–21; Technology Transfer Office and, 121
Trautwein and Associates, 44
Trevas, Robert, 58
Trisolini, Anthony, 73
Tucker, Joseph, 18, 114
tuition, 9, 159
Turnage, Martha, 16, 26, 55, 71
Turner, John, 144
Tusculum College, 3, 5, 76

UNESCO (United Nations Educational, Scientific, and Cultural Organization), 150
unionization: Central Michigan University and, 4, 11–12; criticisms of, 13–14; Ohio University vote on, 12–14. *See also* labor relations
United Mine Workers strike, 49–50
University Council, 10, 15, 22
University of Botswana, 141, 144
University of Illinois, 52
University of Kentucky, 44
University of Manchester, 144
University of North Carolina at Chapel Hill, 88–89
University of Oregon, 5
University Planning Advisory Committee (UPAC), 5, 26–30, 87, 150, 162; media praise of, 28–29, 171
U.S. Agency for International Development (USAID), 140–42, 149
U.S. Department of Education, 147
U.S. Department of Transportation, 127
U.S. International Trade Commission, 156
U.S. News & World Report, 90

value added theory, 30
Vedder, Richard, 74, 156
Venable, Ann Shelton Ping, 3, 176
Venable, Sam, 182
Vietnam War, 8
Vines, Lois, 170
Voelker, Donald, 66
Voinovich, George, 53, 129–30, 162–64
Volunteer Center, 97

Wagner, Eric, 66, 81, 174
Wagner, Thomas, 124, 130–31, 153; first gene transfer by, 116–18, 133
Wall Street Journal: UPAC article in, 28–29, 171
Walters, Jim, 87–88
Washington Post, 117, 156
Washington Post/Los Angeles Times news service, 117
Weinberg, Mark, 112
Wen Y. Chen, 133
Wetzel, Richard, 53
White, Marie, 171–72
Wilhelm, John, 152
Wilson, Dora, 25
Wilson, Robert G., 55
Winters, Bob, 53
women: discrimination against, 24; dual-career marriages and, 25; faculty recruitment of, 24–25; study programs for, 24
World Communications Conference, 21, 136
World War II, 4
Wright State University, 9

Xerox Corporation grant, 125
Xian Jiantong University, China, 151

Yale University, 55, 100, 157

Zook, John, 128